D1091277

CULTURAL CAPITALISM
Politics after New Labour

For William Outhwaite

CULTURAL CAPITALISM

Politics after New Labour

Edited by
Timothy Bewes and
Jeremy Gilbert

Lawrence & Wishart
LONDON DECEMBER 2000

'Culture is the meaning of an insufficiently meaningful world.'
Guy Debord

'Culture ... the number of times I've wished that I had never heard of the damned word. I have become more aware of its difficulties, not less, as I have gone on.'
Raymond Williams

Introduction
Politics after defeat

TIMOTHY BEWES AND
JEREMY GILBERT

The present period finds the left in a situation of apparent total defeat. Capitalism is consolidating its grip on modernity; there seems no possibility of throwing off, nor even of disturbing its hold, which is progressively more assured, both economically and ideologically. It is a period which, in recognition of its historical moment and ideological ancestry, may be characterised as 'post-Thatcherism'. In this case 'post-', that ambiguous and ubiquitous prefix of our age, denotes not a moderation of the 'extremes' of the Thatcher era – as seemed to be promised by such watchwords as 'New Labour', 'the Third Way', 'triangulation', 'caring capitalism', and so on – but rather their conclusive and irrefutable hegemonisation.

The radical left has been stymied. While mainstream politics competes on the centre ground, galvanised by an ongoing struggle for the most consensual position, debate on the left seems more fragmented than ever. Preoccupied by idealistic concerns relating to the constitution of the political sphere, or the qualities pertaining to 'radicalism', or the need to recover 'ideology', the left is acting out its own obsolescence. Even the most basic issues seem to have lost their ballast: should radical politics be 'anti-capitalist' or not? Is politics concerned with particular struggles or universal values? identity or society? the recognition of 'difference' or the pursuit of 'totality'? What is the ontological status of class struggle? There is no consensus, nor even real dialogue, on such questions; yet we find one or other position defended with a level of vehemence in direct proportion to its degree of removal from mainstream debates. The rise of 'anti-capitalism' as a movement with no positive content, and no specifiable programme, may yet prove either to be an opening out of the field of possibilities, or a degeneration of radical politics into inarticulacy. What is clear is that 'capitalism', the old enemy, now defines the field of contemporary experience to the extent that even these most visible forms of resistance to it seem trapped in an apparently futile form of *resistance as such*, undertaken in the name of nothing more knowable than an absolute negation.

A close literary and historical analogy, in terms both of the responses of the left and the options apparently open to it, may be found in the situation of the defeated forces of Satan as they are represented in the opening books of John Milton's *Paradise Lost* – languishing upon the sulphuric lake of the infernal world, miserably contemplating their fate. This work by the great Republican English poet was written and published during a period of political defeat and internal exile, in the years following the Restoration in 1660; and it is not far-fetched to read the debate among the elite of Satan's fallen army as a representation of profound political despair.

In Book 2 of *Paradise Lost*, successive leaders intervene to recommend their favoured courses of action. For Moloch, the only acceptable course is 'open war', on the grounds that nothing could be worse than this indefinite present of categorical exclusion from Heaven's bliss; yet the sheer unfeasibility of this course of action is made unambiguous by the poet. Moloch grossly underestimates the material extent and the historical significance of the defeat. For him history is without objective rationality; victory and defeat are matters of contingency and circumstance, nothing more. Thus he believes the proposed recovery and 'ascent' towards heaven, inspired by the desire for vengeance, is quite as conceivable in prospect as the preceding descent is in retrospect.

For Belial, to the contrary, in a speech dripping with sophistry, it is better for the defeated army to endure their torment with grace, in the hope that dignified suffering may abate the Conqueror's anger and thus, eventually, the intensity of the flames; this too is presented by the text as a contemptible position unworthy of consideration. The final two speeches of the debate are the most suggestive, as well as being the more dialectically satisfying. For Mammon, simple retreat from the struggle – a form of 'inner emigration' – is the logical corollary of defeat. He advocates the cultivation of altogether different, interior values – an argument also put forward in the opening book of the poem by Satan, in the famous lines, 'The mind is its own place, and in itself/ Can make a Heav'n of Hell, a Hell of Heav'n.'[1] For Mammon the implication of total defeat is that we seek 'Our own good from ourselves, and from our own/ Live to ourselves, though in this vast recess,/ Free, and to none accountable ...'. (This proposal finds great favour with the hordes of the underworld, exhausted by war, who greet his speech with mass applause – creating a 'murmuring effect', says Milton, 'as when hollow Rocks retain/ The sound of blust'ring winds'.)

Finally Beelzebub sets out the situation with clarity and boldness, and proposes a course of action which will actually be followed. There is an impasse, he argues: Heaven is impenetrable; but Hell is intolerable. Furthermore, the power of God is such that further revolt will achieve no inroads into His Kingdom; on the contrary, it will enable Him rather to extend His Empire into Hell itself; the King of Heaven has an uncanny ability to turn to His advantage every manifestation of revolt against Him. For Beelzebub it is precisely an understanding of this situation that will lead to the formulation of a new strategy. 'War hath determin'd us', says Beelzebub, 'and foil'd with loss/ Irreparable'.[2] This is not a mitigable situation; yet Beelzebub has heard tell of a 'new World', and a 'new Race call'd Man', upon which, perhaps, their forces may gain some purchase. Thus may defeat itself contain the rudiments of a future victory. The alternative, he makes clear, is to 'sit in darkness here/ Hatching vain Empires', and to continue so indefinitely.[3]

It is no doubt easy to think of contemporary occupants of these respective positions. In a recent editorial in *New Left Review*, Perry Anderson systematically examines the possibility of a coherent position for the left in historical circumstances greatly changed from those in which the journal was founded. His description of the current conjuncture is highly evocative of the predicament of Milton's rebellious angels, and the arguments he considers bear explicit analogy with the debate which proceeds in the second book of the poem. For Anderson the contemporary situation is one in which 'open war' against the forces of the hegemony – the strategy advocated by Moloch – is no longer feasible or desirable. Neo-liberalism has become 'the most successful ideology in world history'; the corpus of oppositional Western Marxism – the work of thinkers such as Lukács, Sartre and Marcuse – has vanished from circulation; labour is in a state of stable 'quiescence'. The starting-point for any realistic left project today, says Anderson, must therefore be 'a lucid registration of historical defeat' – this is precisely the situation faced by the forces of Satan in *Paradise Lost*.[4]

In circumstances such as these, continues Anderson, the options for the left are threefold. First there is 'accommodation', justified in the sentiment that 'capitalism has come to stay, we must make our peace with it'. This is a position analogous to that advanced by the perfidious Belial, and it is a false one – not least because it maintains a static conception of the world as limited by its immediate 'givenness'. Accommodation is nothing other than a renunciation of the political obligation to seek to make the world anew, which shrinks from the veneer of the objective world as from an impenetrable mirror.

The second option mentioned by Anderson is 'consolation' – the search for 'silver linings in what would otherwise seem an overwhelmingly hostile environment' (this is the temperament represented by the speech of Mammon in *Paradise Lost*).[5] Consolation is a response now widely canvassed on the British left in particular, not only as a source of 'psychological compensation' in a situation of defeat, as Anderson notes, but also as a form of 'dialectical' thinking which takes the 'end of politics' at face value as a historical resolution of the 'monumental' struggle between capitalism and communism. Thus politics itself, it is claimed, is devolving from the 'external' structures of political institutions towards the interioristic domain of feelings and 'affect'; the new political terrain is one of intimacy, 'spirituality' and ethical well-being. The project for the radical left becomes one of seeking to make a potentially unpleasant but structurally irrevocable domain more habitable; to *temper* the manifestations of 'unlicensed capitalism' (a fiction which has never existed) in the direction of *cultural* improvement. This is not a position which is clearly distinguishable from that of the current holders of political office.

Finally Anderson introduces the stance which he calls 'uncompromising realism' – one which refuses any accommodation with the existing system, and avoids the 'well-meaning cant' which bows to a pragmatic sense of the inevitability of official hypocrisy, but finds it possible to support modest strivings for a better life in the dialectical acknowledgement of a certain immediate reality: a world-historical capitalist system. 'If the human energies for a change of system are ever released again,' writes Anderson frankly, 'it will be from within the metabolism of capital itself. We cannot turn away from it. Only in the evolution of this order could lie the secrets of another one.'[6]

Like Satan's forces at the opening of Book 3 of *Paradise Lost*, or like Adam and Eve at the conclusion of the poem, we face a situation in which a new world is all before us. This new order has been evolving for a long time, but its disciplinary and conceptual borders are beginning to appear remarkably static. Here is where the question of *culture* is revealed as one of the most important political-theoretical issues of our time; its urgency is greater now, we would contend, even than during the period of its most intensive theoretical formulation in the first few decades of the twentieth century. 'A culture is most alive when it is the subject of conflict' writes Kenneth Allan.[7] Yet a version of 'culture' is currently in the ascendant which is indissociable from the emergence of 'Third Way' politics, and which seems, furthermore, to have an ideological role of enforcing consensus – *denying* conflict, that is to say, rather than giving expression to or genuinely resolving it.

*　*　*

The notion of culture is a product of the dynamic of modernity itself, a dynamic classically conceived in terms of a progressive conflict between the individual and society. Culture, as Terry Eagleton points out in his recent book *The Idea of Culture*, is 'symptomatic of a division which it offers to overcome' – between selfhood and the 'autonomous' objective world. Quoting Raymond Williams, Eagleton observes that culture 'emerges as a notion from "the recognition of the practical separation of certain moral and intellectual activities from the driven impetus of a new kind of society"'. Culture thereby becomes 'a sort of premature utopia, abolishing struggle at an imaginary level so that [it] need not resolve it at a political one.'[8] Thus culture – potentially, at least – is a dialectical concept, *even as it proposes a resolution of the dialectic* (or, to use a different register, culture is an exemplary 'deconstructive' concept, even in its 'quasi-transcendentality').[9] Consider the following propositions:

- Culture is inseparable from ideology, yet irreducible to it. Culture spans *and bridges* the divide between base and superstructure (materiality and consciousness) in the Marxist description of the operation of ideology, since culture is precisely the vehicle of that operation.
- Culture implies the equal redundancy of 'determinist' and 'voluntarist' theories of individuality, since (as ideology) it presupposes the mutual embeddedness of each.
- The concept of culture encapsulates the inadequacy of mutually exclusive 'idealist' and 'realist' – Kantian and Hobbesian – theories of political action. As the works of Marx and Engels, Freud, and Nietzsche imply – particularly when inflected through the continental tradition of post-structuralism – culture as ideology is not the removal of individual agency but precisely its material embodiment.

The ideological 'interpellation' of individuals implies not the 'death of the subject', or anything like it, but the constitution of individuals as subjects, and vice versa.

It is in these senses that 'culture' promises to construct the emergent 'new world' of a *post-capitalist* epoch. In a situation in which, supposedly, there is nothing other than capitalism, how meaningful can the term 'capitalism' be? The boldest move is to recognise that the question of 'culture' – what it is, its relation to politics, its potential for radicalism – is the most important area of political contestation at the present time. To ignore its current impact on politics, with the deluded and parsimonious justification that culture is not part of the political sphere 'proper', is, as Milton puts it, to condemn oneself to 'sit in darkness here/ Hatching vain Empires'. This is something which traditional 'political' critique was guilty of – in its liberal as often as in its Marxist forms – before the cultural studies 'revolution', and it is a position which – in the unreflective objection to the 'cultural', for example – has continued to be upheld in some quarters; Judith Butler is among those who have recently diagnosed this tendency.[10] Its result must be that the sphere of culture is abandoned to the attentions of reactionary political forces, which continue to invest huge amounts of energy into consolidating something called 'culture' – a commodified and reified structure quite different from the dialectical concept outlined above.

On the other hand, in the last thirty years or so, culture has become an object of academic study, intense theorisation, and methodological contestation, in the context of the evolving field of 'cultural studies'. Perry Anderson's analysis provides a means of seeing this, retrospectively, as both an inevitable and a necessary process. The cultural studies tradition has constituted a political response to the 'emergent new world' of culture and, furthermore, a structure that has helped to bring that world into being. More recently, however, this still-evolving discipline has begun to exhibit considerable anxiety over its political identity and its disciplinary status. This reflexive anxiety has been a feature of debates within the discipline for nearly a decade; yet practitioners and theorists of cultural studies have rarely, if ever, addressed the precise question of the institutional and intellectual relationship between cultural studies and political studies. While cultural studies has constituted an interdisciplinary meeting point between literary criticism, cultural history, philosophy, anthropology, linguistics, sociology, media studies, film theory and a few strands of political theory, there have been few efforts to acknowledge the interdisciplinary relevance of the professional concerns of most people working in university politics departments. The lazy assumption that everything is 'political' has frequently resulted in 'politics' disappearing altogether as an object of concern or theoretical attention. At best, the assumption of political or ideological significance remains an invisible backdrop to what is, in effect, the straightforward aesthetic investigation of – or philosophical meditation upon – 'cultural objects'.

This process of disciplinary sedimentation is indissociable from the 'dialectic of modernity' described above; perhaps it signals nothing other than a further stage in the emergence of culture itself in the modern age. Yet – as if aware of the essential instability of the concept of culture – the discipline of cultural studies has lately been encountering a wide range of attempts to rethink its founding assumptions. George Steinmertz, in a recent book of essays on the relation between culture and the state, writes of 'the Scylla of essentialism found in the Weberian and national culture traditions and the Charybdis of ignoring cultural difference, characteristic of the utilitarian and Marxist traditions'.[11] For Steinmertz the contemporary moment is one in which this polarity – within the Western conjuncture at least – has attained a critical urgency.

It has been the task of the best work within this still comparatively recent discipline to steer a path successfully between these two extremes, while recognising the essentially chimerical nature of each. At its worst, however, cultural studies has simply counterposed identity politics (say) to a kind of vulgar liberal or revolutionary 'universalism' – an approach which has resulted in work of crudeness and predictability, even (as Meaghan Morris has written) of 'banality'.[12] As a celebration of diversity, 'heterogeneity' and 'visceral' pleasures, against the totalitarianism and 'cerebral' bias of Marxist criticism, on one hand, and the patrician 'elitism' of the old-style aesthetic criticism on the other, cultural studies too willingly renounces the desirable, albeit increasingly difficult task of comprehending its objects of study within a meaningful historical narrative.

This book presents a series of differing inflections of the relationship between politics and culture. Common to all of them, however, is the recognition that the conception of culture as the sole territory and constitution of political activity is now that of the political establishment itself. Culture, as a hinterland somewhere between radical individualism on one side and radical politics on the other, is the site of the contemporary consolidation of the globalising world order – *and is currently being sold as such*. Culture, said Chris Smith, the Secretary of

State for Culture, Media and Sport, in a speech soon after the 1997 Labour election victory, 'is what gives us a sense of identity both as individuals and as a nation'. Culture is not simply about 'image and history', but about presenting 'a hard commercial edge'. Culture, he affirms, 'lies at the very heart of [the] mission' of the new government. Elsewhere he acknowledges that creativity – for Smith a byword for culture – is especially important 'in a mature industrial economy such as ours'.[13] In other words, the centrality of 'culture' to 'politics' is for Smith an effect of forces of modernisation which it is beyond our wherewithal to manage. History – conceived in the most monumental of terms – has a dynamic of its own; and culture is merely the static product of these forces, a plateau at which the dynamic of history comes suddenly to a halt.

*   *   *

The timeliness of this book, we believe, is due to its embodiment of a series of tensions which define the present conjuncture to a greater degree than any currently identifiable consensus – and certainly more than the position of historical complacency described above. These tensions, none of which is near a point of resolution, are located around the following sets of polarities: (i) cultural studies and political studies, which seem – independently at least – unable to deal with the indisputably changing nature of the relation between culture and politics; (ii) continental philosophy and political theory – bodies of work which inform, respectively, these distinct disciplines; (iii) 'aesthetic' and 'materialist' theories of culture, which – even within Marxist theory – have always constituted twin poles of contestation; (iv) identity as an organising principle of politics, and the kinds of universal values associated with a model of politics which emerged in the Enlightenment, and which was radicalised by the Marxist tradition.

Despite the different aims and objects of the individual essays contained in this volume, a number of significant theoretical, political and methodological themes emerge across the book as a whole. The first of these is the attempt to respond to the political conjuncture brought into being by the enormous success of New Labour. While debate over the political 'character' of New Labour has tended to focus on its differences from 'Thatcherism', or the absence of them, the essays in this book are more concerned with the relationship between New Labour and earlier projects for 'modernisation' which have emerged from the British left. One possible position implied in several contributions[14] is the argument that New Labour is not, as some on the left continue to claim, merely a logical extension of the tradition of thinking which ran from the first New Left through the period of the Greater London Council under Ken Livingstone and into the analysis of 'New Times' pursued by the magazine *Marxism Today* in the 1980s. Rather, the very identity of New Labour is constituted at the moment of a specific *rejection* of that tradition and its desire for a democratising modernisation of British society. This observation demands both an interrogation of the ideological status of terms such as 'modernisation' and 'efficiency' in New Labour discourse, and the posing of a specific question: what resources might there be in the tradition of the 'modernising left', or in society at large, for the articulation of an alternative discourse of modernisation?

A second thematic is identifiable in the work of those who, in attempting to delineate the contours of Labour's project, take their cue from Anthony Barnett's characterisation of its agenda as one of 'corporate populism'.[15] In particular, the emergence of 'managerialism'– what Geoff Andrews has described as 'a new form of governance'– is the object of essays by Alan Finlayson, Tiziana Terranova and Jeremy Gilbert. The emergence of a 'technocratic' discourse which insists on the redundancy of any political goal beyond that of the maximisation of profit through the efficient management of flows of goods and information is central to the emergence of New Labour, and to the hegemony of a managerial-technocratic elite. Moreover, this discourse has resonances which go way beyond Millbank, Westminster and even the city of London. Across a range of spheres – management theory, public sector administration, the digital economy, cultural policy – technocratic ideologies are both mobilised and challenged in the struggle to define the nature and determine the future of social life. Such discourses, with their constitutive refusal of all political explanations for historical phenomena, are shown to have correlates even amongst prevailing trends in recent historiography, as in the work of those writers who characterise that defining event of English modernity, the revolution of 1649, as nothing more than a historical 'accident'.[16] A homologous tendency may be found even in a sphere of activity as far removed from historiography as modern-day management theory, as Karen Salamon shows in her anatomisation of the disturbing prevalence of holism in contemporary business discourse.

Thus – and this is a third theme – all of the contributions to this volume can be understood as critically taking issue with tendencies – historical, political and theoretical – towards depoliticisation. Not only is the refusal or inability to think politically the most debilitating characteristic of the 'common sense' of our time; it is also manifest in certain *intellectual* trends which come under critical scrutiny here – from reductive sociologies of culture, with their inability to think the discursive as the site of contingency and agency, to the orthodoxies of certain self-styled guardians of the Marxist 'legacy'. 'Post-Marxism' is one answer to this particular polarity – a genealogically and semantically rich notion as put forward by Martin McQuillan in his essay, where he counterposes it to a defensive and patrimonial 'Real Marxism'. 'Post-Marxism' derives partly from deconstruction and the work of Laclau and Mouffe, but also from a recognition that conservatism may pertain to the revolutionary left as much as to the establishment right, that it is always an *anti-political* dispensation, and that – as a claim to the 'true inheritance' of Karl Marx – it can only ever do a disservice to the thought of that most subtle of 'post-Marxist' thinkers, Marx himself.

A question arises here in relation to the 'tensions' which converge upon this book – and it betokens the epistemological and dialectical interpenetration of, respectively, 'culture' and 'politics', 'individuals' and 'society', 'discourse' and 'reality', 'truth' and 'appearance': has the smouldering and sometimes bitter history of contention between the defenders of deconstruction and the upholders of the materialist dialectic ever been more than a struggle between competing brands of *fundamentally* identical products? To use such a provocative metaphor is to imply, at the same time, a certain perspective upon the contemporary world – a perspective indissociable from the realisation that neither of these traditions – 'deconstruction' or 'Marxism' – can avoid being implicated in the contemporary consolidation of market capitalism which both, albeit in quite different registers, are directed against. While contributions to this book range from strident expressions of commitment to deconstruction and 'post-Marxism' on one hand, to equally determined defences of the continued relevance of the Hegelian Marxist tradition on the other, the conclusions they draw are often remarkably similar. It has long been assumed that these traditions are implacably opposed; the evidence of the work presented here suggests that such an assumption is itself a symptom of the penetration of intellectual life by the processes of commodification and enforced competition which now shape so much of 'cultural' life. It is upon the essential ambiguity of these processes – which are both liberating and formative of political subjectivity in the present day, and potentially corrosive of it – that politics is presently riven; furthermore, it is on the basis of this ambiguity that we believe the new critical and political formation must be founded.

Finally, what emerges in this book is a common field of enquiry for a number of writers from very different philosophical and disciplinary backgrounds. If the outlines of an (inter)discipline are discernible here, what name should we give it? Some might argue that there is nothing contained in this volume which falls outside the remit of 'cultural studies'. Others might suggest that, given the concern of several essays here with issues normally associated with the discipline of 'politics', a new field of study located somewhere between the two is being delineated. 'Cultural politics' would be a heterogeneous field of study governed by the recognition that all politics is cultural politics. Not only is all 'culture' political (as the most incisive work within cultural studies has always maintained), but all politics is, by definition, 'identity politics' (what was the international class struggle, in all its monumental 'idealism', if not a contest over the relative significance of different social identities?). Cultural theory, therefore, is a practice of irresponsibility, even complicity, if it is not always also political theory. Capitalism – as Weber, Adorno and Gramsci showed decades ago, and as writers as different as Ernesto Laclau and Gillian Rose have argued in recent years – does not simply *have* a culture; it *is* a culture.[17]

Thus, to name the field defined by these observations 'cultural politics' may be self-defeating, even potentially reifying of the very categories ('culture', 'politics') it sets out to destabilise. If all politics is cultural politics, what could be the logic of such a phrase, other than an obfuscation of the simultaneity of the two concepts? 'Culture', 'Politics', 'Society', 'Individuality', etc, are not pre-existing categories to be brought into contact by the agency of a contrived interdisciplinarity; they are interdependent aspects of social reality, the boundaries of which are drawn, erased and redrawn by, precisely, political struggle. These points of apparent instability and contestation are also therefore points of agency and change, moments when the promise of a better future may be realised, and when politics must make its interventions. The area of engagement circumscribed – or not – by this book is nothing more nor less than politics, in all its formal and historical mutability.

*   *   *

The book opens with four essays directly exploring the questions of methodology touched on here. In the opening chapter Timothy Bewes argues that a version of 'cultural politics' already infuses the ideological agenda of the present government, and that it rests upon a well-rehearsed theoretical narrative of the evolution of 'culture' in modernity. His essay traces this dialectic from its inception in the Renaissance, when an integrated, 'autonomous' individuality and a thoroughly 'instrumental' politics first come into contact with each other; through the rise of industrial capitalism, a deeply anxious stage at which individuality and politics appear mutually corrosive and distressing; to the latest phase in which the concept of 'culture' holds in place an inverted relation between the 'subjective' and 'objective' worlds, which it keeps at indefinite remove from each other – a situation of conceptual, institutional and political stasis. This prevalent form of 'culture' threatens to exclude the concerns of politics completely from what Williams called the 'lived system of meanings and values' of people's social reality. At a time when capitalism is rapidly and efficiently reinventing itself as a purely 'cultural' phenomenon, the need to mediate every manifestation of the 'cultural' within New Labour rhetoric has become an urgent task of political critique, even while the emergence of culture as a political form is granted a certain historical necessity.

Jeremy Gilbert defends the approach to the study of politics and culture exemplified by the work of Stuart Hall and practitioners of 'discourse analysis'. From within the cultural studies tradition, Gilbert writes against those who argue for a turn away from that tradition to studies of 'policy' and 'production', a methodological shift which risks the depoliticisation inherent in any merely descriptive sociology. Comparing tendencies in writing on subjects as apparently dissimilar as music and voting behaviour, he identifies in both an inattention to the performative power of discourse which can only result in a blindness to the contingent political dimensions of all such phenomena. Following Derrida and Laclau, Gilbert argues for a deconstructive attention to the constitutive power of rhetoric and for the indissolubility of 'cultural', 'political' and 'social' formations. As an example of the latter, the music media phenomenon 'Britpop', he suggests, clearly prefigured the emergence of New Labour and its constitutive exclusions by several years. He identifies in prevalent left responses to New Labour a failure to address this range of issues, resulting in a misplaced concern to contest the 'truth' of New Labour's statements on matters such as the inevitability of economic globalisation. A more appropriate and effective response, argues Gilbert, is the strategic mobilisation of alternative discourses and structures of feeling.

In a polemical intervention, Paul Smith looks back specifically at the cultural studies revolution, charting its evolution on both sides of the Atlantic. For Smith the difficulty which cultural studies has in intervening politically is an institutional one – due, in other words, primarily to its status and self-image as a 'hybrid' discipline. Cultural studies has become a merely interpretative rather than prescriptive paradigm, the eclectic nature of which – subsisting under the sign of 'openness' – has resulted in methodological imprecision, and thus a kind of interminable suspension of the political. The vagueness with which cultural studies conceptualises even such vital concepts as 'culture' means that it is simply unable to deal with the new quasi-totalising narratives such as globalisation; nor has it provided any tools with which to resist the political reification of the concept of 'culture'. Paul Smith's deliberately provocative essay – a critical reading of an earlier text by Stuart Hall, which itself 'looks back' at cultural studies from the perspective of 1989 – presents the case for a reinvention of this disciplinary paradigm by means of a 'return to Marx', a process which must necessarily involve a rigorous re-theorisation of the concept of culture itself.

In a vigorous counter-attack on behalf of a theoretically-inflected cultural studies, Martin McQuillan critically opposes the Marxist tradition to deconstruction. For McQuillan, the narrow conception of history implied in the question of the 'success' or 'failure' of the left is deeply suspect – and has been best challenged by the body of work collected under the rubric of post-structuralism. It is absurd, implies McQuillan, to distinguish between Marxism as *theory* and Marxism *as it has been practised*, a distinction which the revanchist defence of Marxism *against* deconstruction necessarily reiterates; indeed to do so is an idealist, that is to say non-dialectical, procedure. More to the point, it is in effect an anti-politics, closer to the transcendental demands of a religious sensibility than to the immanence of a political one. To ignore at once the specific circumstances and the irreducible undecidability of the political Event, as the left did in large measure on 1 May 1997, says McQuillan, is the height of political irresponsibility. His case is for a Marxism – reformulated as 'post-Marxism' – that is paradoxically *more* dialectical and historicist – more 'Marxist' – as a result of its encounter with post-structuralism. At a time when 'theory' is coming under attack from all sides for political 'quietism', McQuillan demonstrates the case for a politically and theoretically conscious cultural criticism in his reading of *Star Wars 1: The Phantom Menace* as a film about Clintonian 'triangulation'.

Matt Jordan takes as his starting point Tony Blair's citation of John Milton – 'our great poet of renewal and recovery' – in his 1997 conference speech, and asks just how close these two visions of a new Britain really are. Milton, along with Shakespeare, was the great narrator of Britain's entry into modernity, and he remains our best record of the fact that this was a condition defined from the beginning by the possibility of an inclusive and participatory democracy. It is both ironic and instructive, therefore, that in *Areopagitica*, the very text which Blair quotes, Milton explicitly reviles the anti-intellectual, the anti-democrat and the man of business with no interest in other aspects of existence – a position arguably at odds with that represented in Blairite politics. Jordan discerns a deeper pattern, highlighting the intellectual affinities between New Labour and the revisionist school of seventeenth century history. Both tendencies are characterised by an insistence on the validity of a Middle English 'common sense', according to which events are never anything more than discrete accidents, subject to no wider social and historical processes. While acknowledging the value of revisionism's emphasis on the contingency of events, Jordan also draws attention to the political potential of a text like Milton's, understood as a performative act of 'creative fantasy'. Appealing to Benjamin and Gramsci, as well as to Milton himself, against the pessimism of Richard Rorty's 'weak pragmatism', Jordan asserts that we must retain a sense of history as a discontinuous field of potential intervention if we are to avoid succumbing to 'the currently dominant version of the present'.

Tiziana Terranova's examination of theories and practices of systematicity offers a perspective on the politics of cultural production far removed from any simplistically defined 'political economy'. Although Terranova describes her use of the work of Jean-Francois Lyotard as 'idiosyncratic', it might be better understood as a long-overdue application of Lyotard's most influential work *The Postmodern Condition* to precisely the issues which it set out to address. Using Lyotard to illuminate the difference between cybernetic and postmodern system models, including their different epistemological and political implications, Terranova offers a framework within which to understand the politics and culture of a range of institutions, from universities to digital companies. Her study exposes the gap between the bureaucratic management models imposed on the public sector by administrations such as that of New Labour, and the more fluid models typical of the new 'digital economy' which the same governments claim to lay such store by. A reading of Lyotard illustrates the redundancy of the former models, even on their own terms – not merely because of their obsession with efficiency as an end in itself but because their definitions of efficiency are derived from outmoded techno-scientific paradigms. As such, her contribution provides the basis for a powerful attack on the rise of 'managerial' governance.

Karen Salamon offers a fascinating anthropological account of a recent encounter between two apparently incongruous discourses, in the form of the growing influence of holistic spirituality upon contemporary business management. Salamon's material illustrates a 'cultural-political' phenomenon *par excellence*. In holistic business management, a discourse of extreme 'subjectivity' and one of extreme 'objectivity' – spiritual self-realisation and cold business rationality, discover and construct a curious mutual affinity. For Salamon, holism in business is a politically paradigmatic discourse, both a metaphor of and a vehicle for the real exercise of power in postmodern societies. In this version of holism, discipline is internalised as a unifying ideology aimed at employees, customers and even managers. Its ideal is not so much that of an efficient management structure, following the old 'bureaucratic' model; rather, it is one of a 'corporate religion'. Far from a real synthesis of values, however, Salamon's analysis reveals a radical, unresolvable contradiction underlying this latest ideological form, which seeks to recruit workers at the level of subjective identification at precisely the point at which their objective disposability is most acute. The language of worker 'alienation' has become obsolete, implies Salamon; it is the mission of spiritually 'integrating' workers which is the new focus of the modality of power.

Part Two of the book examines the New Labour phenomenon, both as a political orientation and a particular cultural moment. The view through the lenses of classical cultural theory and liberal political theory, however, is curiously obscure. Timothy Bewes analyses the contemporary conjuncture as one characterised by two specific, closely-related anxieties: the idea of the 'end of politics' and the idea of the predominance of 'appearance' over 'reality' in contemporary culture. These ideas are indebted to liberal political theory, on one hand, and the sociology of culture on the other – each of which puts forward a particularly static conception of the relation between politics and culture. For the first, a categorical definition of 'politics' operates as a torsion on the possibility of political action in the present; while for the second, a similarly categorical teleology of 'modernity' becomes a privileged concept which is unable to provide a foothold for any critical grasp of the contemporary moment. The prevalence of the concept of spin is exemplary of these twin anxieties, symbolising a fetishistic relation to 'truth' in politics, and presupposing a certain conceptual topography of mediation, according to which 'representation' – both electoral and semiotic – is by definition an interruption of an earlier pristine authenticity. 'Spin' as a cultural phenomenon is simultaneously corrosive and chimerical. It is an incoherent notion which is subjected here to scrutiny in order to challenge the topographical model of truth and appearance, and to attempt to yield up the truth of the contemporary moment. In such a context, argues Bewes, the remobilisation of categories from the Hegelian Marxist tradition – in particular, the concept of mediation – promises to reunite political intervention with truth, indeed to reconstitute politics as an essentially truthful activity.

Alan Finlayson offers a detailed analysis of the politics of New Labour, its techniques of governance, and its conditions of emergence. Writing against simplistic accounts of New Labour as either bereft of any project, or as a mere continuation of Thatcherism, Finlayson maps out the co-ordinates of New Labour in government: its sources, aims and means. Finlayson accepts New Labour as a response to the 'New Times' analysis forged in the pages of *Marxism Today* in the 1980s, but it is a response, he argues, that shows little commitment to the democratising goals of that journal. Its objectives, rather, are to secure the conditions for the development of a dynamic knowledge economy through the implementation of a new set of relationships between individuals and government. This new 'exhortatory state' seeks to 'encourage' rather than control its citizens (an analogue, perhaps, of the shift in emphasis from 'ownership' to 'regulation' of public utilities), eliciting forms of behaviour on the part of individuals and institutions which will encourage the innovation and independence required of participants in the 'weightless economy'. As such, *culture* becomes not a peripheral concern, but the central mechanism of governance, by which the ideal subjects of this 'Schumpterian workfare regime' are to be produced.

Jo Littler conducts an analysis both of the cultural policies and discourses of New Labour, and of the terms in which critiques of these policies have been articulated from the left. In particular, she argues, the recurring themes of 'style over substance' and 'dumbing down' threaten to reproduce the uninterrogated and undemocratic category of cultural 'greatness' which prevailed in the nineteenth century. It is more productive, suggests Littler, to locate New Labour's apparent collapse of culture and the market in relation to the history of British cultural policy, an approach exemplified in the work of Raymond Williams – in the light of which the 'aestheticisation' and 'autonomisation' of culture are inseparable from the rise of representative democracy. Littler goes on to look at the cultural policies of New Labour, and its patronage of particular cultural artefacts, such as the *Sensation* and *powerhouse::uk* exhibitions. In contrast to predecessors such as the Greater London Council in the 1980s, New Labour's cultural discourse is fundamentally contradictory; its combination of aestheticism and instrumentalism is comparable to the 'shock aesthetics' of *Sensation* and Oliviero Toscani's Benetton advertising campaigns, each of which produces a cataleptic consumer rendered utterly passive by a visually overwhelming rhetoric of 'immobilising pessimism'. New Labour's discourse, likewise, is characterised by the systematic obfuscation of history and context, and thus the marginalisation of precisely the political consciousness invoked in Williams's concept of culture, or the concept of taste as it is anatomised in the work of Pierre Bourdieu.

In the final chapter of the book, Jeremy Gilbert characterises New Labour as the hegemonic project of a technocratic elite, and suggests possible routes beyond its dominance of British political culture. Like Finlayson and Terranova, Gilbert identifies a managerialist agenda as central to New Labour discourse. This anti-political ideology, he argues, has resonances with wider cultural and political discourses on 'Cool Britannia' and 'reflexivity'. He explains the nature of this formation partly in terms of the inherently anti-political tendencies of any hegemonising discourse, and partly in terms of the specific interests of the class fraction which is central to it. Arguing that a realistic assessment must understand New Labour managerialism as at once non-Thatcherite and wholly anti-democratic, while making a clear distinction between 'New Labour', 'the Labour Party' and the Blair government, Gilbert asks what strategies the left might follow in order to re-articulate the field of British politics in democratic directions. He concludes with a survey of contemporary popular culture, attempting to identify certain formations and tendencies ('Girl Power', dance culture) which embody progressive political potential, and others ('Britpop', 'New Lads') which indicate what the greatest obstacles to democratising projects are likely to be in the new century.

The idea for this book arose from the contributions to a conference, 'Cultural Politics/Political Cultures', which was organised by the editors at the University of Sussex in September 1998. The chapters by Tiziana Terranova, Paul Smith, Karen Salamon, Martin McQuillan, Jeremy Gilbert and Timothy Bewes all had their germination as presentations at that conference. The intentions of this book, as we hope will be apparent, are to represent the full range of current progressive thinking on the question of cultural politics, to juxtapose essays which take conflicting positions, and thereby throw into relief the difficulties experienced by the left (both inside and outside the academy) in describing and characterising the latest phase of capitalist expansion. The fact that such polar arguments as those of Paul Smith and Martin McQuillan can coexist in close *political* proximity, and appear in the eloquent and robust forms that they do here is – we suspect – symptomatic of the transitory period we find ourselves in, and of the intense demands this makes on the existing disciplinary, even 'interdisciplinary' structures of intellectual life.

The photograph of Peter Mandelson on the cover was commissioned from Snowden by *Vogue* magazine for a special issue on 'British style' which appeared in July 1998. We salute the efforts of everyone involved in its production for an image which so captures, with a poetic level of economy, the current 'political' fascination with all things 'cultural'. We would like to express our thanks to Lawrence and Wishart for their willingness to take on this project; to our contributors and everyone who came to the initial *Cultural Politics/Political Cultures* conference; and to the institutions in which we currently work as academics – specifically, the Department of Cultural Studies at the University of East London and the Department of Literature and Cultural History at Liverpool John Moores University – both of which have in different ways pioneered the structural facilitation of interdisciplinary work over the last few years.

NOTES

1. *Paradise Lost I.*, pp254-5. (Note: The epigraphs to this book are from Guy Debord, *The Society of the Spectacle*, trans. Donald Nicholson-Smith, Zone, New York 1995, p131; and Raymond Williams, *Politics and Letters: Interviews with New Left Review*, Verso, London 1981, p. 154.)
2. *Paradise Lost* II. 330-1.
3. *Paradise Lost* II. 377-8.
4. Perry Anderson, 'Renewals', *New Left Review* 1 (January-February 2000), p16.
5. *Ibid.*, p14.
6. *Ibid.*, p17.
7. Kenneth Allan, *The Meaning of Culture: Moving the Postmodern Critique Forward*, Praeger, Westport, Connecticut 1988, p110.
8. Terry Eagleton, *The Idea of Culture*, Blackwell, Oxford 2000, pp31, 7 (Eagleton is quoting from Raymond Williams, *Culture and Society: Coleridge to Orwell*, Hogarth, London 1987, pxviii).

9. For a pertinent and defining use of the term 'quasi-transcendentality', see Rodolphe Gashé, *The Tain of the Mirror: Derrida and the Philosophy of Reflection*, Harvard University Press, Cambridge, Mass. 1986, pp. 307-18.
10. Judith Butler, 'Merely Cultural', *New Left Review* I/227 (January/February 1998).
11. George Steinmetz (ed.), *State/Culture: State-Formation after the Cultural Turn*, Cornell University Press, Ithaca and London 1999, p33.
12. Meaghan Morris, 'Banality in Cultural Studies', *Discourse* No. 10; also in John Storey (ed), *What is Cultural Studies? A Reader*, Arnold, London 1996.
13. Chris Smith, *Creative Britain*, Faber and Faber, London 1998, pp57, 50.
14. See Alan Finlayson, 'New Labour: The Culture of Government and the Government of Culture'; Tiziana Terranova, 'Of Systems and Networks'; Jo Littler, 'Creative Accounting'; and Jeremy Gilbert, 'In Defence of Discourse Analysis' and 'Beyond the Hegemony of New Labour'.
15. Anthony Barnett, 'Corporate Control', *Prospect*, February 1999. Barnett has recently clarified the meaning of 'corporate populism' to give due weight to the first term in the phrase. Corporate populism is an approach to democracy 'modelled on the behaviour of corporations', which treats the country as a company, government as business management, and policy as a consumer durable. See Anthony Barnett, 'Corporate Populism and Partyless Democracy', *New Left Review* 3 (May-June 2000), pp86-7.
16. See Matt Jordan, 'Determined Dissent: John Milton and the Future of Political Culture', in this volume.
17. The sense of capitalism as a culture is quite removed from the 'merely formal' concept of culture which exists in isolation from subjectivity, say, or the domain of politics – a concept interrogated by Timothy Bewes in the opening chapter of this book. Cultural capitalism, to paraphrase Gillian Rose, would imply 'a series of formative experiences in which ... [capitalist] consciousness's definition of itself comes into contradiction with its real existence.' See Gillian Rose, *Hegel: Contra Sociology*, Athlone, London 1981, p116. See also Ernesto Laclau, *New Reflections on the Revolution of Our Time*, Verso, London 1990.

Cultural politics/political culture

TIMOTHY BEWES

INDIVIDUALITY AND POLITICS: A SHORT GENEALOGY

Ever since Jacob Burckhardt described in a beautiful image the 'common veil' beneath which, in the Middle Ages, lay dreaming or half awake the two sides of human consciousness – that which was turned within and that which was turned without – modern thought has been profoundly aware of a historical association between the development of the individual and the rise of the modern state. It was in Italy, writes Burckhardt, that this common veil, woven of 'faith, illusion, and childish prepossession', first 'melted into air', making the Italians 'the first-born among the sons of Europe'. By the end of the thirteenth century, Italy was 'swarming with individuality', as the restrictions imposed upon human personality by the powers of family and race began to dissolve. Man becomes a spiritual *individual* at the same time as the world and the state begin to be treated objectively; at the close of the century 'a thousand figures meet us', announces Burckhardt, 'each in its own special shape and dress.'[1]

In Burckhardt's highly speculative account, this newly-liberated subjectivity and the objective world of the Renaissance have not yet come into any sort of conflict. Private life is capable of thriving despite, and largely because of, the political despotism under which men and women live. A firm divide between individuality and the political sphere ensures that each subsists in isolation from the other. 'The Italians of the fourteenth century knew little of false modesty or of hypocrisy in any shape,' says Burckhardt; 'not one of them was afraid of singularity, of being and seeming unlike his neighbours' (p82). A footnote adds that by the year 1390 'there was no longer any prevailing fashion of dress for men at Florence, each preferring to clothe

20

himself in his own way.' Compared with the progressive alienation of the industrial era, this period described by Burckhardt is a golden age, the cusp on which modern subjectivity was created, with individuals for the first time enjoying an intimate, unmediated relationship with their own interiorities, even though debarred from control over political and economic reality. If fashion, which signifies the subordination of individual 'taste' beneath the values of a disseminated public culture, wields little influence over men's style of dress, this is because, for Burckhardt at this moment in history, individuality and the objective world enjoy dual sovereignty over entirely separate domains.

In the dialectic of modernity, needless to say, this is a very short-lived moment, insofar as it ever really existed at all. The pressures of the objective world have not yet penetrated the space of the individual, and vice versa. The dawn of the Italian Renaissance would seem, from Burckhardt's account, to be a stage prior to the *constitution* of the subject, in the modern sense. It is this unique circumstance that facilitates the great currency of learning in the Renaissance, which can free a man from all ties to race, people and family. 'Wherever a learned man fixes his seat, there is home,' says an unnamed humanist writer quoted by Burckhardt; and Dante's famous words 'My country is the whole world', uttered in exile, have a similar significance (pp84, 83). Such learning is not regulated according to academic discipline. The 'many-sided man' of the Renaissance is a symbol of the fact that learning had to serve the practical needs of daily life, rather than being delimited within the abstract categories of knowledge forged in the later Enlightenment period. For the conservative Burckhardt, political despotism does not impinge on the freedom of the intellectual, who, in his interiority, retains an autonomy that is even expedited by conditions – external to the individual – of political despotism. 'The private man,' he writes, 'indifferent to politics, and busied partly with serious pursuits, partly with the interests of a *dilettante*, seems to have been first fully formed in these despotisms of the fourteenth century.' In its pure state, politics for Burckhardt *is* despotism, and despotism is never more splendid than when it is employed with the ruthlessness and ingenuity of Ludovico il Moro, of whom Burckhardt writes that 'no one would probably have been more astonished ... to learn that for the choice of means as well as ends a human being is morally responsible' (p26). The exemplary politician is a figure concerned solely with instrumentality, with 'ends'; as in Machiavelli's political theory, the moral consideration of means is simply a category error, of no concern to the archetypal *principe* of the Italian Renaissance.

Politics at this stage, then, has no relation to morality, not even an antithetical one; politics is not moral, but neither is it immoral. The morally beautiful individual, as well as the morally repugnant one, is by definition someone (a man) without access to the political sphere – or at least, his moral stature is irrelevant to his political status. Burckhardt's exemplary Renaissance individual is Leon Battista Alberti, who lived from 1404-72, and was a great gymnast, musician, painter, poet, philosopher and inventor, as well as an architect who designed the churches of San Francesco at Rimini and S. Maria Novella at Florence. But the 'deepest spring' of his nature, writes Burckhardt, is

> the sympathetic intensity with which he entered into the whole life around him. At the sight of noble trees and waving corn-fields he shed tears; handsome and dignified old men he honoured as a 'delight of nature', and could never look at them enough. Perfectly formed animals won his goodwill as being specially favoured by nature; and more than once, when he was ill, the sight of a beautiful landscape cured him (pp86–7).

Alberti is a simple man by modern standards, uncomplicated by hidden agendas and ulterior motives, and capable of being shamelessly moved to joy or tears. Despite this embodiment of what later came to be thought of as feminine characteristics, Alberti is not effete; his openness is the mark of an integrity which entirely correlates with his masculinity: 'an iron will pervaded and sustained his whole personality', says Burckhardt; 'like all the great men of the Renaissance, he said, "men can do all things if they will".'

Burckhardt's chapter on politics in the same work is entitled 'The state as a work of art', the sense which he gives to this phrase being primarily that of an artefact, a thing constructed, 'the fruit of reflection and careful adaptation'. In the writings of the most representative Renaissance political theorist, Machiavelli, we see the state treated in an entirely objective fashion. Machiavelli, as is well known, was no 'Machiavellian', and Burckhardt's presentation of him emphasises this: 'He treats existing forces as living and active, takes a large and an accurate view of alternative possibilities, and seeks to mislead neither himself nor others. No man could be freer from vanity or ostentation' (pp57, 55). According to Burckhardt, it was completely possible for Machiavelli to forget himself in his analysis; the Florentine political system is laid bare in the *Discourses*, in all its intrigues and corruption, with an objectivity that Burckhardt describes as 'appalling in its sincerity'.

This objectivity is a characteristic not only of Machiavelli's political theory, but also of the practices of the Italian states themselves. 'The purely objective treatment of international affairs, as free from prejudice as from moral scruples, attained a perfection which sometimes is not without a certain beauty and grandeur of its own. But as a whole it gives us the impression of a bottomless abyss.' What is presented in Burckhardt's idiosyncratic vision is a 'subjective' private world and an 'objective' public world separated from each other and therefore intact. The contrast is obvious (and indeed Burckhardt makes it himself) with the culture of the nineteenth century, in which the relationship between private or artistic integrity and the world of commerce and industrial expansion is a frayed and mutually distressing one. 'Virtuous indignation at his expense', he writes, indicating Machiavelli, 'is thrown away upon us who have seen in what sense political morality is understood by the statesmen of our own century.'

The implication of Burckhardt's thesis is that the extremes of private morality and political expediency have not yet come into conflict in the Renaissance, but exist in complete isolation and freedom from each other. Ethics and politics are entirely separate affairs; a transformation takes place in the relation between the two only when politics begins to be seen as the realm of expediency, of debased necessity, as opposed to ideality. At this moment, explains Benedetto Croce writing much later, the concept of self-interest is 'unconsciously substituted' for the political concept of what is useful. Individuality comes into contention with the State; a dualism is set up in which politics is seen as a realm of 'sad necessity'.[2] By the nineteenth century, when Burckhardt was writing, it is not just the individual and the State which stand in opposition to each other, but, in the more abstract formulation of Georg Simmel, life itself which has come to be threatened by all forms of representation, both political and semiotic. Modern mental life is characterised by the anxiety arising out of a radical disjuncture between individuality and 'social forms' such as the law, religion, marriage, and social etiquette.[3] These anxieties are played out repeatedly in the nineteenth-century novel: Melville's *Billy Budd* is concerned with the tragically unbridgeable gulf between Billy's subjective innocence and his objective guilt, that is to say, his *internal* moral innocence, against his unambiguous *external* guilt according to martial law. Stendhal's *Le Rouge et le Noir* is the story of an apparently pious young man, Julien Sorel, who adopts a strategy of wilful, perpetual hypocrisy as a way of dealing with the disjunction between the external forms of religious belief and his own restless intensity. In Stendhal's nineteenth-century world, the pressures of objective culture are such that it is only Julien's hypocrisy which guarantees his subjective integrity, since (as he realises), 'Progress in the knowledge of dogma, in Church history, etc. counts in appearance only.'[4] The troubled narrator of Dostoevsky's *Notes From Underground* asserts the value of acting irrationally, even when to do so is against one's own interests, merely for the sake of proving one's subjective volition.

This narrative, as described by Burckhardt, is theoretically and methodologically flawed, dependent as it is on a simplified, linear model of history, according to which the past is apprehended unproblematically with the tools of the present. Both in his lectures on Greek civilisation and *The Civilization of the Renaissance in Italy*, Burckhardt looks back through the lens of his own time and finds evidence of a spontaneity and individuality which he deems to have been lost in his own period. As if in recognition of this retrospective lapse, which undermines the very innocence of Burckhardt's ideal of Renaissance individuality, twentieth-century philosophy has entirely replaced the model of the autonomous individual with that of the 'subject', an entity the very existence of which is *brought into being* by the objective world. As the work of Lacan and others have made clear, subjectivity begins with the child's perception of itself 'as other'– in a mirror, for example.[5] For Althusser we are hailed or 'interpellated' as subjects by the objective world, a process of ideological construction without which we would be unable to operate as subjective agents. There is no subjectivity 'outside the text', or outside the subject's inscription by the social 'forms' talked of by Simmel. Burckhardt's evocation of the Italian Renaissance as a golden era of individual freedom and integrity is, in the end, a regressive thesis, not only because of its tacit apologia for despotism, but also because of the ahistorical categories of individual freedom and moral beauty which it imposes upon the past. Burckhardt makes too much and at the same time not enough of a distinction between the emergent individual of the Italian Renaissance and the 'debased' culture of the nineteenth-century bourgeois subject. For all his precocious theorisation of the heterogeneity of individuality and the world of politics, he fails to acknowledge the complicity of the *concept* of individual self-identity – including his own theorisation of it – with the fact of its disappearance. The loss of individual integrity, indeed, is the dialectical precondition of the intellectual capacity to grasp what it means to be an individual; conversely, identity is an ideological, reified structure which, if it is politically enabling, is also – for that reason – an instrument of domination. Adorno and Horkheimer call this the 'dialectic of enlightenment'; it is the lesson of Milton's *Paradise Lost*, as it is of all the great cultural products of modernity, and what it prohibits is any account of history as a simple increase or a decrease in the quality of – or any attachment to a particular historical moment as the epitome of – individuality.

CULTURE: THE CONVERGENCE OF SUBJECT AND OBJECT

It might be pointed out that this critique of Burckhardt substantially fails to dent his thesis; in fact, it does more to confirm the general trend identified in *The Civilization of the Renaissance in Italy*, since it may be seen to enact its final stages. The replacement of *repressive* by *ideological* 'state apparatuses' described in Althusser's famous essay is a movement of the convergence of 'individuality' and 'politics' – or the encroachment of the latter onto the terrain of the former. The same may be said of the historical break which Foucault locates, within the discourses of judicial administration, between modes of punishment directed against the body and the appearance of 'discipline', an ideological mode of self-regulation in which individualisation is as implicated as rationality itself.[6] In the modern age, says Foucault, 'opposing the individual and his interests to [the state] is just as hazardous as opposing it with the community and its requirements.'[7]

Subjective and objective culture, in the guise of 'individuality' and 'politics', are set on a collision course as early as the fourteenth or fifteenth century; by the late twentieth century, they are thoroughly inseparable. Towards the later stages of this trajectory of mutual involvement, psychoanalysis, historical materialism, social theory itself, dialectics and semiotics, even feminism and deconstruction, appear as complementary theoretisations of the progressive indissociability of subject and object. In *The Human Condition*, Hannah Arendt mobilises the concept of *society* to account for this same convergence.[8] In the modern world, society emerges to replace the political as such; the respective autonomy of public life and private life is submerged beneath a new ethos of 'husbandry'. In society, politics becomes administration, an activity determined by the needs of subsistence, which from that moment on defines and delimits both spheres. The supreme power of Burckhardt's glorious despot is superseded by the ideological principle of conformism and its corollary, fashion. In this way, 'objective culture' comes into being, conclusively taking hold of and dominating individual subjectivity. For Arendt, this situation is most perfectly realised in totalitarianism, which erodes the possibility of creative solitude, and makes the homology between inner and outer life a structural principle.[9] Modern totalitarianism is the precise opposite of Burckhardt's Renaissance despotism, therefore, in which the significant divide is located not between the internal and external faculties of the individual, but outside the self, as an unbreachable social boundary between ruler and ruled.

Thus the concept of culture arises with the perception of, and as a solution to, the social inequality of the early modern period, and it presupposes the continuity of Burckhardt's narrative by default. Ideology appears at the dawn of 'culture', along with the possibility of self-disciplining subjects. The earliest theoreticians of culture made constitutional use of the parameters established in Burckhardt's valorising account of the Renaissance. For Georg Simmel, 'the whole history of culture is the working out of [the] contradiction' between life – described in terms of 'restless rhythms', 'infinite fruitfulness' and 'incessant divisions and reunifications' – and forms, meaning 'those self-sufficient crystallised structures' without which no representation, institutional or semiotic, would be possible.[10] Culture 'comes into being [...] by the coincidence of two elements: the subjective soul and the objective intellectual product.'[11] Elsewhere, Simmel articulates this opposition in the most elevated metaphysical terms: culture, he writes, 'moves constantly between death and resurrection – between resurrection and death.'[12] As a mediation of these two transcendental moments (death, objectivity, representation, form – exterior; resurrection, subjectivity, will, life – interior), culture is also unthinkable without them. Even in its claim to abolish, mediate or supersede them, culture differentiates the two extremes evoked in *The Civilization of the Renaissance in Italy*: on one hand, an external pole of 'nihilistic', contentless *politics* as *pure form* – instrumental rationality or 'purposeless purposiveness' as Adorno and Horkheimer conceive of it in *Dialectic of Enlightenment*;[13] on the other hand, an internal pole of *intimacy* and *individuality,* pure content without form, an authentic, apolitical mode of being that is *realisable* only in the sublimity of aesthetic experience, or the propensity to be 'shamelessly moved to tears'. In any form except an adulterated one, each of these poles is seen to be unattainable in the modern age.

In affirming the impossibility or redundancy of such experiences, however, culture establishes their conceptual (and historical) legitimacy. Thus, at one pole, Fredric Jameson writes of the 'disappearance' of an Archimedean point of 'genuinely aesthetic experience' from which the ideological truth of certain cultural products may be critically unmasked.[14] At the other pole, the editorship of the *Observer* newspaper – in an entirely different register – writes of the 'cold economic rationality of capitalism' and the need for its 'worst excesses' to be restrained, avowing earnestly that 'we are social as well as economic beings'.[15] Both Jameson's intervention and the *Observer* editorial are written in the name of 'culture', and from a position that presupposes the 'subjective' and 'objective' polarity. That the subjective sphere is inaccessible except through the fixity of the cultural forms – an insight that is central to Simmel's theory – is immaterial. The emergence of 'culture' is a moment of reification in which 'individuality', 'culture' and 'politics' are respectively rationalised into existence.

For Adorno, the poles of subject and object not only converge in that moment of 'rationalisation', but have changed places, a fact exemplified for him in the pejorative sense given to the word 'subjective', as in the 'scientific' or 'rationalistic' reproach that a particular statement or opinion is 'too subjective'. In *Minima Moralia* he writes:

> Objective [has come to mean] the non-controversial aspect of things, their unquestioned impression, the façade made up of classified data, that is the subjective; and they call subjective anything which breaches that façade, engages the specific experience of a matter, casts off all ready-made judgements and substitutes relatedness to the object for the majority consensus of those who do not even look at it, let alone think about it – that is, the objective.[16]

The absent word here, but one which is implied at every moment in the above sentence, in all its Hegelian complexity, is 'spirit' *(Geist)*. Where *Geist* for Hegel denotes the objective process of historical progression, infusing that process with the consciousness of human intelligence as a creative and epoch-making force, in the modern era 'spirit' has been rendered radically subjective and consigned to the interior, private or domestic sphere. With the term 'objective', the world is rendered factual, non-contentious, immediate, and alienated from the human consciousness that creates it. The term 'culture' *preserves* these inverted senses of subjective and objective by proposing itself as an intermediary between them. Culture as a privileged sphere severs the subjective and objective worlds, where dialectics – to which 'culture' is opposed and with which it is incompatible – would conjoin them.

In the academic sphere, this narrative has a disciplinary form, in the emergence since the 1960s of the field of cultural studies. The continuing power of the polarity of subjective and objective culture is implied in the very evolution of this field *as distinct from* the study of art or literature on one hand – disciplines which, in their purest, most 'traditional' form, are founded on universalist assumptions – and political science and economics on the other – which, in their most 'empirical' forms at least, purport to examine the human world at its most objective. Insofar as practitioners of the newer discipline avoid paying attention either to the subjective 'experience' of reading Dickens, on one hand, or to the 'economistic' elaboration of contemporary cultural objects in terms of capitalist relations of production and commodification on the other, their work enacts a sense of the obsolescence of those older fields of critical activity. The disciplinisation of cultural studies represents both a mediation between and a respective moderation of the Leavisite 'Great Tradition' (which presupposed the autonomy and subjective 'authenticity' of art) and the reductive, purely materialist analysis of culture, exemplified in the 'vulgar Marxism' evoked in the founding texts of the cultural studies tendency (or earlier, in Engels's 1890 letter to Joseph Bloch – an important text for cultural studies theorists).[17]

As presented in Hegel's *Phenomenology of Spirit*, 'culture' is an inherently ambiguous, or rather dialectical concept, which is threatened with the loss of this ambiguity by its institutionalisation – not only as a discipline within the Academy but simply by means of its stabilisation as a concept. The meaning of the German word *Bildung* is much closer to that signified in English by 'cultivation', 'formation' or 'education' (as verbal actions rather than the ossified, institutional products of such actions).[18] Kojève, for example, translates *Bildung* simply as *le travail*. 'On the one hand,' he writes, elucidating Hegel's analysis, work *(Bildung)* 'forms, transforms the World, humanises it by making it more adapted to Man; on the other, it transforms, forms, educates man, it humanises him by bringing him into greater conformity with the *idea* that he has of himself, an idea that – in the beginning – is only an *abstract* idea, an *ideal*.'[19] For Hegel, the 'externalisation' or 'alienation' of the individual implied in the process of culture is *at once* the realisation of his or her 'original nature', and the development of culture itself as the 'universal objective essence'.[20] Culture is not, in other words, a *moderation* of the two extremes of individuality and universality, a category midway between them, but the simultaneous embodiment of those extremes; culture is neither, and both, the subjective expression and objective materialisation of spirit. Culture as spirit represents the realisation of the individual, its bringing to fruition, as simultaneously the *end* (in both senses) of the individual and the vehicle of the historical evolution of the collectivity. Culture is both a 'materialist repudiation of idealism and its ideologies', as Jameson says, and a potential point of resistance towards the mobilisation of such relentless materialism in the service of 'objective social processes' – that is to say, the forces of capitalism.[21]

The most successful theorisations of culture have been those – generally prior (or peripheral) to the emergence of cultural studies in the academy – that have affirmed the structural ambiguity of culture presupposed in the concept of *Geist*. Nothing exemplifies this more than the work of Raymond Williams, whose precise, genealogical attention to the concept of culture anatomises this ambiguity at the same time as it enacts a refusal of the concept as a homogeneous social form. Adorno's *Minima Moralia* is a text more explicitly saturated by Hegel's influence, although Adorno uses the term *Kultur* in preference to the Hegelian *Bildung* – perhaps, as Jameson suggests, because of the bourgeois connotations of the latter, more traditional term.[22] In a well-known paragraph of *Minima Moralia* which I shall return to through the rest of this chapter, Adorno vigorously reproaches materialistic interpretations of culture, which analyse culture simply as ideology, for bringing about the 'barbarism' which culture, *in all its ideological delusion*, may yet be trying to escape.[23] To reduce culture rigorously to material interests, proposes Adorno in his title to the fragment, is to throw out the 'baby with the bath-water'. On the other hand, to forget that culture is a relatively modern invention which cannot be separated from instrumental rationality, from the ideological operations of power, from the demands upon an expanding, modernising society to produce self-disciplining individuals, is to revert to a 'bourgeois' conception of autonomous subjecthood, which understands art as nothing other than the subjective, creative expression of free individuals.

Is it inconceivable to suggest that this idea has more or less entirely lost its currency, that it is no longer believed in by anybody? Certainly it is not part of any dominant cultural ethos pertaining in turn-of-the-millennium Britain – rather the contrary. One need only go through the chapter headings in the most coherent cultural policy manifesto yet published by New Labour, Chris Smith's *Creative Britain*, to see that the language (although not of course the analysis) of Frankfurt School Marxism is now more hegemonic than that of Matthew Arnold or the Earl of Shaftesbury: 'The creative industries in Britain'; 'Culture, business and society'; 'Culture, creativity and social regeneration'.[24] Such a situation has serious implications for the materialist critique of culture;

capitalism here demonstrates by how far it will always outpace the materialism of the most vulgar Marxist.

To his paragraph in *Minima Moralia* Adorno adds the following, paradoxical comment: 'To identify culture solely with lies is more fateful than ever, now that the former is really becoming totally absorbed by the latter, and eagerly invites such identification in order to compromise every opposing thought.'[25] To apply such a sentence, from a quite different context, to the contemporary political world would demand substantial historical licence, particularly since debates within Marxist aesthetics do not carry the heady sense of urgency they once did; yet, with the increasing recourse on the part of New Labour to arguments that were once regarded as belonging properly to the private sphere, Adorno's insight seems suddenly pertinent. New Labour is taking political discourse ever further into the 'cultural' hinterland between pure individuality and pure politics. Its rhetoric unstintingly mines the subjective sphere – in the unprecedented, highly effective attention to 'cultural' matters; in the talk of 'humanitarian intervention' in international affairs; in the emphasis upon 'sincerity' and 'ordinariness' in media presentations of the Prime Minister; in the unashamed mobilisation of moral categories in the fight against 'sleaze' and corruption; and in the reiterated exhortations to the public and press to participate in the 'spirit' of the New Labour project. Yet, adjoined to the sometimes hectoring tone is a blissful magnanimity, an explicit commitment to a 'nurturing' rather than dictatorial approach to 'creativity' – meaning a hands-off approach to the *content* of cultural artefacts – and an emphasis upon the incompatibility of 'excellence' in the arts with their traditional 'elitism'.

NEW LABOUR AND CULTURAL POLITICS

That the relation between culture and politics requires analysis in the specific context of what we might call 'post-Thatcherism' is indicated above all by the high visibility of 'culture' in contemporary political life. In an assessment of the Royal Academy *Sensation* exhibition in *The Times Literary Supplement*, the former Conservative MP George Walden recalls what he represents as an extraordinary, unprecedented statement by Virginia Bottomley, the outgoing Tory Minister for National Heritage, in which she acclaims contemporary British art as 'the most exciting and innovatory in the world'.[26] This, observes Walden, was the first official recognition of avant-garde art ever given by a government minister; it is a sentiment that has since been echoed and refined by the New Labour government, and infused with a tone of liberal benevolence that declines to take offence at any recalcitrant gestures by the fêted artists and popstars themselves. The apparent expansiveness of this new attitude of officialdom notwithstanding, Walden is not the only commentator to have evoked the Soviet era of socialist realism in describing the Labour government's approach to the arts.[27] Such a comparison, however, misses the fact that the relationship between politics and culture has become one defined by the absence of any cultural or ideological vision *distinct from* the economistic one; this homology between the 'cultural' and the 'political', or between subjective and objective, is in fact its dominant characteristic.

Creative Britain, a collection of speeches by the Secretary of State for Culture, Media and Sport, is the most explicit statement yet on the importance of culture for New Labour; there, culture is affirmed repeatedly as having the potential 'to uplift people's hearts and at the same time to draw in a major economic return to the country'.[28] Culture, that is to say, gratifies people's need for subjective affirmation at the same time as, *and inasmuch as*, it gratifies the economic order of things. Needless to say, either of these without the other would be unacceptable. In a speech in Los Angeles on the British film industry, Smith observes:

> There has been an arcane debate among some of our European colleagues in years gone by about the theology of what film is. Is it cultural product, to be protected and defended, or is it economic opportunity, to face the brisk winds of commercial activity around the world? The answer, of course, is that it is both; and if you make good movies you will have successful movies.[29]

It is difficult to imagine a successful 'economic opportunity' that would be disparaged at the aesthetic or 'cultural' level by the Labour government's ethos of cultural entrepreneurship, however. To read Smith's book is to find oneself recoiling from the word 'culture' in all its possible usages. *Creative Britain* constructs an ideal consumer in whom 'subjective' and 'objective' success – individual integrity and economic profitability – are in *inevitable* harmony. Appreciation of 'cultural' products is impossible, therefore, without affirmation of the particular dispensation that evaluates the good entirely according to success in the market. The opposition between aesthetics and economics is not reconciled by Smith's cultural philosophy; rather, the 'cultural product' is recreated as an object that *by definition* affirms the values of the capitalist world. If its apparent straddling of the aesthetic and the economic gives to the ethos an aura of reasonable benevolence, this is as illusory as the idea that the Third Way is a tempered, 'managed' or 'socially conscious' form of capitalism. In truth, there has *never* been any such thing as 'unmanaged' capitalism – just as there has never been any such thing as an economic opportunity deprived entirely of aesthetic concerns (besides currency speculation perhaps, or 'futures' trading). The Third Way represents the extension of the values of capitalism to the sphere of subjectivity and the commonality, just as 'culture' – specifically, the cultural philosophy outlined in *Creative Britain* – represents the assimilation of everything that *by definition* cannot be accounted for economistically, to the economic.

Power no longer 'excludes' and 'represses', says Foucault; thus its effects should cease to be described in such negative terms. Rather, *power produces reality* – a process which includes the production of the individual as such.[30] This is a very Hegelian insight. In the case of New Labour, produced reality is a culture saturated by materiality, and purveyed to a generation of *self-styled* consumers. This is 'Utopia as a shop window', as one commentator has written, in relation to the first significant 'cultural-political' project of the incoming Labour government, the *powerhouse::uk* exhibition on Horse Guards Parade.[31] The politics of New Labour are precisely, *cultural* politics as never before. If the archetypal form of cultural politics is fascism – on the basis that it proposes a homology between inner and outer life – its present form is a more rarefied, consequently less immediately offensive version in which, nevertheless, this structural principle is fully and successfully realised.

CONCLUSION: TOWARDS POLITICAL CULTURE

In another prescient statement on the relation between politics and culture, in 1955 Adorno wrote the following:

> Culture has become ideological not only as the quintessence of subjectively devised manifestations of the objective mind, but even more as the sphere of private life. The illusory importance and autonomy of private life conceals the fact that private life drags on only as an appendage of the social process. Life transforms itself into the ideology of reification – a death mask.[32]

That contemporary politics, even in its own terms, is *cultural* politics means that it has successfully accommodated the threat to the order of things that is posed by the incongruity between subject and object in modernity, as represented in the nineteenth-century novel. Yet the tension between individual and society, a prevailing theme of bourgeois realist and early modernist fiction, is a register not of the *divergence* of subject and object but their *convergence*. The implications of this, as Adorno points out, are that private life is increasingly a creation of the ideological sphere, 'an appendage of the social process' – as is true of its conceptual opposite, instrumental rationality, in the phantasmic form of 'unregulated global capitalism', or those purely imaginary aesthetically-unmediated 'economic opportunities'. Subjective and objective culture are produced by the category of 'cultural politics' as its unacceptable alternatives. The idea that culture has a 'tempering' influence upon the Hobbesian operation of capitalism on one side, and apolitical aestheticism on the other, is an effect of this *spatial* conceptualisation of the relation between individuality and politics.

In carving out a political role for culture and what he calls 'creative activity', Chris Smith acknowledges the convergence of the cultural and the political described by Adorno, a convergence which, in the form of the progressive entanglement of individuality and politics, has been a prognosis of cultural theory ever since Burckhardt. In an interview before the 1997 election, Smith spoke of his vision of culture as *primarily* a means of fostering a sense of collective identity. Culture, he emphasises, is not just 'high art' – the music that is produced or the literature that is written – but 'part of everyday life'. Smith's examples of this 'progressive', democratising approach to culture include an imminent project 'to transform a number of carriages on the Gateshead metro into travelling art galleries', and a proposal to introduce jazz bands into airports, 'so people can go and listen to music for a while … And let's not stop at airports. Why don't we do it in bus stations, shopping malls and so on? Let's make our culture part of people's everyday experience, that's what I mean about getting a sense of identity as a community.'[33]

Despite the resemblance of these sentiments to Lenin's idea of proletarian culture,[34] it is obvious that such a vision, within a capitalist framework, is utterly opposed to Marxist revolutionary politics; its general acceptance, even acceptability, further denotes an understandable and no doubt justified belief that the more radical objective of social revolution is an unrealistic, unattainable goal. For the French philosopher Alain Badiou, however, the 'cultural' in this sense is categorically distinct not just from revolutionary politics but from politics *per se*. The political aspires to the transformation of the totality of the social order, not – as is the case with cultural categories – merely to the recognition of *particular* claims 'in a determinate relation of forces'.[35] Badiou's philosophy, which disavows all ideas of 'cultural politics' (or in any case, refuses their claims to the category of the political), represents one possible response to the situation diagnosed by Adorno and ratified by Chris Smith: that of *denying the validity* of this move into the cultural hinterland. Badiou has called for an end to the project of 'cultural politics', described as a form of attachment to the *mediate* as such, to 'culture' as a realm *between* virtual and actual, between subject and object – between (for example) pure aesthetic decadence and pure political ruthlessness.[36] For Badiou, the cultural 'identities' and 'differences' traded in by all forms of cultural politics are part of the debased currency of the logic of capital.[37] The time has come, he implies, when cultural politics predicated upon identity has lost its 'universalisable' character. If such cultural movements are 'commendable', even at certain periods and places 'necessary',[38] cultural politics in the sense in which we see it operating today is utterly complicit with 'worldly' interests; there is nothing whatever of truth in it. It should come as no surprise to learn that the book in which Badiou most recently makes these Damascene pronouncements is about St Paul.[39]

Badiou is right to identify 'cultural politics' as exemplary of the logic of capital; his refusal of the category of culture is a refusal of the hegemony, the 'lived system of meanings and values' which for Raymond Williams constitutes the 'sense of reality for most people in the society'.[40] It is also a refusal of the relativisation of the world which Badiou ascribes to the 'linguistic turn' of postmodernism, a moment in which the world is rendered subject to the 'total jurisdiction' of language.[41] This is not the place for a detailed discussion of Badiou's thought; yet the implication of the refusal of culture and of the postmodern 'linguistic turn', on the basis of their complicity with the 'logic of capital', is a fetishisation of immediacy, the commitment to a 'Truth-Event' which, in Slavoj Žižek's words, 'shatters the predominant symbolic texture' by an intrusion of the 'traumatic Real'.[42] Such a refusal of culture would seem to replicate the spatial logic of 'cultural politics' itself – a logic which counterposes individuality to the 'purposeless purposiveness' of instrumental rationality, and which is therefore at least as 'worldly' in origin as the capitalist logic which Badiou wants to displace.

Culture itself gives every impression of having become what Lukács, as early as 1922, attributes to the culture of bourgeois society: 'the horizon that delimits the totality that has been and can be created'.[43] Yet narratives which oppose mediation to immediacy, which fetishise the immediate and authentic, replicate the recursive logic of capitalism itself, for which culture is a 'sad necessity' rather than, as it is for Hegel, the vehicle of the realisation of human individuality in the direction of universality. Any theory of culture *as such*, which Badiou's philosophy is by default, must fail to delimit this Hegelian notion of culture *(Bildung)* from the idea of culture as a merely intermediate sphere; the latter concept is not implicated in the totality, but constructed solely by differentiation from the individual and the political. Culture *as such* labours in ignorance of the fact that the 'cultural aspect' of what exists emerges only as a negative relation to the universal.

Badiou, 'openly anti-Hegelian' as Žižek notes,[44] refuses the dialectical notion that the meaningful historical event is embedded both in the history that precedes it and the history that succeeds it; that the Truth-Event can be turned into a lie by historical events, for example, or – conversely – that a historically-specific lie can also tell the truth. The Truth-Event, says Žižek paraphrasing Badiou, 'is simply a radically new beginning; it designates the violent, traumatic and contingent intrusion of another dimension not "mediated" by the domain of terrestrial finitude and corruption.'[45] In the name of the Truth-Event, Badiou is thoroughly opposed to 'culture' in all its forms; he would presumably have no sympathy for Adorno's insistence upon the always potential truth-telling possibilities of culture, even in its most severely 'ideological' manifestations. 'In face of the lie of the commodity world,' says Adorno elucidating this complex, 'even the lie that denounces it becomes a corrective. That culture so far has failed is no justification for furthering its failure, by strewing the store of good flour on the spilt beer like the girl in the fairy-tale.'[46] Yet, so long as one maintains an understanding of 'culture' which exceeds its presentation by modern-day cultural politics – a dialectical understanding which, like Adorno's, is prior to and unbounded by the disciplinary limits of cultural studies – even Badiou's unorthodox Marxism, characterised by an explicit rejection of the economic, and which aligns political matters with those 'of thought, of statements, of practices',[47] might be represented as a form of 'cultural politics'.

The qualified detraction from Badiou is not to say that the contemporary mobilisation of the category of the 'cultural' is not an utterly morbid one. In modern-day 'cultural politics', we see the extension of this deadening process, described by Adorno with characteristic virtuosity: 'Even what differs from technology in man is now being incorporated into it as a kind of lubrication.'[48] By means of 'culture', capitalism demands the interiorities of men and women at the very point at which their social objectification is most pronounced. In a footnote to his discussion of Badiou's book on St Paul, Slavoj Žižek indicts 'the notion and practice of "cultural studies"' for its unambiguous complicity with this state of affairs: 'the basic feature of cultural studies', he writes, 'is that they are no longer able or ready to confront religious, scientific or philosophical works in terms of their inherent Truth, but reduce them to a product of historical circumstances, to an object of anthropologico-psychoanalytic interpretation.'[49] Cultural studies, in other words, is a discipline which is particularly accommodating to the structures of contemporary capitalism, simply on account of its absolute and exclusive preoccupation with *what exists*. Modern-day cultural politics is the *political wing* of this cultural-institutional situation. Shakespeare's Troilus, observing Cressida's infidelity, declares, 'But if I tell how these two did co-act,/ Shall I not lie in publishing a truth?'[50] Intellectual and artistic work that faithfully reflects the world as it is likewise colludes in a lie. The 'cultural' sphere hereby shrinks from the activity and essence of what is required in any political engagement with the world.

What cultural political practice could and should represent, rather, is a dialectical refusal to privilege the cultural sphere; such a refusal implies the activation of a 'political culture' in which the word *culture* retains all the ambiguity of its Hegelian meaning. The constitution of a political culture must begin with a suspicion towards every mobilisation of the cultural *as such*, in tandem with an acknowledgement of the fact that 'culture', a modern invention, is more ideologically important than ever – not only to the institutional political domain, but to all political activity. Political culture retains a methodological, even philosophical faith in the non-institutionalisability of 'culture' – either as an expression of 'identities' or as a tool of instrumental (meaning ideological) rationality. Political culture, a dispensation at odds with modern-day cultural politics, valorises cultural production that refuses to accept the domination of the world of exchange value – a world which, in its very freedom and honesty, as Adorno recognised, is itself a lie. Culture, in a sense held onto by thinkers as different as Hegel and Raymond Williams, preserves in the possibility of lying the very possibility of truth.

NOTES

1. Jacob Burckhardt, *The Civilization of the Renaissance in Italy*, trans. S.G.C. Middlemore, Phaidon, London and Oxford 1945, p81. Henceforth, page numbers appear in brackets in the text.

2. Benedetto Croce, *Politics and Morals*, trans. Salvatore J. Castiglione, George Allen & Unwin, London 1946, pp7-8.

3. See, for example, Georg Simmel, 'The conflict in modern culture', in *On Individuality and Social Forms*, ed. Donald N. Levine, University of Chicago Press, London and Chicago 1971.

4. Stendhal, *Scarlet and Black: A Chronicle of the Nineteenth Century*, trans. Margaret R.B. Shaw, Penguin, Harmondsworth 1953, p194.

5. See, for example, Jacques Lacan, 'The mirror stage as formative of the function of the "I"', in *Écrits: A Selection*, trans. Alan Sheridan, Routledge, London 1989.

6. Louis Althusser, 'Ideology and ideological state apparatuses (Notes towards an investigation)', in *Lenin and Philosophy and Other Essays*, New Left Books, London 1971; Michel Foucault, *Discipline and Punish: The Birth of the Prison*, trans. Alan Sheridan, Penguin, Harmondsworth 1979.

7. Michel Foucault, 'Politics and reason', in *Politics, Philosophy, Culture: Interviews and Other Writings 1977-1984*, Lawrence D. Kritzman (ed.), Routledge, New York and London 1988, p84.

8. Hannah Arendt, *The Human Condition*, University of Chicago Press, London and Chicago 1958, p40.

9. See Hannah Arendt, 'Ideology and terror: a novel form of government' in *The Origins of Totalitarianism*, Harcourt Brace Jovanovich, New York and London 1973, pp460-79.

10. Georg Simmel, 'The conflict in modern culture', *op. cit.*, pp375-6; 'The concept and tragedy of culture', trans. Mark Ritter and David Frisby, in *Simmel on Culture*, David Frisby and Mike Featherstone (eds), Sage, London 1997, p58.

11. 'The concept and tragedy of culture', *op. cit.*, p58.

12. 'The conflict in modern culture', *op. cit.*, p376.

13. Theodor W. Adorno and Max Horkheimer, *Dialectic of Enlightenment*, trans. John Cumming, Verso, London 1979, p89.

14. Fredric Jameson, *Late Marxism: Adorno, or, The Persistence of the Dialectic*, Verso, London 1990, p142.

15. 'The great game begins' (editorial comment), *Observer*, 2 January 2000.

16. Theodor W. Adorno, *Minima Moralia: Reflections from Damaged Life*, trans. E.F.N. Jephcott, Verso, London 1978, pp69-70.

17. See Frederick Engels, 'Letter to Joseph Bloch', in John Storey (ed.), *Cultural Theory and Popular Culture: A Reader*, Harvester Wheatsheaf, Hemel Hempstead 1994, pp199-201. Engels's letter is quoted by Moyra Haslett in her *Marxist Literary and Cultural Theories*, Macmillan, London 2000, p21. Haslett also observes, pertinently, that the degree to which cultural studies 'over-compensates' for the 'vulgar Marxist' condescension

towards the pleasures of consumption 'is beginning to seem absurd' (p148). Her target here is primarily academic analysts of popular culture who celebrate the 'spontaneous' and 'natural' pleasures of television game show audiences, or those of the (mostly female, teenage) fans of performers such as Madonna.

18. Raymond Williams points out several times in his writings that, until the eighteenth century, 'culture' was likewise a noun denoting a process: 'the culture *of* something – crops, animals, minds.' See *Marxism and Literature*, Oxford University Press, Oxford 1977, pp11-20; see also the entry 'Culture' in *Keywords: A vocabulary of culture and society*, Fontana, London 1983.

19. Alexandre Kojève, *Introduction to the Reading of Hegel: Lectures on the Phenomenology of Spirit*, trans. James H. Nichols, Jr., Cornell University Press, Ithaca and London 1980, pp52-3.

20. G. W. F. Hegel, *Phenomenology of Spirit*, trans. A.V. Miller, Oxford University Press, Oxford 1977, §§489-90, pp298-9.

21. Fredric Jameson, *Late Marxism, op. cit*, p124.

22. *Ibid.*, p143-4.

23. Theodor W. Adorno, *Minima Moralia, op. cit.*, §22, pp43-4.

24. Chris Smith, *Creative Britain*, Faber and Faber, London 1998.

25. Theodor W. Adorno, *Minima Moralia, op. cit.*, §22, p44.

26. George Walden, 'Leave your weapons at the door: Democracy, state modernism and the official embrace of the arts', *The Times Literary Supplement* No. 4930 (26 September 1997).

27. See, for example, Andrew Brighton's playful essay 'Towards a command culture: New Labour's cultural policy and Soviet Socialist Realism', *Critical Quarterly* Vol. 41, No. 3 (Autumn 1999).

28. Chris Smith, *Creative Britain, op. cit.*, p6.

29. *Ibid.*, p86.

30. Michel Foucault, *Discipline and Punish*, op. cit., p194.

31. Jonathan Romney, 'Cabbages and cool things', *Guardian* 17 April 1998.

32. Theodor W. Adorno, 'Cultural criticism and society', in *Prisms*, trans. Samuel and Shierry Weber, MIT Press, Cambridge, Mass. 1981, p30.

33. Brian Cox and Colin MacCabe, Interview with Chris Smith MP, *Critical Quarterly* Vol. 38, No. 1 (Spring 1996), p100.

34. 'Art must have its deepest roots in the very depth of the broad masses of the workers', wrote Lenin. 'It must be understood by those masses and loved by them. It must unite the feelings, thoughts and will of the masses and raise them up.' Quoted by Andrew Brighton, 'Towards a command culture', *op. cit.*, p25.

35. Alain Badiou and Peter Hallward, 'Politics and philosophy: an interview

with Alain Badiou', *Angelaki* Vol. 3, No. 3, p119.

36. See Peter Hallward's very lucid introduction to Badiou's thought, 'Generic sovereignty: the philosophy of Alain Badiou', in *Angelaki* Vol. 3, No. 3, esp. pp101a-b.

37. See Alain Badiou and Peter Hallward, 'Politics and philosophy', *op. cit.*, p120b.

38. *Ibid.*, p119a.

39. See Alain Badiou, *Saint Paul: La fondation de l'universalisme*, Presses Universitaires de France, Paris 1997, pp12-13.

40. Raymond Williams, *Marxism and Literature*, Oxford University Press, Oxford 1977, p110.

41. Quoted by Peter Hallward, in 'Generic sovereignty: the philosophy of Alain Badiou', *op. cit.*, p101b.

42. Slavoj Žižek, 'The politics of truth, or, Alain Badiou as a reader of St Paul', *The Ticklish Subject: The Absent Centre of Political Ontology*, Verso, London 1999, p142.

43. Georg Lukács, *History and Class Consciousness: Studies in Marxist Dialectics*, trans. Rodney Livingstone, Merlin, London 1971, p120.

44. Slavoj Žižek, 'The politics of truth, or, Alain Badiou as a reader of St Paul', *op. cit.*, p146.

45. *Ibid.*

46. Theodor W. Adorno, *Minima Moralia, op. cit.*, §22, p44.

47. See Alain Badiou and Peter Hallward, 'Politics and philosophy: an interview with Alain Badiou', *op. cit.*, p117b. Badiou's rejection of an economistic grounding of politics is on the basis that 'every proposition that directly concerns the economy can be assimilated by capital. This is so by definition, since capital is indifferent to the qualitative configuration of things.'

48. Theodor W. Adorno, *Minima Moralia, op. cit.*, p230.

49. Slavoj Žižek, 'The politics of truth, or, Alain Badiou as a reader of St Paul', *op. cit.*, p167 n5.

50. William Shakespeare, *Troilus and Cressida* V. 2.

In defence of discourse analysis

JEREMY GILBERT

WHAT'S IN A NAME?

Terminologies are funny things. Anyone who has followed the twists and turns of the generic classifications of 'dance' musics during the 1990s will have a sense of this. Signifiers such as 'techno', 'trance' and 'garage' have floated like Mary Poppins on a windy day, each of them designating several very different types of music for different people at different times. The 'techno' of Detroit 1988 and the 'techno' of Frankfurt 1993 bore only the most tangential relationship to each other, while basically the same type of music has been referred to as, variously, 'progressive house', 'trance', 'epic house' 'Euro', and 'trance' again by UK commentators and compilation-marketers in the space of eight years.

In academic circles, a similar process can be seen at work if one considers the fate of the term 'discourse analysis'. For some, this term still designates a specific branch of socio-linguistics concerned with the precise, grammatically-informed analysis of the language of social actors in given situations. The most important contemporary exponent of this method is probably Norman Fairclough, whose erudite and prolific work demonstrates a keen and welcome awareness of the many ways in which other writers understand the phrase 'discourse analysis.[1] Foremost amongst these others are those writers connected with the Ideology and Discourse Analysis group at the University of Essex, for whom the latter term has a quite different inflection. For them, 'discourse analysis' is a method for the study of politics specifically informed by the methodologies and ideas of Foucault, Derrida, Lacan, Gramsci, and Laclau. In other words, they practice under the name 'discourse analysis' a particular version of what most of the Anglophone world has recognised for some time as 'post-structuralism'.[2]

What will most strike the reader is the fact that this roll call of key-theorists is much the one which most people would reproduce if asked to name the most important influences on cultural studies since the 1970s. Indeed, ask someone working in a department of Media Studies what they would call an approach to the study of media culture, or anything else, which drew on the work of Foucault, Derrida, Lacan, Gramsci, etc., and they would almost certainly tell you that you were describing a 'cultural studies' approach. On the other hand, if we were to ask somebody working in a literature department the same question, we would probably be told that we were describing the basic intellectual co-ordinates of 'cultural materialism'. (To make matters still more confusing, it is worth reflecting that despite the frequency with which the names of these theorists have been associated with 'Cultural Studies', it is relatively difficult to locate more than a few actual studies of contemporary culture ever to have made serious use of them.) The Essex theorists, whose work is on the whole profound and incisive, do make the occasional reference to key thinkers in cultural studies, such as Stuart Hall, but often seem to write as if entirely oblivious to the existence of the discipline itself, and they certainly never refer to the existence of 'cultural materialism'.

I would suggest that the most accurate way of describing what is happening is as follows. A particular methodology for the study of what is now referred to, very broadly, as 'discourse', has been being developed from a number of sources since the 1970s. When applied to instances of contemporary culture, but not 'Politics', this methodology is understood as exemplary of 'Cultural Studies'. This is not necessarily an accurate description, as such work is not actually typical of most of what has been published under that name. It is however typical of the work on culture and politics of Stuart Hall, who is widely regarded as the central institutional and intellectual figure of cultural studies since the death of Raymond Williams, but whose ideas, while remaining constant points of *reference* within published 'Cultural Studies' work, are not actually explicitly engaged with or drawn on as often as might be expected.[3] This methodology has also been developed with some success under the rubric of 'cultural materialism' by literary scholars since the early 1980s. Again, however, this much-discussed term[4] seems upon examination largely to refer to the work of Alan Sinfield[5] and his closest associates, rather than to a really coherent movement within literary studies. This methodology has recently been developed by analysts of political discourse working under the direct tutelage of Ernesto Laclau, who are consequently more explicitly engaged with the direct theoretical sources of the methodology; but they are cut off from the intellectual tradition to which the work of Raymond Williams is central, and which underpins the work of both Hall and Sinfield. For them, the methodology is named simply 'discourse analysis', although Jacob Torfing's recent introduction to this field prefers the more precise term 'discourse-theoretical analytics'.[6]

For convenience, I will name this methodology 'post-Marxist discourse analysis.' I take its main co-ordinates to be the structuralist and 'post-structuralist' semiotics of Saussure and Barthes, Foucauldian genealogy, Derridean deconstruction, the post-Gramscian theory of hegemony developed by Laclau and Mouffe but arguably prefigured in some senses in the work of Raymond Williams, and Lacanian and post-Lacanian psychoanalytic theory. It is characterised by an attention to the socially-constitutive nature of discourse, and consequently tends to deploy various forms of textual analysis as its core methodology.

I want to do several things with this observation. Firstly, to point to the fact that 'post-Marxist discourse analysis' exists as an implicitly unified field of practice, even if it does not always recognise itself as such, and that it has already demonstrated its worth as a general methodology for the study of 'culture' and 'politics' (even, arguably, economics, as in the recent work of Angela McRobbie, referred to below) – with these being conceived of as part of a more-or-less continuous field rather than as separate entities. This should not be a radical insight for many people, but it might encourage people working in cultural studies to pay more attention to the ways in which 'discourse analysis' is being used by writers working in the field of 'political studies', and it might encourage those 'political' writers to pay rather more than lip-service to the observation that the implication of their own ways of working is that the sphere of 'culture' is a key site of political engagement (and not only insofar as it is traversed and circumscribed by 'social movements'). Secondly, I am going to attempt here to demonstrate the continued importance of discourse analysis for overcoming certain problems which still exist in both political and cultural studies. Finally (yet firstly) I want to note the irony that just when it is gaining recognition as a powerful methodology within political studies, this particular constellation of theories and methods so long associated with cultural studies is itself under attack within its own 'home' discipline.

POLICY OR POLITICS?

Tony Bennett, Stuart Hall's successor as Professor of Sociology at the Open University, has recently consolidated several years of speculative writing on the possibilities and actualities of a turn to 'Policy' in cultural studies with his book *Culture: a Reformer's Science*. In this strangely uneven work, Bennett takes a militantly reformist hatchet to what he perceives as the revolutionary pretensions of most hitherto existing cultural studies. Pursuing what can be called a 'right Foucauldian' agenda, Bennett argues that a recognition of the validity of Foucault's concern with the micro-mechanisms of power implies a turn away from the grand ambitions of the Gramscian moment, informed as they were by an implicit commitment to communism, towards a more realistic, localised, explicitly reformist agenda.

Citing himself in the book's opening chapter, Bennett defends his earlier assertion that 'Cultural Studies might usefully envisage its role as consisting in the training of cultural technicians : that is, of intellectual workers less committed to cultural critique as an instrument for changing consciousness than to modifying the functioning of culture by means of technical adjustments to its governmental deployment'.[7] He dismisses as no longer – if ever– relevant the hope of intellectuals such as Stuart Hall and Fredric Jameson that cultural studies might be allied to emancipatory social movements and political projects wider than those of academy-bound intellectuals.[8]

There are a number of issues at stake in this argument, and a number of reasons why I believe Bennett to be mistaken. Firstly, he posits an illegitimate polarity between his extreme pragmatism and its perceived others. Bennett portrays his position as the only alternative to one which sees cultural studies as producing 'a stratum of intellectuals who will prepare the way for an emerging historical movement to which that stratum will then attach itself in a moment of organicity'.[9] It is unclear exactly who has ever espoused such a ludicrously romantic conception of cultural studies' political role. Bennett implies that this is the view of Jameson and Hall, but how Hall's complex neo-Gramscianism can be interpreted in such vanguardist terms is a mystery. Bennett supports his characterisation thus:

> [Cultural studies] was a project shaped by the will or hope that intellectual work might be aligned with an emerging historical movement and was therefore predicated, as Hall put it, on 'living with the possibility that there could be, some time, a movement that would be larger than the movement of petit-bourgeois intellectuals.'[10]

It seems to me that Bennett's caricature of Gramscian cultural studies rather misses the point of this remark of Hall's. It comes from a passage in which Hall is reflecting on precisely the issue raised by Bennett – the fact that cultural studies alone obviously cannot constitute a transformatory political project.[11] The point of Hall's remarks here is not to imagine cultural studies as the intellectual vanguard of some future movement, but simply to recognise that if a practice of cultural studies is to be thought of as having any politics worth the name, it must be a politics which cannot ultimately be reduced to its own institutional and intellectual project. To be committed to the goals of social and political movements which exist outside as well as inside the academy is not necessarily to imagine oneself as *leading* some grand coalition of such movements, just as Gramsci's 'organic intellectual' is not necessarily the vanguard intellectual of the Leninist party;[12] but it is these two pairs of differing positions which Bennett conflates in his characterisation of any approach which hopes that cultural studies might help to produce critical subjects who are not wholly complicit with the technocratic agendas of state institutions and corporations. This is not to overlook the importance of Bennett's remarks on the importance of attending to the function of teachers of cultural studies as 'specific intellectuals';[13] these remarks are well-made and well-taken, and are a healthy corrective against the romanticism and sheer egocentrism which can attend many attempts to imagine what it should mean to be a progressive worker in higher education. Nonetheless, the terms of Bennett's critique are revealing. For Bennett, the move 'towards a pragmatics for cultural studies' involves a specific turn away from that tradition represented by the work of Hall and Laclau and Mouffe (most notably in Bennett's entirely unsubstantiated claim that Laclau and Mouffe's intellectual project has 'evidently failed),[14] and a turn towards explicitly technocratic agendas. It is this tradition of post-Marxist discourse analysis and its present manifestations which I want to defend.

In order to carry out such a defence, one could simply remark that Bennett's programme for cultural studies assumes a situation – as may well have obtained in Australia during the time that Bennett was working there and writing his book – whereby there are more-or-less transparent channels through which 'policy' ideas will be successfully transmitted from institutions of higher education to those elements of the reforming state capable of implementing them; we might point out that such a situation clearly does not obtain in the UK today or at any time in the past. One could also question the pragmatic utility of

Bennett's programme for students who, like many of mine, are single mothers from ethnic minorities – and thus subject to and participants in a complex range of socio-political struggles on a daily basis, and who are unlikely ever to find employment as the kind of cultural technocrats Bennett wants to train. One could also point to the fact that Bennett nowhere makes clear what *kind* of reformist programmes his new generation of cultural-studies-trained technocrats would be trained to implement, or in the name of what politics these pragmatists would practice. If Bennett were to suggest that these pragmatic reformers might be trained in such a way as to enable them to undertake reforms amenable to, say, a specifically *democratising* agenda, then we might have an answer; but Bennett would then be delineating a programme which neither Laclau nor Hall would be likely to consider controversial, or even novel. However Bennett does not advocate such a turn. Rather, like New Labour, he ends up appearing to advocate reform for the sake of reform, a technocratic approach to government – or, more accurately, *management* conceived of as a kind of government-without-content – which explicitly rejects the notion that 'reform' should have any long-term goal.

Bennett deploys some specifically loaded terms to describe his position and to mark its difference from the tradition he rejects – 'prosaic politics', 'pragmatics'. It is not hard to see where this leads; Bennett advocates a 'new realism' for cultural studies not at all dissimilar in its rhetoric from the 'new realism' which paved the way for New Labour in the British labour movement during the 1980s. The key term here is, of course 'reality'. In marked similarity, Angela McRobbie, another of cultural studies' leading figures since the 1970s, titled her recent edited collection *Back to Reality: Social Experience and Cultural Studies*.[15] By contrast, however, her recent study of cultural production and its economic and discursive contexts, *British Fashion Design: Rag Trade or Image Industry*, manages to provide a detailed account of its subject which generates firm policy suggestions, whilst keeping faith with the tradition of Hall and Laclau and Mouffe.[16] Nonetheless, McRobbie's rhetoric is in places similar to Bennett's, and together they mark a distinct turn in commentary on cultural studies by some of its senior practitioners.[17] According to the advocates of both cultural policy studies and cultural production studies, of whom Bennett and McRobbie are only the best known representatives, what cultural studies needs is a healthy dose of reality.

This is an entirely understandable view. It is now more than twenty years since the publication of the paradigmatic text of British cultural studies, *Policing the Crisis*,[18] a text which, despite its reliance on Gramscian and Althusserian models, Bennett himself refers to as exemplary.[19] In this work, Stuart Hall and his colleagues undertook an analysis of the media construction of a moral panic about black youths mugging innocent passers-by on British streets, and emerged with an account of the hegemonic crisis of the British state and its response which managed to delineate much of the shape of Thatcherism as it was to emerge over the subsequent decade. A theoretical account of a specific discursive phenomenon as produced by the media gave rise to an entire analysis of the emergent political conjuncture. The analysis of Thatcherism pursued so famously and influentially in the pages of the magazine *Marxism Today* in the 1980s appears to have begun, if anywhere, here. One might have had high hopes for cultural studies.

But there has not been another *Policing the Crisis*. Despite the massive institutional dissemination of cultural studies over the past two decades, here and in Australia and North America, cultural studies has yet to produce a single study of contemporary culture which attempts such a serious political intervention. There was no analysis of the culture of late Thatcherism, there have been no fully conjunctural readings of the moral panics over Ecstasy or AIDS. Instead, the effect of postmodernism and post-structuralism, the collapse of the organised left, and the global hegemony of neo-liberalism has been to leave cultural studies apparently bereft of political purpose or identity. Given the forms which 'Cultural Studies' has subsequently tended to take, it's perhaps not surprising that it has received so much criticism from both inside and outside its own camp. All too often, cultural studies appears to generate purely aesthetic engagements with contemporary culture, merely descriptive accounts of current discourses. Ironically enough, this might be a reason both for the (depressingly sectarian) complaint made by the Derridean philosopher Geoffrey Bennington – that cultural studies fails to deliver anything more than mere journalism, a problem for which he inexplicably blames Williams, Hall and Pierre Bourdieu,[20] – and for that of Stuart Hall himself in a recent interview, when he stated that 'a formal deconstructionism which isn't asking questions about the insertion of symbolic processes into societal contexts and their imbrication with power is not interested in the cultural studies problematic'.[21]

It's understandable then, that in their different ways both McRobbie and Bennett want to get away from this type of aestheticised practice, this obsession with texts and texts only, to return to a concern with societal contexts and their imbrications with power. But when such a programme is implemented according to the terms set out by Bennett, a whole new set of dichotomies are in danger of being produced (or rather, a very ancient set is reproduced), which are at least as damaging as they are productive, and which involve a rejection of the possibility of producing just those types of political analysis which cultural studies has the potential to deliver.[22] What I would like to argue for in the long term, although there is not the space to go into detail here, would be a rejection of 'a formal deconstructionism which isn't asking questions about the insertion of symbolic processes into societal contexts and their imbrication with power' – not in favour of a turn to ethnographic or technocratic approaches to such problems, but precisely in favour of a formal deconstructionism which *is* asking questions about the insertion of symbolic processes into societal contexts and their imbrication with power. Such a practice would therefore remain as committed as ever to the cultural studies problematic as conceived by Hall.

DISCOURSE ANALYSIS *CONTRA* SOCIOLOGY (I): THE POLITICALITY OF SOUND

The problem with arguments like Bennett's is that they tend to return to old ideas about the social production of meaning. Looking for the meanings of culture not in its products themselves or in the ways which they are used or understood, but in the ways they are produced, looking for solutions to political problems which locate all potential power with the reforming state – these approaches run a severe risk of reproducing the idea that the truth of culture is always to be found elsewhere, in the relations of production, in the state, in the always-elsewhere site of true power. The field of symbolic activity is thus de-emphasised as a site of power and struggle, reduced to a mere surface expression of some underlying reality. This is not the only implication of Bennett's approach, attentive as it is to the institutional immanence of power. However in any attempt to get 'back to reality' in cultural studies there is an implicit approach to the problem of the relationship between power and discourse which is characteristic of those versions of Marxism which posit the cultural as an expression of the underlying reality of the socio-economic base – or of more sophisticated Marxist models, such as Raymond Williams' notion of culture as an expressive totality; such an approach is also characteristic of a range of other writers who address this problem across a number of apparently disparate fields. Consider two examples, one from the general field of cultural studies, one from the area of political science.

First, consider the ways in which popular music has tended to be treated as an object of study within the cultural studies tradition. One of the key strands which fed into the development of cultural studies as we have come to know it was the sociology of youth subcultures generated at the Birmingham Centre for Contemporary Cultural Studies in the 1970s. It is one of the peculiarities of the development of British cultural studies that the study of popular music culture has tended to become conflated with the study of youth subcultures, such that to this day no course reading list on popular music is complete without reference to Dick Hebdige's *Subculture: the meaning of style*.[23] Hugely important as this book remains, it actually says almost nothing about music (unlike, ironically enough, some of Hebdige's other work). In fact, very little at all has been written about popular music as such from within cultural studies, although there is an increasing body of work, such as that of Richard Middleton and John Shepherd, which incorporates cultural theory and critical musicology to provide a substantive account of the social meanings of musical texts. Until the emergence of such work – which had not achieved widespread dissemination until relatively recently – it remained an assumption of research inspired by 1970s subculture studies, and by the influential work of Simon Frith, the original sociologist of rock, that musical texts were virtually inert in and of themselves, entirely neutral markers to be deployed at will by subcultural groups and individuals in order to mark out their differences from either the dominant social order or the other groups around them. The actual *sounds* of records appeared to make very little difference at all to the social meanings they acquired: context was everything, text was nothing.

In what amounts to a fascinating critique of his own earlier work, Simon Frith begins the conclusion to his latest and arguably most important work *Performing Rites* thus:

> The academic study of popular music has been limited by the assumption that the sounds somehow reflect or represent 'a people'. The analytic problem has been to trace the connections back from the work (the score, the song, the beat) to the social groups who make and use it. What's at issue is homology, some sort of structural relationship between material and cultural forms. As the semiotician Theo van Leeuwen puts it, 'Music can be seen as an abstract representation of social organisation, of the geometry of social structure.'...
>
> The problem of the homological argument, as van Leeuwen himself notes, is that 'music not only represents social relations, it also and

simultaneously enacts them'; and too often attempts to relate musical forms *to* social processes ignore the ways in which music *itself* is a social process. In other words, in examining the aesthetics of popular music we need to reverse the usual academic argument: the question is not how a piece of music, a text, 'reflects' popular values, but how – in performance – it produces them.[24]

The concluding chapter from which this passage is drawn is titled 'Towards a Popular Aesthetic'. What is vaguely unsatisfying about this chapter, and the book as a whole, is that it never really gets around to delineating the terms of the 'aesthetic' which it so rightly argues for. This is also the substance of the critique of Frith made by Negus and Pickering.[25] In their closely argued analysis, Negus and Pickering point to the ultimate failure of *Performing Rites* to resolve the key theoretical problem which it elaborates at great length: that of the relationship between the aesthetic and the sociological dimensions of musical experience, between the observation that, *pace* Bourdieu, cultural tastes can be understood as wholly determined by social location, and the counter-observation that music, like other forms of cultural experience, can itself constitute (rather than merely reflect or express) social experience, and can thus be an agent of personal or socio-political (if those two things can ever be separated) *change*. Negus and Pickering castigate Frith for closing his book with a meditation on the capacity of music to 'take us out of ourselves', which appears to undermine the basis for that explicitly sociological understanding of musical effectivity which they want to defend. Frith, in turn, has responded with a brief defence of his evocation of the 'mysterious' power of music.[26]

I would suggest that in fact both parties to this quasi-quarrel are entirely right, but that what is missed in the debate between them is the dimension of analysis which has the capacity to mediate between their two sets of concerns, a dimension which we might name, simultaneously, 'the political', 'the rhetorical' or 'the discursive'. Within these terms we can understand that music, or any other form of discourse, itself has determinate political effects on the people who hear it, and on the social context into which it emerges, but those effects cannot be understood simply as 'mysterious' or as somehow inherent in the music as such. Music has effects which are context-specific, but which are not wholly explicable in terms of, or reducible to, its social location or function. Any attempt to understand these processes must attend to the details of the ways in which particular pieces of music mediate the contexts from which they come and into which they emerge. So yes, musical value is entirely dependent on social context, but yes, music can 'take us out of ourselves' by problematising as well as merely reproducing our psychosocial contexts. Yes, one needs to deploy detailed aesthetic analysis in order to have any understanding of this process. Yes, one needs detailed social and historical analysis in order to have any understanding of this process. But it is precisely at the level of *politics* that these different elements can be seen to interact and present themselves for evaluation.

The question which Frith and Negus and Pickering fret over, the question of the cultural value of music, can be finally resolved in these terms. The problem of whether one can or should attempt to ascribe *value* to popular music, and if so in what terms, is the principle theme of *Performing Rites*. Frith, largely concerned with demonstrating the significance of questions of value for most participants in popular music cultures, spends a great deal of time *describing* the various social functions which different evaluative practices have within popular music culture, but never commits himself to an opinion as to whether we, as sociologically-informed critics, ever can or should ourselves evaluate such practices. Negus and Pickering tut-tut over Frith's prevarication, but themselves offer little that is more substantial.

Considered at the level of the political, however, this problem is not a difficult one; we will in the future, as critics since Plato have done, always ultimately evaluate musics on the basis of their specific socio-musical effects *and* our politically-informed opinion as to the relative desirability of those effects. The value of the sociology of music, as practised by all three of these writers, is precisely that it provides us with the necessary understanding of those effects and their contexts. Its weakness is that it can never, as Frith (sometimes inadvertently) demonstrates, furnish us with the capacity to articulate an aesthetics, any more than a purely formal account of musical structures can tell us anything about their effects in a given social context. What must always mediate between these two modes of description is a political evaluation.

This lack of attention to the precise level of 'the political' in the analysis of music culture is also characteristic of Sarah Thornton's study of UK 'club cultures', with its specific modification of Bourdieu's concept of 'cultural capital'. In an illuminating and original study of British youth culture in the 1990s, Thornton gives the name 'subcultural capital' to the accumulated sets of shared values and knowledges according to which distinct groups of young people distinguish themselves from outsiders.[27]

Sociological accounts of youth subcultures tend, like the discourses which circulate in subcultural spaces themselves, to present such formations as inherently oppositional, resisting the dominant bourgeois culture and bravely defending their autonomy from the encroachment of the hegemonic 'mainstream' which – usually via the agency of the capitalist media – seeks to 'incorporate' them back into itself. Thornton reverses this account, demonstrating that far from being concerned with opposing the dominant culture of the parent society, youth cultures are largely concerned with establishing hierarchies and distinctions amongst and between young people themselves, thereby exposing the elitism which defines much of 'youth culture', and in particular dance culture. At the same time, Thornton demonstrates the extent to which subcultural groups exist in a symbiotic relationship with the very 'mainstream' media they usually claim to wish to remain autonomous from.

However, Thornton's model has a central weaknesses in its implication that all cultural practices are equally apolitical; however 'radical' a group may consider their particular practice to be, in truth they are merely trying to accumulate subcultural capital at the expense of the unfashionable. This account pays no attention to the specific content of given cultures and given moments, and therefore refuses to make any political distinctions at all between different cultural formations. This is also a mistake. What is needed is not a model of culture which simply refuses to read it politically, any more than one which reproduces the romantic delusion of a single dominant 'mainstream' culture 'opposed' by the heroic guerrillas of the subcultural subaltern. What is needed is an approach to the politics of 'culture' which attends in detail to the range of complex political relationships which can obtain between different formations at different times.[28]

Thornton, like Negus and Pickering, appeals to the work of Pierre Bourdieu in her defence of a 'sociological' approach to the study of music culture. This is understandable. Bourdieu is the great critic of aesthetics for our era.[29] It is actually unlikely that this most subtle of intellectual barbarians would himself advocate an approach which did not attend to the constitutive power of symbolic action,[30] but this question need not concern us here. What is more interesting is the precise way in which his name is used by Negus and Pickering and by Thornton. In both cases, it is an excess of romanticism which is feared and which Bourdieu's name is evoked in order to ward off. In the case of Negus and Pickering this excess is manifested as an inappropriate attention to 'aesthetics' on the part of Simon Frith. In the case of

Thornton, it is an excess of politics itself that she seeks to overcome –
a too-hasty willingness in the analyses of her intellectual predecessors
to read youth subcultures as possessing a clearly legible and clearly
oppositional politicality. Taking these two cases together, we can see
that 'aesthetics' and 'politics' are placed in a similar position of opposition to 'sociology' and 'history'.

These writers are not wrong in their implicitly shared assessment
that an analytical turn towards the realm of aesthetics and a turn
towards the realm of politics each constitute a turn away from the
realm of 'the social'. I would argue, in fact, that the role of politics for
cultural studies is always to *mediate* between the sociological and the
aesthetic, and that it can never dispense with either of the two without
collapsing into either 'a formal deconstructionism which isn't asking
questions about the insertion of symbolic processes into societal
contexts', or a sociology aspiring to the be nothing more than descriptive (mere journalism). However, it is undeniable, as Frith points out,
that in the specific context of Anglophone studies of popular music
culture there has been a notable bias towards the sociological side of
this ideal equation. In this context, a necessary turn towards the question of politics must also involve a turn towards the questions of
aesthetics. Herein lies the ultimate importance of Frith's intervention.

I don't want to deny for a moment that the sociology of popular
music has been and remains a fruitful approach. We can compare this
to the excesses of *Screen* theory in the 1970s, which tended to posit the
cinematic spectator as a mere effect of the ideological filmic text, and
we might well conclude that the political effects of such a textual determinism were ultimately far more debilitating than those of the
sociological contextualism which has characterised popular music
studies. Nevertheless, this approach has produced some remarkable
absences in pop music studies. For instance, as Jason Toynbee pointed
out in an excellent article on the subject some seven years ago, very
little work indeed has paid the slightest attention to popular music
media, and in particular to the ideological projects of the music press –
a remarkable blind-spot indeed for cultural studies, but one which
largely subsists.[31] This suggests that the problem is not merely a failure
to address the specific effectivity of music, but a wider failure to grasp
or attempt to analyse all of the discursive dimensions of this region of
cultural experience. What tends to be implied, to put it very simply, is
that the records we buy and listen to are a pure expression of our existing social location, a function of cultural or subcultural identities
whose effective determinants are located firmly elsewhere. The idea

that the discourses which circulate both through records themselves and through the media which generate cultures around them might actually be *constitutive* of social identities is routinely overlooked in all but the most adventurous of studies (such as Robert Walser's brilliant *Running with the Devil*).[32] This is despite the fact that the really radical gesture of that key text of the field, Hebdige's *Subculture: the Meaning of Style* was, from the outset, a turn away from notions of culture as possessing a homological relation to the social, and towards an idea of culture as signifying *practice*.

DISCOURSE ANALYSIS CONTRA SOCIOLOGY (II): ELECTORAL HEGEMONIES

A similar logic, I would like to suggest, operates within most accounts of one of the most crucial but nevertheless under-examined aspects of contemporary political life: voting behaviour. The idea that political identification is largely a function of social location is hardly a new one, and for most of the history of electoral democracy in the industrialised world it has been self-evidently true. On the other hand, this has never been a fully adequate formulation, but despite its inadequacies most accounts of patterns of voting behaviour, be they static or changing, tend to posit a more-or-less simple expressive relationship between social location and political identification. Even the most flexible of such models must be presented with a serious problem when faced with the event of the 1997 General Election. Whatever changes may have taken place since 1992, the social structure of the British population can hardly have changed sufficiently during that time for such changes on their own to account for the massive shift in voting patterns which occurred in the UK during that time. Given the relatively slight changes in the policies offered by any of the main parties, it is also difficult to see this as a major determining factor, although it obviously had an effect. John Curtice and Michael Steed, trying to analyse the detailed voting statistics from the election, conclude that 'Almost every explanation of the Conservatives' performance which refers to political developments or social changes in the two or three yeas before the election seems to be found wanting.'[33] Ultimately accounting for the Conservative collapse with reference to nothing more specific than 'a long-standing nationwide political disenchantment with the incumbent government', the authors reject economic explanations for changes in voting patterns – on good grounds – and are particularly interested in the fact that the Tory vote fell most in areas where it had previously been strongest. The success of Labour and the Liberal Democrats is explained largely in terms of anti-Tory tactical voting *and* the willing-ness of voters to switch straight from Tory to Labour, which is itself explained partly in terms of an overriding willingness to get rid of the Tories and partly by the apparent political closeness between Tories and Labour. Taken together, what is striking about the collection of phenomena which Curtice and Steed so astutely identify is the fact that, as they themselves acknowledge, they are highly resistant to explanation according to any of the usual frameworks of political science: from the changing allegiance of the press to shifting social structures, a range of possible causal factors is carefully evaluated and found to be inadequate on its own or even as part of a constellation of overdetermining causes.

The reason for this, I propose, is that the scale and significance of the New Labour victory, New Labour's success in winning over swathes of Conservative voters in previously safe Tory areas and in inspiring an effective campaign of tactical voting of which it was the greatest bene-ficiary, can only be fully explained in terms of its successful mobilisation of a new political imaginary. What standard psephological models, rooted as they are in a statistically-driven sociology, are unable to address properly, is the capacity of a project like New Labour actu-ally to re-shape the political landscape, to call into being a new political nation, to interpellate various sections of society, the identities of which are always by definition unstable and incomplete, and by addressing them to name them, forging them into a new unity, re-creat-ing them in its own image; in short, to constitute a new hegemony.

This is in no way to disparage the work of social and political scien-tists. It would be impossible to make this kind of analysis without it, and if the terms of such statistical research are inherently self-limiting then they are no more so than those of discourse analysis. Both the book in which Curtice and Steed write – the latest in the long-running series of studies of UK general elections produced in association with Nuffield college Oxford – and the similar volume *Labour's Landslide*, edited by Andrew Geddes and John Tonge,[34] are very strong on their capacity to explain both the detailed mechanisms by which the Tory electoral machine fell apart and the detailed picture of how New Labour successfully addressed particular groups of key voters. However, it is worth reflecting that both lack any ability to explain such phenomena in terms which require us to understand the extent to which New Labour may have caused groups and individuals to *re-imagine* themselves rather than simply respond to New Labour's attempts to address them in pre-defined terms.

Finally, when considering Anglo-Saxon psephology's treatment of such issues, what can one make of a book published as late as 1994 by as respectable a publisher as the University of Michigan Press – *Ideology and the Theory of Political Choice*[35] – which demonstrates no greater awareness of the theoretical literature on 'ideology' than to define it as 'an internally consistent set of propositions that makes both proscriptive and prescriptive demands on human behaviour',[36] and which can open its concluding chapter with the banal observation that 'In every society, there is a basic tension between altruism and egoism as a motivation for the actions of citizens'?[37] The value of rational choice theory, which sees voters and other social agents as rational atomised agents pursuing clearly defined interests, has been ruthlessly interrogated by critics such as Barry Hindess, who shows that there is no absolute logical correlation between 'actors' social locations and the techniques and forms of thought they employ in deciding on courses of action'.[38] Unfortunately, this does not prevent such models from being uncritically reproduced in this and similar works. This should not lead us to write off the whole field of empirical political science or psephology, but it is indicative of the kinds of conceptual weakness which I am drawing attention to here.

What is missed by standard sociologically-oriented models of political identification, individual and collective, is the *performative* dimension of politics as a discursive practice. I would argue, following the logic of writers such as Laclau and Mouffe and Judith Butler, that hegemony is always a performative operation, and one which cannot be understood without attention to the constitutive effectivity of discourse. One way of putting this might be, as I have suggested, to follow Dick Hebdige, who towards the end of *Subculture* suggests that the subcultural style of the punks should be understood not simply as expressive of a particular social condition, but as a deliberate signifying practice, an intervention in the world of meanings. Perhaps the key move which Stuart Hall, Hebdige's colleague at the Birmingham centre, made in the 1980s was to try to get people to understand that in fact politics itself is just that – a signifying practice. This recognition of the importance of signifying practice in the constitution of social reality seems to me to be the key point of connection between the politically-informed cultural studies of Stuart Hall and the theoretical programme of 'discourse analysis' pursued by Ernesto Laclau and his followers within the field of political theory. Opposed to the depth models of naïve realist sociology, which tend to see both politics and culture as merely surface effects of the social, the discourse-analysis approach emphasises the constitutive and contingent nature of signification in both fields.

This emphasis has some serious implications, both theoretical and practical. Firstly, I would point out that these implications do *not* include a commitment to extreme ethical relativism or epistemological nihilism. What I do take them to include – and this does not, I reiterate, imply either relativism or nihilism – is an affinity with the philosophical programme of deconstruction. Despite Hall's fully appropriate concern to distance cultural studies from an aestheticised deconstruction, the destabilisation of the terms of western metaphysics enacted by Derrida and those whose work has been inspired by his is a precondition for any effective understanding of the status of signification in western culture. It's worth considering here the distinction which Laclau makes between the social – which he defines as 'the sedimented forms of "objectivity" ' – and the political – which he describes as 'the moment of antagonism where the undecidable nature of the alternatives and their resolution through power relations becomes fully visible'. According to Laclau, 'social relations are constituted by the very distinction between the social and the political', between social reality as the effect of the hegemonisation and sedimentation of established discourses, and the political as the field of possibility opened up by the realisation of the very contingency of those discourses and their sedimentation.[39] There is no coincidence to the similarity between this conceptual opposition, and those highlighted and – usually – deconstructed by Derrida in his detailed considerations of the history and fate of western metaphysics: speech and writing, presence and absence, inside and outside, and so on. We could well map this distinction between the social and the political onto the series of terms which Derrida has identified as excluded or marginalised by western metaphysical thinking. A thinking of the social which regards its object as a self-present entity, a thinking of culture or politics which concerns itself with the social reality beneath the surface of the discursive constitution of political projects, an approach to cultural forms which seeks out the underlying forms of objectivity which they 'really' express: all could be seen as reproducing an essentialist, metaphysical approach at the expense of a deconstructive one which would understand the contingent dynamics according to which such phenomena were actually constitutive of their own moments. The classical expression of this opposition would be the argument between Plato and the Sophists: the argument between philosophy and rhetoric. Against the science of the politico-discursive manipulation of the field of signification, Plato proposed a pure knowledge of the reality of which even our immediate perceptions are only a representation, and as such debased.[40] There is truth, and there is the cynical manipulation of language, and the one must be kept resolutely uncontaminated by the other. Nietzsche is the first major critic of this distinction, but it is Derrida who in recent times has considered its implications in the most detail:

> This is an undoubtedly philosophic, and certainly Platonic, ideal, an ideal that is produced in the separation (and order) between philosophy or dialectic on the one hand and (sophistic) rhetoric on the other, the separation demanded by Plato himself. Directly or not, it is this separation and this hierarchy that we must question here.[41]

For Laclau, in a recent essay on the work of Paul de Man, this questioning becomes central to the understanding of the specificity of the political:

> Why should a political theorist like me, working mainly on the role of hegemonic logics in the structuration of political spaces, be interested in the work of a prominent literary critic such as Paul de Man? I could suggest at least two main reasons ... Against all attempts to differentiate between 'appearance' and 'saying', between a primary text whose message would have been mediated by the materiality of the signs, of the figural, and a language of inquiry governed by reason, de Man had always insisted that any language, whether aesthetic or theoretical, is governed by the materiality of the signifier, by a rhetorical milieu which ultimately dissolves the illusion of any unmediated reference. In this sense a generalised rhetoric – which necessarily includes within itself the performative dimension – transcends all regional boundaries and becomes coterminous with the structuration of social life itself...
>
> As for the second reason for a political theorist to be interested in de Man's work, it has to do with something related to the political field itself. Gone are the times in which the transparency of social actors, of processes of representation, even of the presumed underlying logics of the social fabric could be accepted unproblematically. On the contrary, each political institution, each category of political analysis, shows itself today as the *locus* of undecidable language games. The overdetermined nature of all political difference or identity opens the space for a generalised tropological movement ... In my

work this generalised politico-tropological movement has been called 'hegemony'.[42]

For Laclau then, an attention to the constitutive dimension of the political is more-or-less synonymous with a turn to the significant dimension of the rhetorical and a deconstruction of the traditional privilege accorded to 'reality' over the modes of its signification. Contrary to popular belief neither deconstruction nor most of those influenced by it advocate the simple overturning of such conceptual hierarchies; Derrida is not *opposed* to metaphysics: partly because he believes that it remains impossible to think wholly outside of it; partly because, despite the problems with it which he identifies, he does not regard it simply as a 'bad thing'. Neither deconstruction nor Laclau's discourse analysis would advocate a simplistic valuation of rhetoric at the expense of truth, of attention to texts at the expense of attention to the social. However, these approaches do seek to draw our attention to the dangers of a metaphysical obsession with reality at the expense of a concern with the field of signification, and at their most radical would problematise the possibility of always distinguishing between them (such is the effect of Derrida's 'thought of the trace'). The danger of such an approach is that in seeking to *describe* the real, one fails to recognise its contingency, and misses the opportunity of intervening in the very process of its constitution. To use the language of J.L. Austin, if one speaks only in constatives, one may find oneself incapable of thinking the performative.[43] In other words, to understand the fields of either 'cultural' or 'political' discourse as merely descriptive (accurately or inaccurately) or expressive of 'deeper' social realities, is to risk losing sight of the crucial capacity of discourse to intervene in and constitute social reality.

THE RHETORIC OF 'MODERNISATION': DECONSTRUCTING THE THIRD WAY

We have recently seen one example of such an outcome from perhaps the most unlikely source imaginable. In 1998 Chantal Mouffe, Laclau's co-writer and co-theorist, published a critique of New Labour and its emergent philosophy, the so-called 'Third Way' which suffered from precisely this weakness. In her article, Mouffe writes passionately and eloquently against the insubstantiality of the Third Way. Blair and his key ideologist, Anthony Giddens are, she insists, making a terrible mistake. Globalisation, the international hegemony of neo-liberalism, is not necessarily inevitable. The persistence of inequitable structures of power and irreconcilable differences of interest between the power-less and the powerful means that the distinction between left and right politics remains as crucial as ever. Blair and Giddens are wrong to imagine that a purely consensual politics is possible; there can be no politics without enemies.[44]

Of course Mouffe is right in all respects, and her analysis in this article is invaluable. However, what her essay, typical of the response of many left intellectuals to New Labour – in particular those writing in the special 1998 issue of *Marxism Today* whose cover famously declared Tony Blair to be simply 'Wrong' – implicitly overlooks is the fact that politics is not simply about being right. Blair et al are not engaged in a struggle only to *describe* current social reality as accurately as possible, but to *define* it, and thereby, on the political level, to constitute it. Their claim to transcend old political distinctions is not to be understood as a simple statement about the nature of contemporary politics, but as the hegemonic gesture *par excellence*. It is a basic insight of Gramsci's that the moment of hegemony is the moment at which one group in society manages to generalise the idea that its interests are coterminous with those of all or most members of that society.[45] A politics without enemies is, of course, technically impossible, but the articulation of such a politics is nonetheless the logical goal of any hegemonic strategy. As Laclau puts it, 'political victory is equivalent to the elimination of the specifically political nature of the victorious practices'.[46]

There are several interconnected issues at stake here. One is the importance of attending to the performative dimension of political discourse. Another is the issue of how we understand the status of New Labour as a political project. What I am suggesting is that those features of New Labour's discourse which Mouffe so astutely identifies are in fact indicative not of its 'mistaken' view of democracy but of two key aspects of its historical and social specificity. On the one hand, they are indicative of its profound effectiveness as a hegemonic project. New Labour has produced a powerful and persuasive narrative accord-ing to which its policies appear as the only possible set of responses to an implacable present, characterised by inexorable global forces, rather than political decisions taken within a field of contingency. This is not a strategy unique to New Labour. Thatcherism, which Mouffe distin-guishes from the Third Way on the basis that it was explicit about who its enemies were, frequently legitimated its position by means of the assertion that there was 'no alternative' to neo-liberal monetarism. It is, however, a strategy being deployed with remarkable effectiveness by New Labour.

Secondly, it is simply not true that, even at the level of rhetoric, New Labour does not designate its enemies, producing 'frontier effects'[47] which aim to articulate the floating elements of the social according to hegemonic logics. New Labour's rhetoric of 'modernisation' has been mobilised (in a manner consistent with that of earlier Labour administrations) precisely in order to define all those who oppose it, either from 'Left' or 'Right', as simply outside the scope of rationality. What makes Mouffe's appeal to Blair and Giddens, addressed more or less as comrades who have gone sadly and mysteriously astray, so very poignant, is her apparent failure to realise that their enemy, their constitutive outside, is in fact exactly that political and social formation which traditionally aspires to the implementation of the type of redistributive democratic programme which Mouffe herself advocates – Old Labour. In the precise language which she uses, describing New Labour as 'disingenuous' and 'mistaken',[48] Mouffe addresses the statements of New Labour as if they were simple constatives, descriptive contributions to the general conversation of the left. In fact they are *performatives* whose aim is the rhetorical and actual marginalisation of any kind of recognisable left discourse.[49] This process having begun with the production of a frontier between New Labour and 'Old Labour'[50] (an entirely imaginary construct), it has been continued and intensified with Blair's recent attacks on 'The forces of conservatism',[51] a term which Blair explicitly uses to define those who oppose him from either 'left' or 'right' as belonging to a fundamentally similar class of irrational elements. As Alan Finlayson has commented (presciently writing before this latest phase in the evolution of Blairite rhetoric), 'The rhetoric of modernisation can be seen as a way of drawing antagonistic lines of exclusion and inclusion. On one side is that which is modernised or attuned to modernisation and this is always good (if sometimes requiring a 'hard choice'). The other side is always, by definition, out of touch and anti-modernisation.'[52]

In fact, the term 'modernisation' has almost acquired the status in contemporary political discourse of what Laclau calls an 'empty signifier'.[53] Such terms – like 'freedom', 'democracy' or 'socialism' – come to be central to political discourse precisely to the extent that they lose any actual meaning. Almost devoid of determinate content, it appears at times to be the case that modernisation is simply whatever the supporters of the project do; whatever they don't do is its opposite, the hopelessly regressive preserve of conservatism. Just as, in Herbert Morrison's words, socialism is whatever a Labour government does, 'modernisation' is whatever Tony Blair does. At the same time, 'modernisation' comes to name the totality of these decisions and interventions as a coherent unity, and to render irrational by definition all that is excluded from that unity. This has a number of effects, one of which is to de-historicise a situation which, looked at over the long term, can be read as a simple case of victory for the Labour right after a seventy-year history of struggle against socialists in the Labour party. Rather than recognising the current situation as the result of political struggle between different sections of the party, naming the project 'modernisation' appears to raise it above the history of sectarian conflict, at once neutralising its specific politicality and allowing it to represent its interests as at one with those of the labour movement – and indeed the country – as a whole.

This process of hegemonisation, whereby one group comes to represent its interests as at one with those of the whole collective, this *emptying* of key signifiers (in this case, 'modernisation'), always involves the suppression of other potential projects, other potential meanings for those signifiers. There is an emptying of the signifier which comes to stand in for the coherence of the collectivity as a whole (in this case, the collectivity of decisions and interventions which characterises 'New Labour'), and at the same time a *filling* of that signifier with a content which is specific to the hegemonising group. This always involves a certain suppression of other potential contents for the signifier in question.

I would suggest that there are two potential meanings of the term 'modernisation'. One of them is very close to the term 'rationalisation' as it is used to justify actions such as the sacking of a substantial part of a company's workforce. Within this register, the term designates a determination to accommodate to the present without in any way challenging that present or its terms. To modernise is therefore to become more efficient, more successful, under circumstances and according to criteria which are not only not of one's own choosing but which there is no imagined possibility of changing. 'Modernisation' therefore means accommodating to modernity conceived as a fixed and permanent present. The obvious manifestation of this in terms of Labour policy was the insistent drive to make Labour appealing to Middle England. Rather than any attempt to disrupt the coherence of that imagined political-cultural bloc, or to offer leadership or a new vision, or even just a new sense of where the interests and loyalties of certain social groups could lie, much of New Labour's agenda has been determined by a desire to conform to the views and wishes of an imagined nation of fundamentally conservative voters. Determining policy on the basis of market research, rather than boldly campaigning to carve out new market spaces for the Labour product, is the ultimate manifestation of 'modernisation' thus conceived.

There is an alternative definition of 'modernisation': not just a specific set of measures aimed at the accommodation of a statically-conceived present, but a perpetual opening-up to modernity conceived as an unfolding process of change. This notion of 'modernisation' would involve a radical openness to the future and its possibilities. This version would embrace the modern not by trying simply to adapt to the present but by seeking to ride those currents of change which might lead in progressive directions. Working with those tendencies and formations at the 'leading edge', it would have a very different set of priorities to those which often seem to characterise New Labour. The de-stabilisation of traditional family structures might not be so feared by this modernisation, but might even, at certain points, be embraced for its liberatory potential. The democratising potential of new digital technologies might here be harnessed to a commitment to de-centralisation of political structures to enable us to imagine new modes of democratic participation. Imaginative responses to the changing needs of industry might allow us to think about re-ordering our still puritan work-culture, allowing for more employee-sensitive working conditions and a shorter working week. Finally, an openness to the possibility of a better future might also allow us to preserve a vision of a society less riddled by poverty and inequality.

What the difference between versions of modernisation really amounts to is a difference in approaching the question of how we deal with the changes which capitalism continues to wreak on all aspects of life. De-stabilising social structures and institutions, breaking down national and international boundaries, de-stabilising communities and identities; these are and always have been the dislocatory effects of capitalism. At exactly what points do we accept, encourage, resist or seek to redirect these processes? This is still the central question of contemporary politics, and our two modes of modernisation present radically different types of response. That form of modernisation which seeks to accommodate the desires and prejudices of Middle England states its belief in family structures based on the two-parent model. At the same time, it seeks to meet the demands of capital by subjecting even single parents to the rigours of the work ethic. It responds to anxieties about social breakdown and disruptive youth with authoritarian rhetoric and the appointment of a 'Drug Czar'. It responds to social insecurity not by implementing a full programme of workers' rights but with an increasing social conservatism. On the other hand, a more radical modernisation project would react to social change with new democratic institutions, with an enabling response to new forms of family life and gendered and sexual identities, with a determined embracing of multiculturalism. At the same time it would resist most determinedly the erosion of those institutions – primarily the local and welfare states and the trade unions – which protect groups and individuals from the oppressive and disabling effects of capitalism.

BRITPOP: THE CULTURAL POLITICS OF BLAIRISM

So we have, I think, two types of modernisation, two sets of responses to capitalist dislocation, and while one can discern elements of both at work in New Labour's often ad hoc implementation of a modernising programme, it seems depressingly clear that it is the former model which predominates. The discourse of modernisation as perpetuated by New Labour must therefore be understood as constituted by, as much as anything else, a specific marginalisation of this idea of modernity as democracy.

However, as the account I have just offered implies, we cannot get much of a sense of the real nature of this project *without* recourse to the strategic realism of sociology. Without understanding which social groups it is that New Labour is trying to coalesce into a coherent political constituency and which it is prepared to marginalise and risk alienating altogether (public sector workers, for instance), we can't know much about the nature of its hegemonic project, and elsewhere in this volume I attend more closely to the socio-political bases for New Labour.

Nonetheless, my main point here remains that we always have to be attentive to the unfinished, incomplete character of all social agents, of all subjectivities (collective or individual) and to the performative role of political discourse in constituting them. And I would like finally to suggest that if at any point in the few years preceding the election of the Blair government someone had wanted to get a sense of the shape of the emergent hegemony of Blairism, they could have done better than to look either at the thoughts of Professor Giddens or the changing contours of the British social structure or the statistical details of the globalised (or not) economy. No; the field which best expressed the nature of Blairism and its constitutive exclusions through the mid-1990s was that of popular music. With the emergence and success of 'Britpop', a music discourse which sought to re-establish the normative hegemony of white male heterosexuality within British popular culture in the face of multifarious threats to it from the polyglot, polysexual internationalism of dance cultures, we saw the articulation of a structure of feeling predicated at once on the rejection of the individualist cultures of the Thatcherite 1980s and on the exclusion of more radical, democratic, multicultural alternatives: a cultural and musical Third Way. Britpop's articulation of a music discourse which placed white masculinity at the centre of British cultural identity was conducted in terms which closely prefigured the non-committal communitarianism of New Labour.[54]

The Britpop moment pulled together a whole range of previously disparate audiences (Adult-Oriented Rock, student-oriented indie, teen pop) to create a supposedly homogeneous audience for a music and an outlook that every suburban white kid and his Dad could identify with. In 1995, at the high point of Britpop, at the moment when Oasis were outselling any British band of recent times and were engaged in their much-hyped rivalry with London Britpoppers Blur, one of the few times since the decline of punk when popular music has been headline news, one could see the shape of New Labour to come. Britpop was clearly an attempt to revive white rock culture after the challenge to its cultural hegemony by the dance explosion of the early 1990s. The rather confused set of movements and tendencies which emerged throughout the 1990s around new forms of dance music presented an immense challenge to the dominant music culture of the time. Dance music culture was pluralist and multicultural, drawing deeply on its roots in the gay black and Hispanic cultures of Disco. It also had egalitarian and democratic tendencies in the forms of its production and consumption: new technologies made music production easy, there were a multiplicity of producers who were all fairly anonymous, and in night clubs the focus of attention was on those listening (and dancing) to the music over those making it. In contrast, the rock culture which Britpop revived was heroic rather than egalitarian: attention at concerts was firmly on the macho guitar hero rather than the audience, fans were offered an imaginary identification with a few charismatic individuals whose lives were given intensive exploration in the press. Furthermore, by emulating bands from the 1960s, Britpop mythologised a homogeneous idea of white Britishness which the social transformations of the previous thirty years had undermined.

Britpop had a powerful affinity with the hegemonic project of New Labour, and it's no accident that the Britpoppers and the Blairites became so publicly enamoured of each other,[55] with Oasis featured in the Labour Party press and their lead singer invited to a soirée at 10

Downing Street. The homogeneous culture which Britpop evoked provided a sense of togetherness and shared experience which was as inclusive and as vague as that offered by Blair's appeals to community, youth and virtue. At the same time, both New Labour and Britpop were concerned with manifesting quite traditional power relations in the face of earlier democratising impulses. The level of participation offered by the star-obsessed culture of Britpop was very similar to that offered by the centralised structures of the New Labour Party; you get to cheer your heroes and leaders while they're up on the stage making meaningless pronouncements ('All you people right here right now – we're gonna be a young country – d'you know what I mean?'), but any deeper form of participation was off the agenda.

This may seem like a trivial set of observations, but it isn't. My point is that the reality and the danger of Blairism as a hegemonic project lies not in the veracity or otherwise of its truth claims about the nature of the world economy, but in its capacity to resonate with such contemporary structures of feeling. Only an attention to the dispersed regularities of discourses both 'cultural' *and* 'political' can ever enable us to comprehend the shape of such emergent formations.

ENDNOTE

I find myself in an ironic position. I couldn't be writing this now without having grown up on the work of Hall, Laclau, Mouffe, et al. It was the historic task of these writers, most notably Hall writing in the pages of *Marxism Today*, to try to shake the British left out of its complacency. While most on the left at the beginning of the 1980s comforted themselves with the view that Mrs Thatcher's view of the world was obviously wrong, that its falsity and its moral repugnance would quickly be its own undoing, Hall told them to wake up and get a grip, to realise that Thatcher knew exactly what she was doing and that what she was doing was to re-make the nation in her own image – that what she had wasn't a set of errors but a hegemonic project. What's more, the resonances of this project had to be read not just in the narrow world of Westminster politics and its mediations, but in the wider culture as a whole. Now I find myself wanting to say just the same thing to the authors and chief legatees of that analysis: Blairism isn't a mistake either. It's a hegemonic project too, and one which already looks likely to be far more successful than Thatcherism ever was. What's more, a mere glance at the discursive terms of both New Labour and the contemporary structures of feeling with which it is most resonant reveals that the Third Way is very far from being, as

Mouffe describes it, a politics without enemies. It knows exactly who its enemies are – anyone who remains committed to the democratising projects of the twentieth century, be they Old Labour or New Left. An obsession with the real, it seems, can only blind us to this truth.

NOTES

1. Lilie Chouliaraki & Norman Fairclough, *Discourse in Late Modernity: Rethinking Critical Discourse Analysis*, Edinburgh University Press, Edinburgh 1999, pp37-53, 120-39.
2. Anthony Easthope, *British Post-Structuralism Since 1968*, Routledge, London 1988, pp23-33.
3. David Morley and Chen Kuan-Hsing (eds.), *Stuart Hall: Critical Dialogues in Cultural Studies*, Routledge, London 1996.
4. See John Brannigan, *New Historicism and Cultural Materialism*, Macmillan, London 1998.
5. Alan Sinfield, *Faultlines: Cultural Materialism and the Politics of Dissident Reading*, Oxford University Press, Oxford 1992.
6. Jacob Torfing, *New Theories of Discourse: Laclau, Mouffe and Zizek*, Blackwell, Oxford 1999.
7. Tony Bennett, *Culture: A Reformer's Science*, Sage, London 1998, p30.
8. *Ibid.*, pp31-3.
9. *Ibid.*, p32.
10. *Ibid.*, p32.
11. Stuart Hall, 'Cultural Studies and its Theoretical Legacies', in Lawrence Grossberg, Cary Nelson and Paul Treichler (eds), *Cultural Studies*, Routledge, London, 1992.
12. Antonio Gramsci, *Selections from the Prison Notebooks*, trans. Quentin Hoare and Geoffrey Nowell-Smith, Lawrence and Wishart, London 1971, pp3-23.
13. Hall, *op. cit.*, p288.
14. Bennett, *op. cit.*, p32.
15. Angela McRobbie, *Back to Reality: Social Experience and Cultural Studies*, Manchester University Press, Manchester 1997.
16. Angela McRobbie, *British Fashion Design: Rag Trade or Image Industry*, Routledge, London 1998, pp1-11.
17. See also, for example, several of the chapters in Marjorie Ferguson and Peter Golding (eds), *Cultural Studies in Question*, Sage, London 1997.
18. Stuart Hall et al, *Policing the Crisis: Mugging, the State and Law and Order*, Macmillan, London 1978.
19. Bennett, *op. cit.*, p24
20. Geoffrey Bennington, 'Inter' in Martin McQuillan et al (eds) *Post-Theory*,

Edinburgh University Press, Edinburgh 1999, p105.

21. Stuart Hall, 'Culture and Power' in *Radical Philosophy* 86, London 1997, p25.

22. McRobbie is again the exception here, her contribution to *Cultural Studies in Question* constituting an explicit and timely refusal to accept the dichotomy between ethnographic and empirical research on the one hand and anti-essentialist discourse analysis on the other.

23. Dick Hebdige, *Subculture: The Meaning of Style*. Routledge, London 1978.

24. Simon Frith, *Performing Rites: On the Value of Popular Music*, Oxford University Press, Oxford 1996.

25. Michael Pickering and Keith Negus, 'The Value of Value: Simon Frith and the Aesthetics of the Popular' in *New Formations* 34 (Summer 1998), pp109, 126.

26. Simon Frith, 'A Note on 'The Value of Value' in *New Formations* 34 (Summer 1998), pp127-9.

27. Sarah Thornton, *Club Cultures*, Polity, Cambridge 1995, pp1-25.

28. For an extended account see Jeremy Gilbert & Ewan Pearson, *Discographies*, Routledge, London 1999, pp158-60.

29. See Pierre Bourdieu, *Distinction: A social critique of the judgement of taste*, Routledge, London 1984.

30. See Pierre Bourdieu, *Language and Symbolic Power*, Polity, Cambridge 1991.

31. Jason Toynbee, 'Policing Bohemia, pinning up grunge: the music press and generic change in British pop and rock' in *Popular Music* 12/3, Cambridge University Press, Cambridge 1993, pp289-300.

32. Robert Walser, *Running with the Devil: Power, Gender and Madness in Heavy Metal Music*, Wesleyan University Press, Hanover 1993.

33. John Curtice and Michael Steed, 'The results analysed', in David Butler and Dennis Kavanagh, *The British General Election of 1997*, Macmillan, London 1997.

34. Andrew Geddes and John Tonge (eds.), *Labour's Landslide*, Manchester University Press, Manchester 1997.

35. Melvin J. Hinich and Michael C. Munger, *Ideology and the Theory of Political Choice*, University of Michigan Press, Ann Arbor 1994.

36. *Ibid.*, p11

37. *Ibid.*, p221.

38. Barry Hindess, *Choice, Rationality and Social Theory,* Unwin Hyman, London 1988, p112.

39. Ernesto Laclau, *New Reflections on the Revolution of Our Time*, Verso, London 1990, p35.

40. Plato, *The Republic*, trans. Desmond Lee, Penguin, London 1974.
41. Jacques Derrida, 'White Mythology' in *Margins of Philosophy*, trans. Alan Bass, Harvester Wheatsheaf, New York 1982, p224.
42. Ernesto Laclau, 'The Politics of Rhetoric', University of Essex Department of Government, Colchester 1998, pp1-2.
43. J.L. Austin, *How to do things with Words*, Oxford University Press, Oxford 1962, pp1-12. See Jacques Derrida, *Limited Inc*, Northwestern University Press, Evanston 1988; Judith Butler, *Excitable Speech: a Politics of the Performative*, Routledge, New York 1997.
44. Chantal Mouffe, 'The Radical Centre: a Politics Without Adversary' in Soundings 9, Lawrence and Wishart, London 1998.
45. Gramsci, *op. cit.*, pp181-2.
46. Ernesto Laclau, *New Reflections on the Revolution of Our Time*, Verso, London 1990, p68.
47. Ernesto Laclau and Chantal Mouffe, *Hegemony and Socialist Strategy*, Verso, London 1985, pp134-7.
48. Mouffe, *op. cit.*, p13.
49. Of course, my critique of Mouffe is entirely vulnerable to exactly the same charge: is not Mouffe herself attempting to make a performative contribution to the strategic re-definition of New Labour itself? Of course, but the likely efficacy of any such strategy is entirely dependent on the fact of key participants in New Labour actually paying the slightest attention to what Mouffe says, which is frankly, though tragically, unlikely. There can be no doubt that Mouffe herself would fully realise this, and more importantly there can be no doubt, despite my argument here, that the rhetoric of truth and honesty deployed by Mouffe will be a crucial resource in forthcoming struggles to re-articulate the fields of global politics.
50. As Mouffe herself acknowledges, *op. cit.*, p23.
51. Tony Blair's speech to Labour Party Conference, 28 September 1999.
52. Alan Finlayson, 'Tony Blair and the Jargon of Modernisation', *Soundings* 10, Lawrence and Wishart, London 1998, p25.
53. Ernesto Laclau, 'Why do Empty Signifiers Matter to Politics', in *Emancipation(s)*, Verso, London 1996.
54. For a fuller account see Jeremy Gilbert, 'Blurred Vision: Pop, Populism and Politics' in Anne Coddington and Mark Perryman (eds), *The Moderniser's Dilemma*, Lawrence and Wishart, London 1998.
55. *Ibid.*

Looking backwards and forwards at cultural studies

PAUL SMITH

As we enter the twenty-first century, how much value is there in spending time looking back over the history of cultural studies and trying to imagine its future? For one thing, the issues involved in thinking about this field, or about what could or should constitute it, have rather been done to death over the last four decades, even if there's not much sign of the activity abating. On the other hand, it seems to be the case that this perpetual defining and redefining, looking backwards and forwards, has often been taken as a sign of the very vitality of the field, and sometimes as an essential and positive part of its nature and task; therefore, insofar as a constitutive claim of that sort keeps being made, it still needs attending to. Cultural studies, we often hear, is what it is and is valuable in part because it doesn't rest or stand still, but continually reinvents itself to adjust to new information and new circumstances. We might argue, on the other hand, that this state of flux is rather more a symptom of confusion and uncertainty than an essential strength in the enterprise. It might be that at this juncture, as before in the history of the field, nobody really quite knows what cultural studies is, and what it will be.

As well as risking the boredom of yet more such rehashing, this essay will probably also be somewhat foolhardy, since in a way it comes to try and bury cultural studies – at least, the cultural studies that I see in front of us right now, as well as some of its central claims or most frequently repeated vanities. And, by that token, it will probably also be a somewhat hubristic essay in that I'll be trying to make some recommendations and even exhortations around the topic of cultural studies. It will be a somewhat difficult project to keep under control as well, at least in part because of my own history, a history that underlines – if not exemplifies – the disjuncture between British and American 'versions' of cultural studies. Having been educated in the British cultural studies vein, I've also spent almost 20 years in the US, working in the first cultural studies undergraduate programme in the country (at Carnegie Mellon) and more lately in one of the first PhD programmes (at George Mason University). Now, returning to the UK, I'm possibly out of touch and my view perhaps parochial. But all these risks seem worth taking because of what still seems to me the most important potential of cultural studies: that is, its promise to be an intellectual endeavour with an overt claim on the political shape of contemporary culture and society.

Real cultural studies junkies will no doubt have noticed that the title for my article refers to – or rather, it repeats almost verbatim – the title of one of Stuart Hall's more extraordinary pieces of writing, a talk he gave first in 1989 and which was published in 1992 in *Rethinking Marxism*.[1] Hall's work is, of course, taken to be seminal in cultural studies everywhere and is consistently understood as definitive in many respects. I don't want to argue with that assessment; rather, I want to use that particular article to follow up some questions which continue to provoke debate within contemporary cultural studies, the central one of which the editors of this volume have explicitly taken up, namely, the relation between politics and culture. In order to approach such issues, I begin with a somewhat sceptical reading of Hall's article.

In his own looking back Hall presents one version of what is by now an almost canonical view of the history of cultural studies. But it's also a history that, for my purposes here, is rather emblematic: in a symptomatic reading, it can show some of the strange leaps and manoeuvres that cultural studies has always made in the past and still makes now. At its beginnings, Hall suggests, cultural studies stood in opposition to positivist social science departments which had seen cultures merely as analysable systems composed of abstract norms and values; cultural studies was equally a corrective to the disciplines of the humanities which had chronically refused to 'name let alone theorise or conceptualise culture'.[2] Then – and here's the first of several of Hall's emblematic moves that I want to point to – he goes on precisely *not* to offer a definition or conceptualisation of culture. Or rather, he falls back on a version of those large nebulosities that cultural studies has been pleased to be able to pull down wholesale from Raymond Williams's altogether more satisfying work, where culture is defined very generally as 'whole ways of communicating ... whole ways of life, where popular culture intersects with the high arts ... where power cuts across knowledge ... where cultural processes anticipate social change.'

This is the first thing I want to point to by way of Hall's article – the propensity in cultural studies to avoid offering up any especially firm definition or methodologically productive view of what culture really is. This isn't the only place where Hall offers such vagueness at the heart of the endeavour. In another well-known article, 'Cultural studies: two paradigms,' he goes further and suggests that in the foundational work of the Centre for Contemporary Cultural Studies – both in Birmingham and in its satellite courses and publications – there had been 'no single, unproblematic definition of "culture"' to be found. What the CCCS operated with was, rather than a logically or conceptually clarified notion of culture, a convergence of what he calls 'interests'.[3]

What I want to suggest here is that this determination not to define the central object of cultural studies has led to what can only be described as a pluralistic tendency at the heart of the project. This is a tendency that has authorised cultural studies to take many forms, of course, and in that sense might be considered a good thing, especially by those who think of cultural studies as an opportunity to escape the perceived rigours of the usual disciplinary structures. But it seems unarguable at this point that the lack of willingness to define the central object of study has also and necessarily implied a lack of methodological and procedural consistency and denied any but the loosest cohesion to cultural studies. We might here consider John Frow's recent claim that, by and large, the cultural studies version of culture is in fact an embarrassment, not only in its lack of clarity and definition but also in its inability to engage properly with other disciplinary and methodological approaches to culture, such as those found in ethnographic and anthropological traditions.[4]

But, as I've pointed out, it's often this very looseness and openness that many cultural studies practitioners have chronically held to be most valuable about the enterprise. Certainly, Hall has been by no means alone in speaking out against the 'codification' of cultural studies and reminding us that there can be no final paradigm for the field.[5] Some of the most prominent names in cultural studies have made analogous claims on the grounds that the flexibility of assumptions and procedures in cultural studies allows for a kind of analytical freedom that can flexibly react to the ever-changing complexities of cultural life. Perhaps the strongest version of these claims is made in the editors' introduction to one of the most influential anthologies in the field,

Cultural Studies. There, Lawrence Grossberg, Cary Nelson and Paula Treichler object to the idea that the field should be policed in any way and recommend a loose and open intellectual approach, one equivalent to a kind of *bricolage*. The line is, in all its glory, that 'cultural studies has no guarantees about what questions are important to ask within given contexts or how to answer them; hence no methodology can be privileged or even temporarily employed with total security and confidence, yet none can be eliminated out of hand.'[6]

This position has been so internalised in the field by now that it's almost an article of faith to say that cultural studies does not need definition, because it is anti-disciplinary or non-disciplinary, and that a large part of its strength lies in its capacity to offer intellectual freedom. Indeed, as the argument runs, any moves towards a 'disciplined' cultural studies would constitute a policing of the project in a discourse where the notion of policing is understood as authoritarian from the start and therefore somehow antithetical to it. This championing of the openness, looseness or unfinished character of cultural studies work thus becomes the sign of a properly liberated intellectual project.

Such a position is exactly what Hall adopts in his article – this is the second move he makes which I want to draw attention to. Armed first of all with only the vaguest definition of culture, Hall goes on to claim that cultural studies gets its specificity from its contingent location, its flexible positions, and its self-reflexivity. There can be no argument: those features have indeed tended to establish the specific character of what we know as cultural studies, but at the not inconsiderable price of rendering cultural studies an at best eclectic, and at worst unprincipled intellectual endeavour. This is a perspective that produces the kind of argument that Lawrence Grossberg makes when he insists that cultural studies is and must always be influenced by its 'outside', or that the nature of work in cultural studies must somehow be dictated by existing concerns.[7] There is clearly a problem with this perspective insofar as cultural studies is perhaps the only current form of knowledge production which explicitly argues that the processes of knowledge production are ideologically and historically contingent. Throwing cultural studies itself at the mercy of existing concerns is to refuse to allow it any possibility of breaking through the ideological construction of what Hall himself has called 'useful knowledges'.

Equally to the point, the assumptions of this somewhat reactive approach – what I'd call a wait-and-see methodology – are that the object of knowledge will automatically make evident the mode of analysis proper to it, or that method and intellection can somehow be pulled from the air in order to deal with changing circumstances and variable phenomena. Such a view mystifies the relationship between object and knowledge, and it seems to me that such mystification is a high price to pay for what the argument intends to buy – namely, the freedom of the individual scholar or researcher to follow their track without the constraint of discipline. Obviously such methodological freedom compromises intellectual results.

From the point of view of intellectual method, this all leaves cultural studies with only one place to go. With no focused definition of the object, and with what amounts to an ad hoc or merely opportunistic methodology, cultural studies can then justify itself only in terms of the topics it approaches. In other words, cultural studies can do no more than become a thematically organised area of study where the choice of specific topic or theme comes to be of more import than the choice of method or procedure. And this indeed is illustrated by the third emblematic move in Hall's essay, which arrives on cue just as his discussion of procedural or methodological issues is displaced onto largely thematic concerns. Cultural studies is visibly transformed, in Hall's account, into a *topical* enterprise. In this particular essay, the privileged topic is race and ethnicity, which emerge as the essential focus of the field. My pointing out this third move on Hall's part is not, I want to emphasise, to say that race and ethnicity are not amongst the proper objects of investigation for cultural studies. It is simply to suggest that, given the history and assumptions that I'm examining, it seems inevitable that this topic, or some topic quite like it, should have emerged as a quasi-definitional element for the field at the same time as any particular or 'codified' way of approaching it is explicitly eschewed.

That is not to say that the way Hall approaches the chosen topic is entirely unfamiliar, nor that he doesn't try to sketch out a recognisable cultural studies approach. The set of bedrock ideas to which he appeals in order to approach the question of race includes a familiar tour around Fanon's phenomenological schemas, borrowings from Lacanian psychoanalysis and side-trips into Freud and Lévi-Strauss. Those points of reference are well-established in the chapbook that cultural studies has been peddling for many years now, and they sit alongside forms of semiotic analysis – deriving mostly from Saussure via Roland Barthes – which have stood unchallenged in the field for decades as tokens of a common methodology. To see how deeply those points of reference have taken root, one has only to look at the kind of work published under the rubric of cultural studies in the last few years. The heady mix of Fanon and psychoanalysis that Hall concocts, a somewhat crude binarism of self and other, has since been taken to its intellectual extremes by Homi Bhabha, and more recently to its purest banality by Nick Stevenson.[8] The persistence of the semiotic model for the analysis of meaning is fully evident even in the kind of work which is currently claimed to be a recasting of cultural studies, like the essays collected in Angela McRobbie's *Back to Reality?* Perhaps the strongest indication of the unreconstructed nature of the influence of the semiotic model is to be found in two recent Open University textbooks: *Representation,* edited by Stuart Hall himself, and *Doing Cultural Studies*, a primer of the field construed around an extended case-study of the Sony Walkman. In each of these three texts, a Barthesian semiotics is taken as read, as it were, with little regard for the numerous critiques of such a model of meaning-production and still less regard for any alternative theoretical models.[9]

Whatever else can be said about what I'm calling the cultural studies chapbook, it's easy to see that its points of reference define a field that is simultaneously eclectic and narrow, and that many of its most frequently deployed components have been pressed into service for many years now without serious renewal or reconsideration. In any case, it would be difficult to regard this set of co-ordinates as anything so systematic as a methodology, even if it continues to guide a majority of cultural studies practitioners. In the face of this situation, it becomes hard to resist the accuracy of Meaghan Morris's observations about what she calls 'banality' in cultural studies, whereby the limited and yet eclectic range of theoretical co-ordinates tends to produce and reproduce a kind of template cultural studies article in which essentially the same thing can be said about any object in the cultural life.[10]

We can now leave Hall's article, having pressed it a little too hard in any case, especially considering its schematic nature. But the points I've tried to draw from it remain for me emblematic of a certain set of problems within cultural studies. If I've stressed the issue of methodology, it's not that I rather simple-mindedly believe that in order to rediscover itself cultural studies needs to establish protocols and procedures which would be more rigorous and more intellectually consistent. I *do* believe that, but I also reckon that the kinds of analysis that remain acceptable and even applauded in contemporary cultural studies have consistently proceeded on the faulty assumption that to address a certain set of thematically construed issues is tantamount to undertaking political analysis and even political intervention. In that sense, politics is understood as an automatic engagement, as the necessary and inevitable outcome of a certain kind of intellection. If we then turn to the question of what relation, if any, cultural studies can claim with existing political projects in theory or practice, we might have to understand that to discover any such relation might not be altogether welcome. For instance, what relation operates between current cultural studies in the UK and the ascendancy of New Labour, a relation going back at least to 'New Times' and the critique of Thatcherism which simply admired Thatcherism too much;[11] or the relation between the policy strain of cultural studies in Australia and the erosion of labour politics in that country; or the relation between cultural studies in the United States and the forms of individualism and identity politics which resonate with a permanent strain of reactionary thought in the history of that republic? These are questions which I won't attempt to answer here, even though they are surely questions which cultural studies needs to be asking.[12] And this would seem especially appropriate where, in the UK particularly, cultural studies not only takes the political for granted but often claims a connection to an 'organic' politics of resistance.

As much to the point in the immediate future would be to try to suggest ways in which cultural studies might reinvigorate its idea of the political, or even begin the task of drawing up a new political agenda for the field. And it might be as well to cut to the chase, as it were, by saying that the way forward seems to me to be a way back. That is, that somewhere in the past of cultural studies is an almost forgotten engagement with Marxism and with the analysis of capital that should, in my view, lie at the heart of any serious consideration of culture. I do realise that for many cultural studies practitioners such a suggestion can only cause a groan of weary recognition or boredom, since it would appear that any debate about the place of Marxist analysis has now given way to what is essentially an absence of Marxism in cultural studies.

The coming about of that absence has, of course, a lengthy history by now. Indeed, Colin Sparks's account of the relation between cultural studies and Marxism points first of all to the relatively weak or sceptical Marxism of the 'founding fathers' of cultural studies, Richard Hoggart, Raymond Williams and E. P. Thompson.[13] Even though Marxism gained some prominence in cultural studies in the aftermath of 1968, particularly with the focus on ideology under the influence of Althusser's work, this was part of a generally eclectic searching around for theoretical tools, and was in any case almost immediately eclipsed by the liberal and selective version of Gramsci adopted by Hall, along with the almost anti-Marxist version of Gramsci promulgated by

Laclau and Mouffe in their influential book *Hegemony and Socialist Strategy*.[14] The influence of Laclau's and Mouffe's work on cultural studies can hardly be underestimated, especially in the USA, where its assault on the supposedly intractable essentialism of Marxism was taken up with great relief by cultural studies practitioners for whom (in a context where red-baiting is still a popular sport) the whiff of Marxism around cultural studies had been an embarrassment.

Inevitably, too, the eclectic tastes of cultural studies have found much to like in the well-stocked kitchen of poststructuralism, and the tendency of poststructuralism to elide Marxism has been easily adopted. The elision is almost total if one looks at recent cultural studies metacommentaries such as *Cultural Studies in Question*, a collection of essays on the current state of the field. There, in the course of more than a dozen supposedly cutting-edge essays, Marxism is mentioned a handful of times, and then as a historical curiosity (in relation to theories of ideology, for instance). Even the contributions of Nicholas Garnham (whose longstanding insistence on the importance of political economy for the study of culture has been more or less ignored within cultural studies) and Douglas Kellner (writing on the use of political economy for cultural studies) appear constrained not to mention the M-word, even while they argue strongly for the use of what are Marxist analytical tools.[15]

The standard or most frequently repeated objection to Marxism in cultural studies is probably the double-headed notion that Marxism is both 'reductive' and 'economically determinist'. Those two charges are still used as a shorthand way of dismissing Marxism, though to them has been added the claim that Marxism's emphasis on class necessarily precludes the dynamic studies of other forms of subjectivity – race and gender in particular. Such claims are mostly rhetorical, pointing to a kind of Marxism that I, for one, almost never see, but which in any case would be far outweighed by other kinds of Marxist theory and analysis. The charges seem in any case particularly problematic when made from within a discourse that has been unwilling really to think about the question of determinations within the processes of culture – this despite promptings from one of the 'founding fathers', Raymond Williams, whose work came to insist on the need to establish 'the real order of determination between different kinds of activity'. 'That there always is such an order of determination cannot be doubted,' he writes. 'This is the necessary, theoretical base for the recognition of genuinely different social orders.'[16]

The understanding of determinations – and, of course, levels of over-determinations – within cultural life is really no more than a single one of the huge gaps in the knowledge produced by cultural studies, but it is an important one. I can recall no cultural studies text that has argued specifically against the 'necessary theoretical base' Williams recommended; and that's perhaps because the mere possibility of thinking through issues of determination disappears once the spectre of Marxism's economic 'determinism' has been raised. More crucially even, the absence of that analytical register from cultural studies authorises the *thematic* selection of cultural elements, and their treatment as isolated, discrete entities whose contextual relations are not significantly to do with the mode of production. In the extreme, such an absence sanctions a kind of reading operation to be performed on cultural objects or events as, essentially, 'texts' with no necessary reference to the place or conditions of their production.

What I'm pointing to is what Fredric Jameson has noted in his understated but ultimately quite scarifying indictment of cultural studies, that is, the tendency of cultural studies to eschew the economic and the whole question of determinations, thence to end up in what he calls 'a kind of forthright anarchistic stance on the thing itself' – a critique similar to what John Clarke has called, even more loudly, 'the abolition of the object' itself within cultural studies.[17] A clear example of what analysis looks like from that kind of anarchist or nihilistic stance in relation to the object is provided by one of the books I mentioned earlier, Paul du Gay's textbook *Doing Cultural Studies*, where all questions of the economic are turned into a mere contextualisation of the object, and where all questions of determinism are rejected as unthinkable. In other words, for work of this sort the role of what are clearly political-economic elements can be no more than instrumental; political-economic elements may be used to help provide 'readings' of particular features of the object, but must not be used to forge an explanation of the logic of the object itself. In this case, the object is a highly successful product, the Sony Walkman, but there is no recognition that its role in the circuits of commodity exchange is a crucial part of its identity as object. The notion that the representational logic of the object itself could be in the end no more than a function of a political-economic logic is always already ruled out of court.

In a more ordered and calm way than I have done here, John Frow has recently addressed some of the kinds of problems that I'm pointing to in cultural studies. His view is that the kind of work I'm criticising, with its emphasis on the production of meaning rather than the production of commodities, will always be at a distance from work that stresses the political-economic elements of culture. Indeed, Frow thinks that, as a field of study, cultural studies is at an impasse with an impossible job of reconciliation on its hands. His position seems worth quoting fully:

> There is no simple way (apart from straightforward reductionism) of squaring a methodological concentration on the productive working of texts with a methodological concentration on the productive work of the [capitalist] system. They are not complementary, and the effect of this tension is a kind of necessary indeterminacy principle. Both positions are 'correct', but there is no way of reconciling them in a single perspective. By the same token, to elaborate a 'correct' position is therefore by definition to fail to perform the countervailing analysis.[18]

In my view Frow's point here is a little pessimistic. It doesn't seem quite or necessarily impossible to produce the kind of cultural studies analysis that would make the connections between the production of meanings and subjectivities and the production of commodities. The important point is to be able to consider and analyse the processes of determination amongst and between the different levels of production. This implies, at the very least, an agreement that it is impossible to think of any kind of cultural form or any kind of cultural artefact or event as autonomous. Rather, cultural phenomena, far from being autonomous texts, are caught in a logic of totality (a totality considered, of course, in all its contradictions). The task of thinking any object whatsoever in that manner has traditionally fallen to Marxism; the particular attention that Marxism has paid to all realms – the cultural, the social, the political, and the economic – still constitutes a more advanced and difficult project than the vagueness of this area called cultural studies, which, it would seem, has shied away from such difficulties, preferring instead a lack of rigour that has somehow come to think of itself as radically democratic and liberating.

In the end, cultural studies has not been a radical intellectual movement that upset existing disciplines, reformulated knowledge, continually interrogated itself and its methods, and opened out onto a thriving area of politics beyond the academy, addressing the public sphere. It's really been none of those things, if we're honest about it. Cultural studies has never managed to fill the gaps it made in itself when it elided Marxism; no other feasible theoretical forms have come to do the job that Marxism did and that cultural studies always claimed it wanted to do. To now rehabilitate a set of ideas and methods which are associated with Marxism would not make cultural studies Marxist per se. But it would mean that cultural studies could no longer afford an antipathy to Marxist theory, an antipathy that has helped lead it into numerous dead ends and crises and held it back from realising its best intellectual and political aspirations.

NOTES

1. Stuart Hall, 'Race, culture, and communications: looking backward and forward at cultural studies', in John Storey (ed) *What is Cultural Studies? A Reader*, Arnold, London 1996. The essay originally appeared in *Rethinking Marxism* 5.1 (1992), pp10-21.
2. *Ibid.*, p336.
3. Stuart Hall, 'Cultural studies: two paradigms', in John Storey (ed), *What is Cultural Studies? A Reader*, Arnold, London 1996, p33. The essay originally appeared in *Media, Culture and Society* 2 (2), pp57-72.
4. John Frow, *Cultural Studies and Cultural Value*, Oxford University Press, Oxford 1995, pp7-8.
5. Stuart Hall, 'On postmodernism and articulation' (an interview edited by Lawrence Grossberg), in David Morley and Chen Kuan-Hsing (eds), *Stuart Hall: Critical Dialogues in Cultural Studies*, Routledge, London 1996, pp149-50.
6. Lawrence Grossberg, Cary Nelson, Paula Treichler (eds), *Cultural Studies*, Routledge, New York 1992, p2.
7. See Lawrence Grossberg, 'Cultural studies: what's in a name?', *Bringing It All Back Home*, Duke University Press, Durham NC 1997 [1995], pp245-71.
8. See Homi Bhabha, *The Location of Culture*, Routledge, London, 1994; Nick Stevenson, *The Transformation of the Media: Globalisation, Morality and Ethics*, Longman, London 1999 (especially the penultimate chapter on the Rwandan genocide).
9. Angela McRobbie (ed), *Back to Reality? Social Experience and Cultural Studies*, Manchester University Press, Manchester 1997; Stuart Hall (ed), *Representation: Cultural Representations and Signifying Practices*, Sage/The Open University, London 1997; Paul du Gay, Stuart Hall, Linda Jones, Hugh Mackay, Keith Negus (eds), *Doing Cultural Studies*, Sage/The Open University, London 1997.
10. Meaghan Morris, 'Banality in cultural studies', *Discourse* 10, pp3-29 (also in John Storey, ed., *op. cit.*).
11. This point is made more fully in my *Millennial Dreams: Contemporary Culture and Capital in the North,* Verso, London 1997, pp152-7.

12. More along the same lines will be found in my forthcoming *Cultural Studies: A Manifesto*, University of Minnesota Press, Minneapolis 2001.

13. Colin Sparks, 'Stuart Hall, cultural studies and Marxism', in David Morley and Chen Kuan-Hsing (eds), *op. cit.*, pp71-101.

14. Perhaps Hall's most productive use of Gramsci is in 'Gramsci's relevance for the study of race and ethnicity,' in David Morley, and Chen Kuan-Hsing (eds), *op. cit.*, pp411-40. See too Ernesto Laclau and Chantal Mouffe, *Hegemony and Socialist Strategy: Towards a Radical Democratic Politics*, Verso, London 1985; and my critique of it along these lines: 'The secret agent of Laclau and Mouffe' in Miami Theory Collective (eds), *Community at Loose Ends*, University of Minnesota Press, Minneapolis 1991, pp99-110.

15. Marjorie Ferguson,and Peter Golding (eds), *Cultural Studies in Question,* Sage, London 1997.

16. Raymond Williams, *Towards 2000*, Chatto and Windus, London 1983, p15.

17. Fredric Jameson, 'On "cultural studies"', *Social Text* 34 (1993), p45; John Clarke, *New Times and Old Enemies: Essays on Cultural Studies in America*, HarperCollins Academic, London 1991, p25.

18. John Frow, *op. cit.*, p70.

Clintonism: the phantom menace

MARTIN MCQUILLAN

'We do not know how it is with the inhabitants of other planets and with their nature, but if we ourselves execute this commission of nature well, we may surely flatter ourselves that we occupy no mean status among our neighbours in the cosmos.'

Immanuel Kant[1]

'Find out who killed Kennedy, and tell me whether there are UFOs or not.'
Bill Clinton to Webster Hubbel[2]

ONCE MORE UNTO THE POST

Why has history been so undialectical as to produce Tony Blair? Why is the new *Star Wars* film so disappointing? These two questions are not unrelated and might be reformulated in a third question, one asked by Jacques Derrida in a recent text on Marxism: 'What is to be said about *philosophy as ontology* in the inheritance left us by Marx?'[3] All three questions are, in different ways, predicated by those familiar thematics of the left: failure, defeat, setback, frustration. For as long as there has been a 'left', there seems to have been an accompanying discourse of defeat. From Danton to Daniel Cohn-Bendit there is endemic in the left a sense that disappointment is not what it used to be. This situation seems to be structural to those political positions and performativities which some continue to feel reassured enough to call 'the left'. This heterogeneous constellation of voices seems to have been troubled with ends, crises, and ruins for some time now. Leaving aside for the moment the significance of the title of this essay and more direct responses to our opening trio of questions, how might we account for this belatedness of the left?

81

If the term 'the left' presents a difficulty of representation, it is because of the desire of the disparate, contradictory and competing voices occupying that space to lay metonymic claim to represent the entire field.[4] A continued unproblematic use of the term 'the left', qua political identity, presupposes the idea of a unified tradition, genealogy or legacy identical with itself, possessing an integrity in aims and methods and working towards a recognisable and knowable end. The fact that this is not the case, and never has been, is demonstrated by the diverse composition of the present volume. However, there remains within a certain idea of 'the left' a resistance to recognising this heterogeneity. This takes the form of a discourse that addresses the assumed unity of a 'we of the left' and imagines its readership as a fraternity, linked by transparent relations of mutual comprehension. Such brotherly accord relies upon the assurance of a legitimate claim to the rights of the legacy 'of the left'. The desire to represent the totality of the left from one 'politically correct' position is a desire to secure the rights to an inheritance, to be the true heir(s) of a hallowed tradition. It is a common presumption on 'the left' that *we* all want the same thing and *we* all know what that thing is, even if present circumstances temporarily stop *us* attaining that thing.

It is on this basis that one member of the leftist family has sought to keep watch over the thoughts of his brothers and sisters.[5] Terry Eagleton, perhaps now only a symbol rather than a catalyst of the presumptive 'Marxism' to which I am referring, has (in a journal of postcolonial theory) recently upbraided his 'fellow-travellers' for abandoning the truth of the Marxist inheritance. Having cited recent mediatic examples of social unrest, he writes:

> One way to stave off the most disastrous consequences of such disruption is for those in the thick of it to produce a coherent programme of demands and plan of action; and this means, among other things, the survival of socialist ideas in an epoch when they are everywhere under threat. 'Postcolonialism' has played its part in suppressing, sidelining and displacing such increasingly unfashionable notions, and thus has a degree of responsibility in this regard. Class struggle is now embarrassingly passé, whereas the affirmation of cultural identity is not. One of the less creditable reasons for the emergence of postcolonial discourse, as indeed of feminism, is that certain other forms of political conflict in the societies which breed these languages are currently proving too hard to crack, and a certain displacement effect has accordingly set in.[6]

Derrida comments elsewhere that 'one can only rub one's eyes in disbelief and wonder where he [Eagleton] finds the inspiration, the haughtiness, the right' to act so proprietorially regarding the legacy of Marx (MS, p222). On this occasion, Eagleton manages the most impressive of political contortions, simultaneously acknowledging 'postcolonialism' (and feminism, as if it did not predate Marxism!) as responding to specific conditions of thought and action, while dismissing them as failures for not adhering to the programme of a socialism which, by his own admission, has failed. In contrast, Eagleton remains the keeper of the flame, awaiting the day when the scales will fall from his colleagues' eyes: '"Postcolonialism" has been on the whole rather stronger on identity than on the International Monetary Fund, more fascinated by marginality than by markets. It finds it hard to accept that the acknowledgement of difference, hybridity, multiplicity, is a drastically impoverished kind of political ethic in contrast to the affirmation of human solidarity and reciprocity, even if the former is of course a sine qua non of the latter.' It is difficult to see how ethics might be the poorer for a consideration of difference rather than the International Monetary Fund, while it might be the task of a 'political ethic' to interrogate such casual discursive formulations as 'human solidarity', given that the officers of the IMF no doubt feel some degree of solidarity in their affirmation of the reciprocity of world debt. Certainly, Eagleton is not the only border-guard of this Marxist discourse; one might think of Aijaz Ahmad, Perry Anderson and Benedict Anderson as figures who also find resources amongst the ruins of post-Cold War politics to protect the boundaries of Marxism, and to presume the right to do so.

The sense of failure ('political conflict … proving too hard to crack') which seems inevitably to accompany political action of 'the left' (and it is not at all clear whether this sense of failure follows behind, picking at the debris or carries a torch directing the way) is related to the desire for purity and propriety which informs a certain Marxist-Socialist discourse. One can only be disappointed with the outcome of a political event if one had expected a different resolution. Expecting a different resolution depends upon knowing what you want, knowing that what has happened is not what you wanted, knowing that what has happened will still not lead to what you want, and knowing that what you want can only be achieved via a determinable path (which is one which has identifiably *not* happened). To know all of this would be to know a great deal, knowledge which seems more than a little precarious, given the absolute unknowability of the future as it arrives in a present non-identical with itself. To be able to identify an event as a 'defeat' or a 'failure', one must assume both a limit to the outcome of that event (the effects of which will have to be recognisable and no longer active) and that this limit does not coincide with the fixed aspirations of the epistemological frame from which the event is judged. In other words, for a certain type of 'Marxism' to denounce either a political event as a 'failure' or a theoretical discourse as 'not properly Marxist', a great deal has to be assumed about the prophylactic integrity of the Marxist tradition and the knowability of what is permissible within such boundaries.

If one starts from this position, that is, from the belief that there is such a thing as Marxism (a programme applicable to all occasions, to be enacted within the social realm to achieve certain determinate results – what Eagleton refers to as 'a coherent programme of demands and plan of action'), and that the mandates of its proprietors must be upheld as a precondition of belief, one is bound to be disappointed by the outcome of history. There is something profoundly contradictory in the assumption that the socio-economic space is so unstable as to lead to a revolutionary situation through the application of a theoretical programme, while that programme is so certain that its propriety will not be affected by socio-economic change. Hence, it is not unusual to find the disingenuous situation of some Marxist theoreticians denouncing the history of the Soviet Union as not being properly Marxist and so dismissing most of the history of Marxism as impure in the name of a pure Marxist idea of History, which by accident of history they have become heirs to.[7] Not that the Marxism of Eagleton, Ahmad or Perry Anderson (to name only the most prominent examples of an idea of 'materialism' which continues to pervade the academic left, at least in Britain) is necessarily recognisable as the Marxism of, say, Althusser or Lukács (to cite similar self-appointed keepers of the flame). It would seem that ensuring the integrity of the Marxist legacy also involves the conscious decision to disassociate the name of 'Marxism' from anything that might be thought of as failure. Consequently, so the argument would seem to run, Marxism has not failed because it has never actually been tried, that is to say, real Marxism has never been tried. It is with the fervour of the spin-doctor that such proprietorial Marxists attempt to protect the boundaries of Marxism by distinguishing between Real Marxism and Marxism Lite, between political failure which, because it has failed, cannot have been true Marxism and a theoretical discourse which retains its purity by disassociating itself from something identified as practical 'failure'.

In this way, Real Marxism occupies the 'win-win' situation of denouncing other discourses of 'the left' as not being 'practical' (one might say ontological) enough, while ensuring its own determinedly theoretical status by (implicitly) defining itself in opposition to the messy business of historical 'defeat'. Such a gesture involves a constant shifting of the goalposts to ensure that Real Marxism can never be defeated, scoring opportunistically against those discourses which refuse to share its dogmatic adherence to the idea of a programme, whilst avoiding coming off the bench and putting itself in play, lest it risk the possibility of sharing in defeat (or blaming something other than itself for mistakes whenever a defeat looks likely). This points to a terrible combination for such theoreticians, namely, avoiding defeat by constantly re-evaluating, in the light of historical events, what constitutes true Marxism (an action which would seem to run contrary to the idea that the tenets of such Marxism are fixed, which is why they are true) and simultaneously sharing in the vocabulary of defeat by bemoaning the failures of the left (which will have been failures by virtue of not having been really Marxist). The result of such a tactic for the directors and supporters of Real Marxism is not so much political quietism (for they will always be the first to denounce in the loudest and most prominent mediatic positions heretic 'Marxisms' such as deconstruction or so-called post-structuralism)[8], but the absolute impossibility of politics as such. Real Marxism retains its purity by remaining above anything like an empirical political space, awaiting the proper moment of revolution, which despite false starts, is yet to happen or at least is yet to be identified by this group of Marxists as having happened to their satisfaction. A text like Eagleton's response to Robert Young, cited above, screens out the transcendentality of its position by complacently gesturing to the identifiable politics of the IMF, rather than participating in the difficult task of thinking through identity, including the identity of 'the left'. Accordingly, this least engaged of discourses negates the possibility of politics by avoiding contestation, change or the unforeseeable intervention of the other, through an insistence on its own transcendent position with respect to historical events, placing itself as the cause, the end and the judge of those events.

This is the Real Marxist calculation, which on May 1 1997 ran as follows: the New Labour government will inevitably be a failure, I will avoid association with that failure by not helping to elect New Labour. Rather, I will cast my vote for a Real Marxist party (which stands by the true tenets of socialism), even though it will never win power. To have done this in order to ensure the inevitability of Labour's failure in government seems to me to be the most scandalous of depoliticising acts. The question on that day was not the justice of a Labour victory and the results it would produce, but the possible indeterminate and unknowable effects of not having a Conservative government. To this end, millions voted tactically in a political affirmation of the possibility of change with a non-Conservative government; voting, where context allowed, Liberal Democrat, Scottish and Welsh Nationalist, or Independent. The consequence of such votes was an inevitable dent in the scale and significance of the Blair victory, but that is secondary to the greater affirmation of a positive non-Conservative vote. Meanwhile, voting for pure Marxism under conditions in which a Real Marxist candidate did not represent the primary opposition to the incumbent or challenging Conservative, was a vote that elevated itself above the political situation of that day (circumstances as specific and localised as any other). Such votes judged the result of the political process in advance without participating in it, absolving the good conscience of the abstainer, whilst embalming the political tenets of Marxism against risk, blame or impurity. A vote of this kind was a pure transcendental, golden vote, which could not be said to be a political event because it never arrived in the present with anything like the weight of an event.

One is bound to be disappointed by historical circumstances if this is one's considered view of history . It might well be asked, how could history be so undialectical as to allow only Terry Eagleton to be correct and everyone else to be wrong? Perhaps the difficulty with patrimonial Marxism (the inheritance of Marx following in a continuous line of legitimate heirs) lies in its very conception of History, assuming (given the above comments) that this conception has been the same through-out the 'tradition'. The 'History' of Marxism (or the idea of 'History' which the custodians of the firm, 'Marx & Sons', have continued to peddle despite the law of diminishing returns and the seeming ruin and bankruptcy faced by consecutive generations within the family business) can allow only for a sense of failure. If, despite one's best political efforts, history results in anything other than the detailed outcome planned for it by the producers of Real Marxism, then those political efforts (as non-identical with intention) will be deemed a failure. Because the historical event cannot be programmed (since it arrives from the future in an unknowable form, and the idea of a history depends on its continuous arrival in this form), any history which does not follow the rhythm of a programme will be a failure according to any programmatic criteria. A 'leftist' programme for history will always fail because history cannot be programmed in this way; those who claim rights as keepers of the programme ought to know this, for their continued existence as keepers depends upon the impossibility of implementing the programme. For this reason, it might be more appropriate to think of history not as dialectical, but as *spectral*. Like the spectre which is haunting Europe in the opening line of *The Communist Manifesto*, history arrives from the future, and it is the unknowable effects of this future arrival which disturb and destabilise the present. Marxism is haunted by its own history of failure. Not only the historical terrors and tragedies of those political events which it disavows as not properly Marxist (this exorcism acting as a persistent form of conjuration), but also its own failures as a philosophical discourse in dialogue with others of 'the left' (those such as feminism or postcolonialism which present it with questions too difficult to answer), as well as its own ineffectiveness as a political discourse. (The inactivity it reviles in others can surely only be a projection of self-loathing, unless Oxbridge and Ivy League professorships are an as yet unrecognised form of revolutionary practice.)

The history of Real Marxism, as a history of failure, is a history of the repression of what I will provisionally call 'post-Marxism'. Let us take the syllables of this term one at a time lest its use here be confused with other invocations of a similar sounding phrase. First, the prefix 'post-' is used in much the same way as Lyotard uses it in 'the post-modern'.[9] 'Marxism' as an unstable non-unitary discourse, open to the effects of historical and epistemological change, contains (within itself) an ethico-theoretical dynamic, which seeks to compel itself into a state other than itself. This would be the meaning of the avowed 'objectives of Marxism' such as emancipation, liberation, class struggle, and revolution. Each of these activities furthers the programme of Marxism and so forces that programme into a re-evaluation of itself in the light of new historical and social conditions, so that a practice of constant re-evaluation could no longer adhere to the name of a programme. Furthermore, the indeterminable effects produced by activities of struggle and emancipation would push Marxism itself into a new and unfamiliar space. What was once called 'failure' might be identified as new conditions of possibility from which the idea of the political must be rethought each time. In this way, the conditions of possibility of a Marxist programme guarantee the impossibility of a Marxism that would take the shape of a programme, so Marxism is compelled by historical circumstances to be in a constant state of otherness to itself.

Marxism as an idea of political change must, as a necessary condition of that change, be 'constitutionally and ceaselessly pregnant'[10] with that Marxism which is not itself. This is a Marxism without Mar*xism*, what I am calling here 'post-Marxism' – not because it is an epistemic configuration which comes after the legacy of Marx, but because it follows the spectral logic of the use of the prefix 'post' as Lyotard and others have used that term.[11] Therefore, post-Marxism is the 'primal scene' of Marxism, and in order for any event (either reading or political activity) to be Marxist, it must first be post-Marxist. To actually participate in a politics of change, it is necessary to be open to the effects of that change and to re-evaluate those politics in the light of those indeterminable effects. Changing politics is the result of changing politics.

Secondly, the proper noun 'Marx' designates a collection of texts covering topics as diverse as political economy, literary criticism, historiography, sociology, and philosophy. This body of work is as indeterminate with respect to its meaning as any other textual corpus, while its heterogeneity and substantial co-authorship makes its reading and analysis – given all that we know about textuality – all the more pressing. In other words, there can be no boundaries to the reading and re-reading of the texts of Marx. Their meaning cannot be fixed by an arcane priesthood of Real Marxists, who (like the humanist New Critics they are said to despise) seek to establish the eternal verities of Marx and defend the great tradition from those perverse enough not to accept their interpretation of Scripture. Insofar as this proper noun names the texts of Marx, it recognises that the history of Marxist hermeneutics constitutes a series of footnotes to those texts, but is not reducible to those texts. In other words, the texts of Lukács, Althusser, or Eagleton are not the same thing as the texts of Marx and/or Engels and there is no intrinsic reason why a reading of the latter must, as a precondition of interpretation, pass through the former. The anxiety caused within patrimonial Marxism by a reading which does not seek permission for its interpretative value through the appropriate channels,[12] demonstrates the desire of the self-proclaimed legitimate heirs of Marx to deny any illegitimate children access to the legacy – whether they stake their claims openly or in secret. In order to open up the question of the meaning and the place of Marx today, in a serious way, it will first be necessary to open up the closed shop of Real Marxism which seeks to keep the discussion of his Legacy within the limits of a predictable vocabulary by a programmed denunciation of outsiders and troublemakers.

Finally, the suffix '-ism', which is by no means peripheral to the concerns under discussion here. Heidegger, at the risk of causing further offence to Marxists, notes that 'every mere "ism" is a misunderstanding and the death of history'.[13] If the syllable 'ism' denotes a fixed system of belief with a closed and limited order of operation (McCarthyism, fascism, Thatcherism, Clintonism, cubism, poststructuralism), then any 'ism' merits its suffix by its inability to recognise the impossibility of its own closure. As a closed system, it must draw up its rules of operation by placing a limit on its actions.[14] This limit (as a limit) must exclude as well as define. Accordingly, the system as a system of universal belief cannot explain or influence that which it excludes and so cannot be universal. On the one hand, this formulation has the status of the most trivial of truisms; on the other hand, it is precisely its standing as an 'ism' which legitimates the policing actions of the heirs of Marx*ism*. The indeterminable effects of history which give rise to the phantom of post-Marxism, and the inability of Marxism as a system to close itself (we might ask, under what circumstances could the reading of Marx not be open?), might allow us an opportunity to move away from a thematics of defeat and failure while attempting to approach the ontological questions of politics posed in this chapter.

A NEW HOPE

In order to respond to some of the issues raised in the first half of this essay, I will now examine two texts which treat the ontological questions of political philosophy in relation to contemporary political developments: Christopher Hitchens's seductive polemic, *No One Left To Lie To: The Triangulations of William Jefferson Clinton*, and the much derided film *Star Wars Episode 1: The Phantom Menace* (a film that was not really that bad, so long as one did not have fixed expectations of it). Opening with the line 'This little book has no "hidden agenda"'(NOL, p.9), Hitchens would seem to be tempting fate in an altogether irresistible manner. A polemicist must build his house on sure foundations and Hitchens is certainly sure of himself: he knows what he wants – socialism – and he knows that he does not yet have it. Assuming such an -ism exists, is knowable and obtainable, Hitchens hopes that in his pages 'some of the honor of the Left can be rescued from the moral and intellectual shambles of the past seven years, in which the locusts have dined so long and so well' (p21 – that metaphor of ruin again). The seven-year itch which Hitchens refers to covers the period of American and world politics since the inauguration of President Clinton. Hitchens's svelte polemic is a heartfelt and convincing enumeration of all the crimes and misdemeanours of the Clinton administration – some familiar, some not so, some shocking, some less so. The book ought to be a port of call for anyone seeking to establish a relation between the 'failures' of the New Democrats and those of New Labour: from 'the People's Inauguration' to President Clinton's promise to connect every classroom in America to the Internet. However, beyond admiration for Hitchens's accumulation of journalistic detail and ear for a fine *bon mot*, what is one to make of this text, which for the most part is content to list the Clintons' failings as a route to a justification, in the concluding chapter, of Hitchens's own deposition to the Office of the Independent Council?[15] My interest (in the context of this book) lies in the persuasive argument Hitchens offers concerning the political practice of Bill Clinton, which, employed in a certain context, might provide a reposte to the comments I made above regarding tactical voting in the 1997 British general election.[16]

For Hitchens, Clintonism is all about 'triangulation'. This term is adopted from Clinton's sometime political adviser, Dick Morris, to describe the ancient political practice 'of the manipulation of populism by elitism' (p23). At a superficial level what Hitchens characterises as 'triangulation' would seem to resemble a certain idea of deconstruction.[17] Think of Clinton's 'affectless equidistance between left and right, Republican and Democrat, white-collar crime and blue-collar crime, true and false, sacred and profane, bought and paid for, public and private, *quid* and *quo*' (p12). However, there is no displacement of the political system that produces such binaries, and so no deconstruction. As Dick Morris explains in his archly entitled *Behind the Oval Office*, 'triangulation is much misunderstood. It is not merely splitting the difference between left and right.' [18] Such a splitting would suggest that the triangulated position was as fixed as the assumed stability of both left and right, as in the dialectic-friendly 'Third Way'. Rather, Hitchens suggests, triangulation allows Clinton to offer 'the Democratic party a devilish bargain: Accept and defend policies you hate (welfare reform, the Defence of Marriage Act); condone and excuse crimes (perjury, campaign finance abuses); and I'll deliver you the executive branch of government' [19] And, in a move by now familiar to Blair-watchers in Britain, Clinton has been able to decouple the office of the chief executive from his party in congress, relying on its support while looking to the Republicans as a foil and source of ideas.

As an analysis of the reductionism of current 'bipartisan' politics in the Anglo-American context this argument has some currency, even if it tells us little about the knowability and achievability of the socialism on which Hitchens grounds his critique, the absence of which (like pest control) has allowed the locusts of the last seven years to grow fat. However, the crux of Hitchens's argument, and the justification of his deposition to Kenneth Starr, comes when he writes:

> The traditional handling of the relation between populism and elitism involves achieving a point of balance between those who support you, and those whom you support. Its classic pitfalls are the accusations that fall between flip and flop, or zig and zag. Its classic advantage is the straight plea for the benefit of the 'lesser evil' calculus, which in most modern elections means a straight and preconditional choice between one and another, or A and B, or Tweedledum and Tweedledee. The most apparently sophisticated and wised-up person, who is well accustomed to saying that 'there's nothing to choose between them', can also be heard, under pressure, denouncing abstainers and waverers for doing the work of the extreme right. (pp26-7)

It is Hitchens's astute contention that the voting-for-Clinton/Blair-as-the-lesser-evil calculation is a precondition for allowing such politicians 'of the left' to rely on a fixed 'leftist' voting-caucus for support, while ensuring political survival by pursuing policies designed to appeal to traditional voters 'of the right'. Words for the left, actions for the right, as Hitchens chooses to describe Clinton's 'right-of-centre' administration.

Hitchens is a sharper polemicist, shrewder thinker and more elegant writer than most of the patrimonial Marxists cited above, and one should be grateful (in a sound-alike Washington press corps) for his adherence to the political value of the contretemps.[20] However, superficially seductive as this argument might be, it continues to suppose that the ontological questions of politics have already been settled, rather than just beginning to be asked. Continuing to rely on a thematics of defeat, Hitchens assumes that the calculation that led to the casting of a vote for Clinton happened within certain definable limits. The 'lesser evil' gambit requires one to be able to make a decision with respect to an option, which if it can be made is not a decision as such (there is no moment of undecidability) but a programmed response, since one *knows* what has to be done. Knowing what has to be done – for example, elect Blair at all costs – does not constitute a choice as such. However, given (say) Blair and Major as a *choice*, there is always more than one option: Blair, Major, neither Blair nor Major, Labour in a general election, Conservative in a local election, and vice versa. Given a *choice* as such, the voter is never confronted by a 'straight and preconditional choice' between A and B, which as Hitchens recognises is no choice at all. Rather, the voter participates in an economy of voting by means of a 'single' vote. The calculation, which negotiates a path through this economy, in order to exercise the least act of violence, does not run by any simple programme. Similarly, the effects of that vote cannot necessarily be calculated in any direct way at the time of voting. Hitchens seems to imagine that the act of voting is in some way determinable (that is, voting for Blair would produce a definite and specific effect in the socio-economic realm and the reason one votes for Blair is to achieve that goal). However, the result of achieving closure on this objective would be that it was no longer necessary to vote with this issue as a consideration. It is a short step from here to achieving a fixed programme of goals from A to Z by voting (which produces fixed effects); very quickly, the end of voting becomes the end of voting because all the knowable and desired issues, A through to Z, have been achieved.

Similarly, Hitchens's approval of abstention works on the same model used here to calculate a voting intention, that is, knowing that voting for Blair (because it is assumed that there is no context in which one would ever vote for Major) will not achieve, say, full employment, regardless of whatever might happen in the future. Hence voting for Blair would be a failure because Blair will not deliver the programme that the 'voter' knows to be both desirable and achievable. However, this is to base any voting consideration on a fixed notion of what would constitute a defeat. Under certain circumstances (and there are as many specific circumstances as there are voters), 1-0, even 10-0 or 100-0, is not a defeat. For example, if one were to lose 10-0 on the last game of a league programme, while one's nearest rival lost 11-0, then 10-0 would not be a defeat (examples could be multiplied). Even being 10-0 down, there is nothing historically to suggest that we are not still in the opening minutes of a process which does not necessarily have a discernible limit. Given this possibility, an abstention of the kind 'Don't vote Blair, it will end in failure' brings a halt to the movement of politics before it has even begun. While voting Blair might not achieve full employment in the short- to medium-term, a vote for Blair in the longer run of history may prove to have effects that bring about the conditions for full employment at a later date. One could argue that if ship-building on the lower Clyde had been saved by a Westminster government there would not now be a devolved legislature in

Edinburgh capable of addressing the singular problems of the lower Clyde. Accordingly, such an abstention manages to denounce the political process as being unable to deliver full employment without having to test the credibility of this policy within the realm of political contestation (ship-building on the Clyde presupposed the markets of empire and later the arms race of the Cold War). The good conscience of the abstainer allows him or her to feel assured that they did not participate in the failure which was the non-achievement of full employment, whilst retaining this policy as a transcendental standard against which to judge the failure of the political process.

Hitchens insists that his 'little book' has no hidden agenda. However, with such an opening it already reveals a series of assumptions upon which it bases its polemic. It would be a truly marvellous 'little book' if it could speak from a transparent position, free of ideology. This is not to question Hitchens's deposition to the Office of the Independent Council, which is a matter of conscience and would require a more detailed analysis of its relation to the law than is possible here. Rather, it is to question the very idea that a book based upon journalistic sources, by a political correspondent and one so intimately related to the Washington milieu, about a juridical-mediatic event in the contemporary political space, could in any way begin to disentangle itself from the mediatic noise it sets out to report on. By the closing chapter of the book, Hitchens has narrated his own complicity in the process; like Ford Madox Ford's narrator in *The Good Soldier* he becomes implicated within the events he relates and so raises doubts concerning the reliability of that narration. However, Hitchens retains a model of transparency between journalistic and political realms, as if the two were not totally integrated and that this was not the primary cause of Clintonism and its 'triangulations'. In an unrecognised 'kettle logic', Hitchens supposes that there are 'real lives' being led outside of the Washington scene, whose reality contrasts and exposes the unreality of Washington (some of Hitchens's angriest and most subtle writing here concerns the fate of poultry workers in Missouri), while continuing to privilege Washington as the ontological site of American politics. One may well argue, against Hitchens, that the Washington he describes (and to which his journalism is inextricably linked) is, in the manner of the mediatic space of contemporary politics, an over-determined site for the spectral effects of politics as hauntology. The phantomatic Clinton described by Hitchens, he of the videotaped evidence and campaign advertising, takes place as an image linked to a structure of reproduction, which 'this little book' itself participates in.

Bill Clinton is a phantom, as spectral as any other mediatic image that uncannily presents itself in the form of a return, never having been properly present in the first instance. From the saxophone-playing Bill on MTV to the sweating and uncomfortable Bill of the Grand Jury evidence (a video played repeatedly on satellite and cable television), the space of politics which Hitchens describes (and which he takes to be the ontological realm of the political) has only ever been active as a spectral event of tele-technology. This is not to deny the reality of the Missouri poultry workers, but to ask a question about the ontological status of what continues to be understood by an astute thinker like Hitchens as the privileged realm of politics. Clinton/Blair may not be a phenomenon unique to the political qua mediatic space; indeed, Hitchens's account of triangulation may well point to a history of hauntological politics at least as old as modernity, perhaps even democracy. However, it is my contention that the 'ontological political realm' of the traditionally understood legislature may be the last place to look today for an answer to the questions that have been raised in this essay. Or at least, if we are to look there, then a new way of seeing is required to read in it a site of hauntological inquiry rather than a metaphysical model of transparency and transmission. Where – picking up the necessary x-ray spectacles – might one begin to look for an inscription of the question of philosophy as ontology in the inheritance of the left? My second chosen text of Clintonism may point to these leftovers.

PERPETUAL PEACE, AGAIN

The meaning (and commercial success) of the first *Star Wars* trilogy was grounded in its historical status as a series of films about the Cold War. The mythic vision of these films as a universal contest between absolute good and radical evil so suited the climate of Cold War America that its vocabulary began to inculcate itself within the terminology of the ontological political realm. We remember Ronald Reagan's 'Evil empire' and the 'Star Wars' 'strategic defence initiative', a spectre revived by the Clinton administration which on 6 January 1999 finally approved a $7 billion budget to build 'Star Wars'. However, a new *Star Wars* film, which fell outside the historical conjuncture of the Cold War, would always struggle to find reasonable grounds on which to base a battle between good and evil. Just as James Bond, the espionage genre, and the US State Department, have laboured to find new post-Cold War enemies, so too the curious shallowness of *Star Wars: Episode 1* might be put down to a change in the political climate that informs its narrative.

There is no Darth Vader (the blackest man in the universe); but his master the Emperor remains. In this prequel he is downsized for the 1990s, not the dark lord who ruled the galaxy and commanded armies of battle cruisers, but, in the guise of Senator Palpatine, a scheming politician within the United Nations-style Galactic Senate. The action of the film is based not upon the subversion and overthrow of a tyrannical empire, but on the consequences of the taxation of trade routes in the outlying regions of the galaxy. It is hard to get as excited by the minutiae of the GATT agreement and the problems of capital within globalisation, as it is by the prospect of nuclear Armageddon. Palpatine hopes to exploit the dispute over galactic free trade in order to further his own universal ambitions, whilst distracting the Senate through procedure and bureaucracy. Indeed, the Senate as the ontological realm of politics bears a similarity to the political intrigue in Washington described by Hitchens. The Senate is also referred to in the film as the Congress of the Republic (all three terms 'Senate', 'Congress' and 'Republic' having specific resonances for an audience familiar with the impeachment of Bill Clinton). The Congress is unable to respond effectively to the crisis that emerges on the planet of Naboo (Palpatine's own planet) when the sinister and ambiguously constituted 'Trade Federation' (walking reptiles with Sino-Japanese accents) blockade and invade the planet (for reasons that are not altogether clear but may have something to do with not wanting to pay tax). Queen Amidala of Naboo escapes the invasion to plead her case at the Congress, confident that the Senate will revoke the trade franchise of those who have invaded her planet.

When held up to any sort of scrutiny, the logic of any *Star Wars* film tends to collapse into absurdity. Here, in *Episode 1*, an entire planet (a self-proclaimed 'democracy' which seems to retain a monarchy with executive powers within a global government without constituent nations) is subdued by a dozen landing craft and a trading company official. However, it may be productive to indulge this analogue for the politics of the contemporary United States. On her arrival at the Senate, Queen Amidala is met by Supreme Chancellor Valorum. Valorum, we are told, has no real power but is 'mired by baseless allegations of corruption', while bureaucrats within Congress ensure endless debate through a strict adherence to baroque procedure. Palpatine tells the Queen, 'The Senate is not what it once was. There is no civility, only politics.' Like Clinton's administration in Washington – as characterised and abhorred by Christopher Hitchens – the Congress of the Republic qua ontological political space fails to produce the necessary and knowable political effects demanded by the Queen. The senator from the trade federation blocks the Queen's demands for intervention by the Senate. Instead, Chancellor Valorum bows to bureaucratic insistence that a commission of inquiry be set up to investigate the validity of her claims. The Queen then appeals to the sensationalism of her cause as a way of screening out this process of investigation. She tells the Senate, 'I will not watch my people die as you discuss this invasion in a committee', and acts on Palpatine's nefarious suggestion to call for a vote of no confidence in Valorum. Palpatine then succeeds Valorum on a platform of controlling the bureaucrats and stamping out corruption, while the Queen returns to Naboo telling Palpatine, 'This is your arena, I must go back to mine. It is clear to me that the Republic no longer functions. I trust you will bring sanity and compassion back to the Senate.'

In this filmic example, the assumptions which inform the Queen's political actions (that the Senate is the ontological realm of politics and a location of failure; that the politics of real lives takes place in a separate sphere; that a knowable and necessary set of criteria cannot be achieved by means of the ontological realm of politics while that realm remains a privileged space of discussion; that, in order to defend the propriety of a certain political discourse of emancipation and struggle, it is necessary to abstain from the ontological realm of politics, whilst making constant reference to it, judging it by your own set of abstemious and transcendental criteria; in short, all Hitchens's assumptions) do in fact work to the benefit of 'the extreme right' (or at any rate, one might argue, 'the dark side of the force'). Having bypassed the Congress and successfully achieved identifiable political ends through heroic struggle against cosmic capital, the film ends with a victory parade. The last word of the screenplay is a triumphant 'Peace!' as the camera picks out the unforeseeable (at least to the characters) 'phantom menace' of now Supreme Chancellor Palpatine and the momentary hero of the Republic, Anikan Skywalker (later to become Darth Vader). One might read this film, in all its mythic clarity, as an allegory for the difficulties posed for a transcendental political discourse (reassured by the sensationalism of its cause) by the absolutely unknowable condition of any event.

However, what interests me about *The Phantom Menace* (apart from its obvious appeal as a Hollywood turkey) is its depiction of the ontological realm of politics through the hauntological medium of film. In his 'First Definitive Article of a Perpetual Peace', Kant states that 'the civil constitution of every state shall be Republican'.[21] Kant's definition of a republic, like that of George Lucas, the director of the *Star Wars* films, seems to follow the example of the American constitution with a separation of powers between legislature, executive and judiciary. Kant is at pains to distinguish a republican state from a democratic one:

> *Republicanism* is that political principle whereby the executive power (the government) is separated from the legislative power. Despotism prevails in a state if the laws are made and arbitrarily executed by one and the same power, and it reflects the will of the people only in so far as the ruler treats the will of the people as his own private will. Of the three forms of sovereignty, *democracy*, in the truest sense of the word, is necessarily a *despotism*, because it establishes an executive power through which all the citizens may make decisions about (and indeed against) the single individual without his consent, so that decisions are made by all the people and yet not all the people; and this means that the general will is in contradiction with itself, and thus with freedom. (p.101)

Republicanism is then a 'representative system' in which the chief executive (Chancellor Valorum, Frederick II, Bill Clinton) is merely the highest servant of the state. Kant concludes that 'the smaller the number of ruling persons in a state and the greater their powers of representation, the more the constitution will approximate to its republican potential' (p101). While it is not clear either in Kant or in *Star Wars* how representation is to be achieved or measured, there remains common to both texts (and to Hitchens's book) a general consideration of the idea of republicanism as the most preferable shape for ontological politics (and a feeling that it is only politicians who tend to spoil it). However, all three texts also acknowledge the impossibility of 'government' by such a model. This is Kant's intention, since non-government (the separation of executive and legislature) will block 'despotism' and prevent war. Hitchens notes the importance of non-government to Clintonism as it silences the Democratic minority in Congress, while allowing a 'triangulated' Clinton to profit from political gridlock, as when the Republicans attempted to shut down government during the early months of 1996. For a cinema audience familiar with a series of 'lame-duck' presidents who have spent most of their second terms pursued by special prosecutors, Chancellor Valorum's plight seems all too convincing. It is the gap between government and non-government, between political office and an inability to pass just laws, which is the moment of crisis in each of these texts. The model of transparency between government and action, which underpins Hitchens's (and the Real Marxists') understanding of the ontological realm of politics, is displaced by Kant and subverted by *Star Wars*.

While it is the desire of all government to end all government by the implementation of successful and definitive policies, the impossibility of this desire is the necessary condition of government as such. Government fails not because the intentions of its custodians are impure (although they often are), but because any act of government (regardless of the propriety of its programme) takes place over the abyss between government and non-government, between a transcendental idea of the law which is always before us and yet to arrive, and the immanent singularity of the moment which happens and so is always already past. Just as philosophy opens up history by defining itself against non-philosophy, and Marxism participates in history by being opened by non-Marxism, so too government actualises history through its relation to non-government. Failure is the *necessary condition* of government. This is a matter of historical record, as well as of the overwhelming experience of culture and politics in Blair's Britain.

NOTES

1. Immanuel Kant, 'Idea for a Universal History with a Cosmopolitan Purpose', in *Political Writings*, trans. H.B Nisbet, Hans Reiss (ed.), Cambridge University Press, Cambridge 1991, p47n.

2. Quoted in Christopher Hitchens, *No One Left To Lie To: The Triangulations of William Jefferson Clinton*, Verso, London and New York 1999; hereafter referred to as NOL. Webster Hubbell was a 'business associate' of the Clintons in Arkansas, later appointed to the Justice Department (where the above remark was made), before being indicted for tax evasion during the Starr investigations.

3. Jacques Derrida, 'Marx & Sons', trans. G. M. Goshgarian, in *Ghostly Demarcations: A Symposium on Jacques Derrida's 'Specters of Marx'*, Michael Sprinker (ed.), Verso, London 1999, p214; italics in original. Hereafter referred to as MS.

4. For an early commentary of this sort see Geoffrey Bennington's 'Demanding history', in *Post-Structuralism and the Question of History*, Derek Attridge, Geoffrey Bennington, and Robert Young (eds), Cambridge University Press, Cambridge 1987, p17, which presages all Derrida's commentary on patrimony and inheritance in 'Marx and Sons', *op. cit.*

5. See Derrida's 'Marx & Sons' for an elaboration of this metaphor, where the

figure of legitimate and illegitimate children arguing over the rights of a legacy is closely related to that of the dead body implied by the pervasive thematics of ruin.

6. Terry Eagleton, 'Response to Robert Young', *Interventions: International Journal of Postcolonial Studies*, Vol. 1, No. 1, (1998-9), p26.

7. For example, Terry Eagleton and Drew Milne (eds), *Marxist Literary Theory: A Reader*, Blackwell, Oxford 1996; Alex Callinicos, *Theories and Narratives: Reflections on the Philosophy of History*, Polity Press, Cambridge 1995; Michael Ryan, *Marxism and Deconstruction: A critical articulation*, Johns Hopkins University Press, Baltimore 1982. However, the situation is widespread well beyond these minimal indices.

8. For example, see Eagleton's review of Gayatri Spivak's 'A critique of post-colonial reason', *London Review of Books* Vol. 21, No. 10 (12 May 1999).

9. Jean-Francois Lyotard, 'Rewriting modernity' in *The Inhuman: Reflections on Time*, trans. Geoffrey Bennington and Rachel Bowlby, Polity Press, Cambridge 1991.

10. Lyotard, *ibid.*, p25.

11. See Robert J.C. Young, 'Poststructuralism: the improper name' in *Torn Halves: Political Conflict in Literary and Cultural Theory*, Manchester University Press, Manchester 1996; and Nicholas Royle, 'Déjà vu' in Graeme Macdonald, Stephen Thomson and Robin Purves (eds), *Post-Theory: New Directions in Criticism*, Martin McQuillan, Edinburgh University Press, Edinburgh 1999.

12. For example, see the responses of Terry Eagleton, Aijaz Ahmad and Tom Lewis to Derrida's *Specters of Marx* in Michael Sprinker's *Ghostly Demarcations*, op. cit.

13. Martin Heidegger, *What is a Thing?*, trans. W.B Barton Jr and Vera Deutsch, Henry Regnery Company, Chicago 1967.

14. For a more detailed commentary on systematicity, see Ernesto Laclau and Chantal Mouffe, *Hegemony and Socialist Strategy: Toward a Radical Democratic Politics*, Verso, London 1985.

15. During Clinton's trial, Hitchens volunteered an affidavit to Kenneth Starr's office testifying that Sidney Blumenthal, one of Clinton's spin doctors, had attempted to 'spin' Hitchens a story that Monica Lewinsky was a stalker and mentally unstable. When both Clinton and Blumenthal denied under oath this very 'spin', Hitchens felt obliged to inform Starr's office – this despite the fact that Blumenthal was an 'old friend' of Hitchens, and that Hitchens's testimony would leave him open to a charge of perjury. Hitchens's account of his actions appears as an afterword to *No One Left to Lie To*.

16. What follows in no way negates Hitchens's helpful accumulation of the

problems with the Clinton regime. For a fuller account of my response to Clintonism, see Eleanor Byrne and Martin McQuillan, *Deconstructing Disney*, Pluto, London 1999.

17. The important word here is 'certain', but anecdotal evidence suggests that Derrida himself was particularly taken by Clinton's notorious line, 'It depends what the meaning of "is" is' and used it as a recurring joke in his Paris seminar in the weeks following Clinton's testimony.

18. Dick Morris, *Behind the Oval Office*, quoted by Hitchens, *op. cit.,* p34.

19. Hitchens is quoting David Frum, a conservative political theorist writing in the Murdoch-owned *Weekly Standard* in February 1999; see Hitchens, *op. cit.,* p29.

20. See Jacques Derrida, *Specters of Marx*, trans. Peggy Kamuf, Routledge, London and New York 1994, *passim*.

21. Immanuel Kant, 'Perpetual Peace: A Philosophical Sketch', in *Political Writings, op. cit.*, pp99-102.

Determined dissent: John Milton and the futures of political culture

MATT JORDAN

One of New Labour's most characteristic rhetorical reflexes has been to portray itself as the protagonist in a heroic struggle against Cynicism, the semi-secularised descendant of Bunyan's Giant Despair. In his first speech to the Labour Party Conference following the election victory of May 1997, Tony Blair concludes by casting his political triumph as an epochal event, in a peroration it is worth quoting in full:

> On 1 May 1997, it wasn't just the Tories who were defeated. Cynicism was defeated. Fear of change was defeated. Fear itself was defeated. Did I not say it would be a battle of hope against fear? On 1 May 1997, fear lost. Hope won. The Giving Age began. Now make the good that is in the heart of each of us serve the good of all of us. Give to our country the gift of our energy, our ideas, our hopes, our talents. Use them to build a country each of whose people will say that "I care about Britain because I know that Britain cares about me". Britain, head and heart, can be unbeatable. That is the Britain I offer you. That is the Britain that together can be ours.[1]

A timid desire to cling to the safety blanket of the past is here set against a hopeful, indeed self-assured – perhaps even, with the benefit of hindsight, smug – openness to future success, an outcome which is presented, almost, as in the gift of our new premier.

However, this orientation toward the future is not predicated on a total suppression of the past, which is not to be left to its own devices, but is instead pressed into the service of the present and future. This urge seems to have been in the air in the Anglophone world. Richard

Rorty, writing the year before Blair's speech and – despite his North American provenance – in terms notably consonant with it, argued that 'The appropriate intellectual background to political deliberation ... is the kind of historical narrative which segues into a utopian scenario about how we can get from the present to a better future'. Rorty characterised the current climate in terms of 'a loss of hope – or, more specifically ... an inability to construct a plausible narrative of progress.'[2] As if in answer to this lament, Blair opens his speech with a brisk history of the British as 'one of the great innovative peoples'. This history spans a period 'from the Magna Carta to the first Parliament to the industrial revolution to an empire that covered the world', and on to 'Britain today ... an exciting, inspiring place to be' which has the potential to be much more, nothing less than a 'beacon to the world'. To sum up the British – 'by our nature and tradition innovators' – Blair turns to 'our great poet of renewal and recovery, John Milton', whom he quotes as follows: 'A nation not slow or dull, but of quick, ingenious and piercing spirit, acute to invent, subtle and sinewy to discourse, not beneath the reach of any point that human capacity can soar to.'

Leaving aside the issue of which nation is under discussion (when he wrote these words in late 1644 Milton was markedly disaffected with the Presbyterian church discipline which the Scots, in the form of the Solemn League and Covenant, were attempting to impose on England as a condition of their support for Parliament against Charles I in the Civil War), *Areopagitica* (the tract from which Blair is quoting) would seem in many ways an appropriate text to seize on. An argument against censorship, in the form of licensing of the press, *Areopagitica* is full of expressions dear to the self-image of Western modernity and, in turning to it, Blair arguably attempts a more daring and radical version of John Major's 'Back to Basics'. The essence to which Blair appeals is not static, enshrined in 'timeless' images, but a tradition of dynamism. Like Blair's speech, Milton's *Areopagitica* expresses distaste for the recent past, and a vigorous confidence in the present and the future onto which it opens. Milton is convinced that the English nation is witnessing a 'new and great period' in the making, in which it will be possible to 'joyn, and unite into one generall and brotherly search after Truth'.[3] Just as Blair calls on his party and the nation as a whole to 'build' a caring yet efficient Britain, Milton conceives of his compatriots as 'wise and faithfull labourers' – especially in London, 'the mansion house of liberty' – engaged in constructive discussions ('opinion in good men is but knowledge in the making') so that 'the house of God can be built' (*CPW* 2: 554-5). The efforts of these 'indus-trious' men are contrasted with 'the gripe of custom', 'eyes blear'd and dimm'd with prejudice', and construed in terms of a nation engaged in 'casting off the old and wrincl'd skin of corruption to outlive these pangs and wax young again' (*CPW* 2: 532, 563, 565, 557).

However, the historical and cultural resonance that *Areopagitica* lends to Blair's discourse derives from a vision which is in many respects much more radical than Blair's, even in today's terms. Perhaps most striking, when the two texts are set side by side, is the reductive and impoverished nature of the collective practice Blair envisages even as he tries to enthuse his constituency. His is a top-down, technocratic vision of 'the Britain I offer you'. Where *Areopagitica* aspires to the creation of a space in which the nation can awake into enlightened debate with itself – England is 'entring the glorious waies of Truth and prosperous vertue destin'd to become great and honourable ... Methinks I see in my mind a noble and puissant Nation rousing herself like a strong man after sleep, and shaking her invincible locks' (*CPW* 2: 557-8) – New Labour instead repeatedly offers 'hard choices' which are a euphemistic new rendering – although not to exactly the same ends, certainly with the same rhetorical/hegemonic intent – of Thatcher's 'There Is No Alternative' to the acceptance of hard economic facts. 'The hard choice,' explains Blair, is 'stay as we are and decline. Or modernise and win' (one of six references to hard choices in the speech). Insofar as there is 'a place for all the people in New Britain, and ... a role for all the people in its creation', a 'task for a whole people, not just a government', a vision of 'all getting involved', it is a matter of 'our energy, our ideas, our hopes, our talents' being harnessed to the demands of an overriding imperative, the development of a 'creative economy'.

It is tempting to say that, by contrast, *Areopagitica* is concerned with an *economy of creativity*. It is far from precious about imagining the truth in commercial terms. Indeed, it models free trade and free speech in terms of an ideal but not inevitable reciprocity. Milton refers to 'our richest Marchandize, Truth', and later asserts that 'Truth and understanding are not such wares as to be monopoliz'd' (*CPW* 2: 548, 535), drawing here on the discourse of those merchants who had objected to the Crown granting exclusive rights over certain trades to favoured companies. However, although there is a degree of imagina-tive consonance between the two in Milton's mind, perhaps even to the extent that he sees the one as easing the way for the other, he does not reduce the stuff of debate to the level of the commodity: a free trade in truth means not leaving others to do your intellectual work for you, as is clear from Milton's contempt for the man so preoccupied with business that he will not give over time to religious (in this context, political) issues, and who instead decides 'to find himself out som factor [commercial agent], to whose care and credit he may commit the whole managing of his religious affairs'. To be a citizen is to be above exchange in this sense.[4] It does, however, mean being extremely open to intellectual exchange, sharing a 'zealous thirst after knowledge' (*CPW* 2: 544, 554). The passage Blair quotes regarding the 'quick, ingenious, and piercing spirit ... suttle and sinewy to discourse' of the English occurs on the same page as, and is contrasted with, 'the forc't and outward union of cold, and neutrall, and inwardly divided minds' (*CPW* 2: 551), and is an expression of that 'democraticall growing spirite' which Sir Cheney Culpeper, writing in 1646, perceived and praised.[5] As Sharon Achinstein remarks, quoting the same passage as Blair, in *Areopagitica* Milton offers his audience a choice as to 'whether they thought ordinary English citizens were capable of participating in politics or not', and promulgates, for his part, 'a revolutionary theory of citizenship as conscientious readership ... Milton designates and constructs an audience that was supposed to be active and *activist*'.[6]

Blair's speech, keen as it is that Britain should be 'the new power of the information age', shows no sign of recognising that *Areopagitica* emerged out of what can justifiably be called an 'information revolution' in the course of which, liberated for a time and to varying degrees from central government control, the people produced and read some 22,000 pamphlets.[7] Blair's repeatedly expressed desire that Britain be a 'beacon to the world' is foreshadowed by Milton's belief that, as he puts it in *Of Reformation*, England has 'set up a Standard for the recovery of lost Truth ... the new Lampe of *saving light* to all Christendome' (*CPW* 1: 525). In 1644, dedication to this end dictated that Milton break the law by publishing *Areopagitica* (Milton disregarded Parliament's Licensing Order of 1643, and made this defiance still more pointed by printing his name in large letters on the title page, when others sought relative safety in anonymity).[8] In 1649 it caused him to be asked by the government to write in justification of the trial and execution of Charles I, an act which set an example 'wherein', Milton claimed, 'we have the honour to precede other Nations who are now labouring to be our followers.'[9] As David Norbrook has recently remarked, 'At the basic level of imagining a political and literary culture divested of monarchy and its attendant trappings ... the mid-seventeenth century can make modern Britain look archaic.'[10] Within this movement of history, *Areopagitica* stands out clearly as a work of an intellectual and political avant-garde of the kind New Labour professes to despise. Its relation to its moment differs profoundly from that of Blair's speech to his.

This might seem merely, if pleasingly, ironic, especially since *Areopagitica* failed in its ostensible, 'practical' purpose of ending licensing of the press, after which Milton lapsed into public silence for five years. However, its apparent failure is suggestive in terms of the way history is narrativised, and with respect to the political implications in the present day of such narrativisation as that employed in Blair's speech. Methodologically analogous to Blair's political outlook is what came to be known in seventeenth-century studies as 'revisionism'. Although it predates New Labour by a couple of decades, revisionism shares New Labour's preoccupation with mainstream or moderate opinion, and mobilises the supposed view of 'Middle England' (England outside London and some other towns such as Manchester) against those who are alleged to have viewed the seventeenth century in terms of a 'High Road' to the English Civil War, or English Revolution, itself construed as a major episode in the development of liberal democracy in England.

These include both Whigs, for whom the Revolution was a battle for the liberty of Englishmen against the absolutism of the Crown, and Marxists, who gave this political account 'a material base in the nature of economic developments and class relationships in England'.[11] Against any sense that these events were somehow inevitable, revisionists seek to show that until relations between Crown and Parliament rapidly deteriorated in 1640 and 1641, there was considerable consensus in the country about how and by whom the country should be governed (although there is a lack of consensus among revisionists regarding what that consensus consisted of). This breakdown of relations tends to be blamed on a succession of contingencies, combined with a small minority of extremists on either side, without whom the moderates would have continued to live in peace.[12]

The problem with this is that it drains meaning from history, and makes the events of the 1640s 'virtually unintelligible': they become 'mere' events.[13] As Ann Hughes remarks, the overall effect of revisionist accounts of the Civil War is a sense that it was 'irrational, unnatural, accidental'.[14] For some this is salutary: as Anthony Fletcher remarked, one lesson that might be learnt from such a view of things is that great events do not necessarily have great causes.[15] But while the immediate causes may seem comparatively trivial (a summary of the different accounts is impossible in the space available here), this overriding emphasis on contingency detracts from an understanding of the wider factors at work. This is not altogether true. Conrad Russell, for instance, has described the various structural weaknesses of the Crown, above all financial, which paved the way for the operation of malign chance.[16] But what is singularly lacking in the revisionist picture of the Civil War is a sense of the long-term combination of economic and ideological developments which provided the conditions in which Charles I ran into such difficulties. Whig and/or Marxist views that a rising gentry or an entrepreneurial class were responsible for the Civil War seem to have been discredited by empirical research. The conflict cannot be explained in terms of an outright contradiction between the forces and relations of production. But what cannot be ignored is that a century or so of rapid economic change had drastically altered the social composition of the nation. Those able to profit from new agricultural techniques and willing to espouse new attitudes to the production of wealth included not only a sizeable proportion of the nobility and gentry, but also large numbers of what had come to be termed the 'middling sort'. Together, and united to varying extents by their consumption of a variety of cultural forms aimed at them as a market, including the new industry of news, these groups constituted a new phenomenon, a 'public', or at least the makings of one. The dawning ideological self-consciousness of this public, which increasingly saw itself as part of a 'Country' which could be opposed to a Court, contributed greatly to Charles's fear of the threat of 'popularity', or proto-democratic tendencies, which in turn led him into promoting an authoritarian and unpopular 'Arminian' regime in the English Church, and seeking to avoid parliaments in which grievances might be raised. When financial necessity forced him to call a Parliament to vote him taxes in 1640, the existence of a 'public' was a vital factor in making a settlement between Crown and Parliament so difficult that, in the event, it proved impossible.[17]

This was by no means apparent to the vast majority of contemporaries. Indeed, it was almost certainly not fully apparent to anyone. The trends simply did not appear to point toward civil war. Conrad Russell is right to describe England in 1637 as 'a country in working order', and the description could probably be extended to 1640.[18] Certainly, the calling of a second parliament in 1640 (the Long Parliament), after Charles had dissolved the Short Parliament in disappointment at the line it was taking, was accompanied by widespread hopes of national renewal. But this was due to a feeling that at last things would start working again as they had used to, or, given the outburst of goodwill, even better than before: some felt that a golden age was at hand.[19] The positive service which revisionism has performed has been to demonstrate the extent to which revolutions are not the culmination of readily perceivable trends, but are often unexpected. Only retrospectively do their causes become sufficiently apparent to become a matter for debate. It is precisely in downplaying the importance of ideas, however, that revisionist historiography has deprived itself of a grasp on the Revolution, for attention to the ideological struggle which led up to and continued throughout and beyond the Civil War reveals the Revolution as having a logic which, while it is not deductive, is not a mere construct imposed by hindsight but something retrospectively apparent: a highlighting of one figure in the carpet, among other possible figures. It is in this sense that it becomes possible to talk of the Revolution as having 'intellectual origins'.[20]

This is not the place to describe that logic in any detail, but it is certain that Hobbes, a contemporary historian of the Civil War, as well as the foremost political philosopher England has produced, believed that the origins of the Revolution lay in intellectual developments. In *Behemoth*, he describes the combination of what appeared to him religious zealotry – 'the interpretation of a verse in the Hebrew, Greek, or Latin Bible, is oftentimes the cause of civil war and the deposing and assassinating of God's annointed' – and a classical education, which furnished people 'with arguments for liberty out of the works of Aristotle, Plato, Cicero, Seneca, and out of the histories of Rome and Greece, for their disputation against the necessary power of kings'.[21] In *Areopagitica*, cast in the form of a classical oration, prioritising above all the divine search for Truth, and engaging closely throughout with classical and biblical texts, Milton seeks to build on these origins and produce 'an idea of the public sphere that matched the political needs of the English Revolution'.[22] In order to do so, he draws not only on the kinds of ideas which appealed to the classically educated or religiously committed (both groups of considerable influence and numbers) but, as discussed earlier, on the language of monopolisation, a particular concern of traders and artisans of the 'middling sort'. The potential scope of the appeal of his rhetoric is considerable, as is suggested by its continuing popularity. For instance, when 'free-born' John Lilburne went on trial in 1649 for allegedly seditious writings, the judges were denounced as 'monopolisers of law' by one of his supporters (Lilburne contended that the jury had the right to adjudicate on points of law as well as of fact, a position indignantly rejected by the judges).[23]

The trial of Lilburne might itself be taken as a mark of how Milton 'erred' predictively. *Areopagitica* concedes that it is necessary – especially in time of civil war – 'to have a vigilant eye how Bookes demeane themselves, as well as men' (*CPW* 2: 492), and so, in principle, allows for such trials. But such concerns about publication as it has are overwhelmingly to do with Royalist – and possibly Catholic – propaganda, and its tolerance is of what can a little misleadingly be called the left, which had the new ideas that depended on print for dissemination.[24] The repression of Lilburne – already a prominent figure, although the Levellers were not yet as clearly defined a grouping as they were to become – is not on the horizon. However, *Areopagitica* is at least as much an act of attempted construction as of prediction, an act of political imagination as much as it is shaped by the exigencies of the time and its apparent tendencies. Written when a Parliamentary victory was by no means certain – indeed, when military events were such as would soon necessitate the formation of a New Model Army which would never know defeat so long as it existed – *Areopagitica* is, like the inception of that army, 'an act of creative fantasy'.[25] In it, Milton conceives the nation in terms of an alliance and convergence of purpose among different sectors of 'the people'. In this respect, *Areopagitica* maps out not only what the Revolution needed at that moment, but the course it might have taken had not the Leveller leaders in the New Model Army been shot at Burford in 1649. This bloody end to the embryonic popular alliance which the Army had – far from unproblematically – embodied appears in retrospect to have made the Restoration of 1660 if not inevitable, then an accident waiting to happen.[26] Milton's position with respect to these developments is suggested by the fact that, despite his acceptance of employment within a revolutionary regime that had turned against the Levellers, radicals outside the government seem to have continued to regard him as a sympathiser. Lilburne, for one, remained happy 'to refer to Milton as a great "patriot", and translate his Latin from the *Defensio.*'[27]

In this respect, *Areopagitica* can be apprehended, from our point of view (but also from that of contemporaries who, like Milton, kept faith with what they regarded as the 'Good Old Cause'), as a part of a larger and more profound – but by no means simply continuous – history than is dreamt of in the philosophy of revisionism. This act of 'creative fantasy' turned out to have a considerable afterlife, one which can be traced in the radicals of the early 1650s, the underground Dissent of the 1660s, the increasingly revolutionary Dissent of the late 1670s, 1680s and 1690s which eventually secured freedom of the press in 1695, and on through the beginnings of the French Revolution, the execution of Louis XVI, Peterloo, Chartism and even the founding of the Greek Republic in 1831.[28] *Areopagitica* adumbrates the principle of what Habermas has called 'communicative reason', as opposed to subject-centred or subjective reason. This consists in a conception of truth as emerging from a process of debate rather than from a confrontation between an individual subject and a given object, and has been intimately bound up with democratisation.[29]

By contrast, Blair's speech seems very much *in keeping* with the spirit of the times, and very much in touch with the trends that are currently shaping the world. Only three years later, Blair's speech also looks rather thin; if Milton's poetry and prose embody 'the energies that the Revolution quelled', Blair's speech shows that no amount of elevated rhetoric can substitute for the existence of revolutionary masses.[30] New Labour now seems – if it didn't then – not only in hock to the present but intent on mortgaging the future, when a concern for fiscal rectitude is held to demand the Private Finance Initiative.

Nevertheless, there was something compelling, and perhaps there still is, about the story New Labour tells about the past, present and future – especially, I would suggest, to those under the age of forty or so, whose primary experience is of defeat after defeat for the Left, and of an increasing hold over common sense of the idea that the global economy is becoming ever more autonomous of nation states and of the popular will they are supposed to express. It may be that this is the overriding reason – over and above dislike of the various morally dubious policies they have implemented – for the extent of the hatred the left feels for New Labour: the sneaking suspicion that they may be right. It would be nice to think that this is also why many figures within New Labour get so upset at criticism from the left: their heart is telling them something different to their head, they are not who they wanted to be.

It may be, however, that the cynicism and gloom which surrounds contemporary political life is the result of a misguided assumption of intellectual mastery, which takes the possibly paradoxical form of knowing that intellectuals have become useless. Richard Rorty laments 'our loss of hope' and 'inability to construct a plausible narrative of progress'.[31] The reason for the current impossibility of a 'plausible narrative of progress' is his conviction that we are stuck with capitalism:

> The leftist use of the terms 'capitalism,' 'bourgeois ideology', and 'working class' depends on the implicit claim that we can do *better* than

a market economy, that we know of a viable alternative option for complex technologically-oriented societies. But at the moment, at least, we know of no such option. Whatever programme the Left may develop for the twenty-first century, it is not going to include nationalisation of the means of production or the abolition of private property.[32]

The apparent agnosticism regarding future possibilities is itself dogmatic (by no means everyone agrees that there are no other options), and rather undermined by the sheer assertiveness of the last sentence quoted, which betrays the conviction that capitalism has won the day. A number of things follow from this conviction. First, Rorty is often extremely gloomy about the future. Rightly convinced that the challenge of globalisation is to ensure that 'political order [can] take precedence over the economic while still leaving room for economic growth', and that this implies 'the need for a global polity', he believes that the chance of achieving such a thing is 'slim'. This is because, in the absence of an alternative to capitalism, he believes that our capacity to 'alleviate misery' depends on our ability to win over the new global elite to our way of thinking by appealing to their sentiments and hoping they will display 'condescension'.[33] According to this analysis – whereby we simply know there is no alternative to capitalism – intellectuals have no particular role to play, since their understanding of the world and capacity to produce proposals to change it are no better than anyone else's: 'We can no longer function as an avant-garde'. There is no longer any scope for the kind of intellectual who makes predictions: 'It would be best, in short, if we could get along without prophecy and claims to knowledge of the forces which determine history – if generous hope could sustain itself without such assurances'.[34]

This emphasis on hope rather than scientistic prediction is welcome, but the trouble is, in Rorty's case, that this leads him, for reasons which we will examine in a moment, to take Václav Havel, and the 1989 revolution in Czechoslovakia, as an example. Admitting that, at the time of writing, 'I have no idea how that revolution is going to proceed or any good guesses about whether the moral and political consensus that swept Havel to power will endure' (the time of writing appears to be, from the dates of the books to which he refers in his footnotes, 1992 or 1993), he lauds Havel for seeming 'prepared to go all the way in substituting groundless hope for theoretical insight'.[35] To expand on the vocabulary of Leninism, the demise of which Rorty is celebrating in this essay, this might be described as a position of passive voluntarism; or, to expand on the tradition of liberal sympathetic reformism to which Rorty is so drawn in the shape of Dickens, a 'political Micawberism': something – and something not really sufficient – will turn up.[36] However, in its principled and total disregard for evidence, this takes on an aspect of whistling in the dark, especially since such evidence as Rorty admits elsewhere, regarding, for instance, the need for the primacy of the political over the economic referred to earlier, could well be argued to highlight the need for a reorganisation of economic relations, the possibility of which he has ruled out in advance. The fact that this state of affairs is apprehended through the filter of the 'can do' spirit of his pragmatist philosophical forebears, above all Dewey, introduces two possible perspectives. The sense that western modernity was, for a long time, a 'good thing', and that things went on getting better until they just stopped, leaves Rorty either at a loss, and hopeless, or keen to latch on to any locatable vehicles of liberal progressivism, such as Havel. In other words, Rorty represents both the dark, despairing twin and the opportunist upside of Blair's brittle assurance that 'modernisation' is the panacea for all ills. This faith in 'modernisation' is the embattled bastard descendant of that ideology of historical inevitability criticised by Walter Benjamin in his 'Theses on the Philosophy of History'. For Benjamin, 'Nothing has corrupted the German working class so much as the notion that it was moving with the current'. This worldview, dominated by 'the concept of the historical progress of mankind', could not, in Benjamin's view, 'be sundered from the concept of its [mankind's] progression through a homogenous, empty time'. Benjamin contrasts this serene conviction with 'the awareness that they are about to make the continuum of history explode ... characteristic of the revolutionary classes at the moment of their action'.[37] The requisite existential stance in the absence of such a moment is evoked in Gramsci's famous dictum, 'Pessimism of the intellect, optimism of the will', a frame of mind distinguished from 'political Micawberism' both by its firm political orientation and by an awareness of history as discontinuous rather than progressive, characterised not only by achievement but by *The Experience of Defeat*, as Christopher Hill entitled his book on Milton and his contemporaries.[38] Writing on the verge of the Restoration of the monarchy, and at mortal personal risk, Milton published two editions of what seemed at the time his swansong to the English republic, *The Readie and Easie Way to Establish a Free Commonwealth*. In it, Milton declares (I quote from the second edition, produced when hope in an immediate, practical sense was as good as lost):

What I have spoken, is the language of that which is not called amiss *the Good Old Cause:* if it seem strange to any, it will not seem more strange, I hope, than convincing to backsliders. Thus much I should perhaps have said though I were sure I should have spoken only to trees and stones; and had none to cry to, but with the Prophet, O *earth, earth, earth!* to tell the very soil it self, what her perverse inhabitants are deaf to. Nay though what I have spoke, should happ'n (which Thou suffer not, who didst create mankind free; nor Thou next, who didst redeem us from being servants of all men!) to be the last words of our expiring libertie. But I trust I shall have spoken persuasion to abundance of sensible and ingenuous men: to some perhaps whom God may raise of these stones to become children of reviving libertie; ... though they seem now chusing them a captain back for *Egypt* ... (*CPW* 7. 462-3)

In his reference to Egypt, Milton evokes a contrast between the choice England seems to be making, a return to regal bondage, and the Israelites' flight from captivity. Soon Milton was to find himself in virtual captivity, hiding in fear of his life while friends of his were hanged, disembowelled and quartered.[39] In *Paradise Lost,* much of it written 'In darkness, and with dangers compassed round, / And solitude' (*PL* 7. 27-8), Milton returns to this trope, as the archangel Michael relates to the recently fallen Adam how, in time to come, the Chosen People will flee from Egypt to liberty 'Through the wild desert, / Not the readiest way' (*PL* 12. 216) – an affirmation, it would seem that, although Milton's efforts could not prevent the return of monarchy, all was not therefore necessarily lost.

If, for Benjamin, the revolutionary class will 'make the continuum of history explode', then there remains a task for the intellectual (in his terms, the historian) other than predicting success – that of 'fanning the spark of hope in the past'. The historian who manages this 'establishes a conception of the present as the "time of the now" which is shot through with chips of messianic time.' This is a conception akin to that of the Jews, for whom 'every second of time was the strait gate through which the Messiah might enter'.[40] If revisionism was in part directed against a Marxism which sought to conjure from the past a confidence-building image of the inevitability of revolution, perhaps its admittedly over-zealous restoration of the contingency of history has given us, if not reasons to be cheerful, then sufficient cause not to be downhearted. Sir Edward Dering, one of the moderate figures whose outlook revisionism is keen to accentuate, describes his state of mind in the build-up to the first battle of the Civil War, at Edgehill, in terms of his desire for 'a composing third way'.[41] To maintain such a position of 'moderation' was soon to prove quixotic, however. Sir Edmund Verney, less pragmatic than Dering, could bring himself neither to fight for the King nor to desert him, and rode into battle unarmed. In this instance, the result was predictable, but, against easy assumptions of what is predictable, Milton's texts and their histories – among many others – might save us from succumbing to the currently dominant version of the present.

NOTES

1. Tony Blair, Speech to Labour Party Conference, 30 September 1997.

2. Richard Rorty, 'Globalisation, the politics of identity and social hope', in *Philosophy and Social Hope*, Penguin, Harmondsworth 1999, pp229-39, 231-2.

3. John Milton, *Areopagitica*, in *Complete Prose Works of John Milton*, 8 vols., Don M. Wolfe *et al* (eds), Yale University Press, New Haven 1953-83, Vol. 2, pp553, 554. Subsequent references will be given in the text in the form *CPW* 2: 553-4, for example.

4. Nigel Smith, '*Areopagitica*: voicing contexts, 1643-5' in James Grantham Turner and David Loewenstein (eds), *Politics, Poetics, and Hermeneutics in Milton's Prose*, Cambridge University Press, Cambridge 1990), pp103-18, 115. Blair Hoxby, who literalises Milton's metaphors, and argues that he conceives of truth as a commodity, would not agree. He reads the moral of the greedy tradesman as being that 'Milton wants men to be enterprisers in *all* aspects of the public sphere – religious, political, and economic – and he objects to the notion that activity of one sort may substitute for toil of another.' See 'The trade of truth advanced: *Areopagitica*, economic discourse, and libertarian reform', *Milton Studies* 36 (1998), pp177-202, 188, 192. In general, Hoxby seems a little sanguine about the intrinsic congruity of intellectual and economic exchange.

5. Quoted from a letter to Samuel Hartlib in David Norbrook, '*Areopagitica*, censorship, and the early modern public sphere' in Richard Burt (ed.), *The Administration of Aesthetics: Censorship, Political Criticism, and the Public Sphere*, University of Minnesota Press, London and Minneapolis 1994, p11.

6. Sharon Achinstein, *Milton and the Revolutionary Reader*, Princeton University Press, Princeton, NJ 1994, pp60, 65.

7. The phrase 'information age' in this context is that of Peter W. Thomas in 'The impact on literature' in John Morrill (ed.), *The Impact of the English Civil War*, Collins and Brown, London 1991, pp123-42, 125.

8. One example of anonymous publication which belongs to the same debate

as *Areopagitica* is the tract attributed to William Walwyn, *The Compassionate Samaritan* (1644), referred to in Abbé Blum, 'The author's authority: *Areopagitica* and the labour of licensing', in Mary Nyquist and Margaret W. Ferguson (eds), *Re-membering Milton: Essays on the Texts and Traditions*, Methuen, New York 1987, pp74-96, 80. The Licensing Order stipulated that all books should have the approval of a Parliamentary Licenser and be registered with the Stationers' Company. A full text of the order can be found in *CPW* 2: 797-9.

9. The quotation is from Milton's response to that request, *The Tenure of Kings and Magistrates, CPW* 3, p236.
10. David Norbrook, *Writing the English Republic: Poetry, Rhetoric and Politics 1627-1660*, Cambridge University Press, Cambridge 1999, p5.
11. Ann Cust and Richard Hughes, 'Introduction: after revisionism' in Cust and Hughes (eds), *Conflict in Early Stuart England: Studies in Religion and Politics, 1603-1642*, Longman, Harlow 1989, pp1-3. For a reference to London and Manchester as homes to a zealotry foreign to other parts, see, for example, John Morrill, 'The coming of war' in Margo Todd (ed), *Reformation to Revolution: Politics and Religion in Early Modern England*, Routledge, London and New York 1995, pp142-54.
12. See, for example, Morill in Todd (ed.), *ibid*., p150: 'While the moderates, as always, talked and agonized, extremists seized the initiative'.
13. Richard Strier, *Resistant Structures: Particularity, Radicalism, and Renaissance Texts*, University of California Press, London 1995, pp6-7.
14. Ann Hughes, 'Local history and the origins of the Civil War', in Cust and Hughes (eds), *op. cit*., pp224-49, 227.
15. See Cust and Hughes (eds), *op. cit*., p9.
16. For a brief account, see Conrad Russell, 'England in 1637', in Todd (ed), *op. cit*.
17. Cust and Hughes (eds), *op. cit*., p34.
18. Russell, 'England', *op. cit*., p118.
19. David Underdown, 'Popular politics before the Civil War', in Todd (ed), *op. cit*., p220.
20. See Christopher Hill, *Intellectual Origins of the English Revolution*, Clarendon, Oxford 1965.
21. Thomas Hobbes, *Behemoth or the Long Parliament*, Ferdinand Tönnies (ed.), University of Chicago Press, Chicago 1990, pp144, 56.
22. Sharon Achinstein, *Milton and the Revolutionary Reader*, Princeton University Press, Princeton, NJ 1994, p60.
23. Achinstein, *ibid.*, p50.
24. Christopher Hill, *Milton and the English Revolution*, Faber, London 1977, p157.

25. Achinstein, *Milton and the Revolutionary Reader, op. cit.,* p59.
26. Christopher Hill, *The English Revolution 1640* (3rd edition), Lawrence and Wishart, London 1955, pp52-3, perhaps overstates a little: 'Cromwell's shooting of the Levellers at Burford made a restoration of monarchy and lords ultimately inevitable, for the break of big bourgeoisie and gentry with the popular forces meant that their government could only be maintained either by an army (which proved crushingly expensive as well as difficult to control) or by a compromise with the surviving representatives of the old order.'
27. Nigel Smith, 'Popular Republicanism in the 1650s: John Streater's "heroick mechanicks"' in David Armitage, Armand Himy and Quentin Skinner (eds), *Milton and Republicanism,* Cambridge University Press, Cambridge 1995, pp137-55, 148.
28. See, for example, Nicholas von Maltzahn, 'The Whig Milton, 1667-1700', and Tony Davies, 'Borrowed language: Milton, Jefferson, Mirabeau' in Armitage *et al* (eds), *ibid.*
29. This is an argument which is developed at length in Donald L. Guss, 'Enlightenment as process: Milton and Habermas', *PMLA* 106 (1991), pp1156-69. Cf. p1156: 'Enlightenment, according to Habermas, presumes what its adversaries think they alone have discovered: that self and world are constituted in language and human interaction, that truth reflects interests and power. But for such an Enlightenment, Habermas has no convincing genealogy, no originating figure to counter the postmodernist's bogeyman, Descartes. For that role, I propose Milton.' Habermas does refer in passing to *Areopagitica* in *The Structural Transformation of the Public Sphere: An Inquiry into a Category of Bourgeois Society* (trans. Thomas Burger with the assistance of Frederick Lawrence), Polity, Cambridge 1989; but on the whole, this work is surprisingly blind to events of the 1640s and 1650s, concentrating instead on the aftermath of the 'Glorious Revolution' and the end to Licensing in 1695.
30. The description of the force of Milton's style is from Terry Eagleton, 'The God that failed', in Mary Nyquist and Margaret W. Ferguson (eds), *Remembering Milton, op. cit.*, pp324-49, 345.
31. Rorty, 'Globalisation', *op. cit.*, p232.
32. Richard Rorty, 'The end of Leninism, Havel, and social hope' in *Truth and Progress: Philosophical Papers*, Vol. 3, Cambridge University Press, Cambridge 1998, pp228-43, 234.
33. Rorty, 'Globalisation', *op. cit.*, pp233-4; 'Human rights, rationality, and sentimentality' in *Truth and Progress, op. cit.*, pp167-85, 181.
34. Rorty, 'Globalisation', *op. cit.,* pp231, 235; 'Failed prophecies, glorious hopes' in *Philosophy and Social Hope, op. cit.*, pp201-209, 209.

35. Rorty, 'The end of Leninism', *op. cit.*, p236.
36. For Rorty on Dickens and social reform by sentimental appeal, see 'Heidegger, Kundera, and Dickens' in *Essays on Heidegger and others: Philosophical Papers*, Vol. 2, Cambridge University Press, Cambridge 1991.
37. Walter Benjamin, 'Theses on the Philosophy of History' in *Illuminations*, Hannah Arendt (ed), trans. Harry Zohn, Fontana/Collins, London 1973, pp255-66, 260, 263.
38. Christopher Hill, *The Experience of Defeat: Milton and Some Contemporaries*, Faber and Faber, London 1984.
39. Hill, *Milton, op. cit.*, p207. Milton was, in the event, exempted from the list of those to be executed.
40. Benjamin, 'Theses', *op. cit.*, pp257, 265, 266.
41. Morrill, 'The coming of war', *op. cit.*, p149.

Of systems and networks: digital regeneration and the pragmatics of postmodern knowledge

TIZIANA TERRANOVA

In a series of interventions posted to the mailing list *nettime*, media theorist and activist Geert Lovink sketched out a short, provocative history of media theory. According to Lovink, 'In the late eighties, the analysis of ownership and power over the media seemed to have ended up in a dead-end street ... Both the academic, 'speculative' media theory and the critical discourse of journalism had had enough of the 'culture of complaint' about the ongoing concentration of power. People no longer believed in the conspiracy theory of the media as the propaganda tool of capitalism.'[1]

This impasse, according to Lovink, spurred a wave of theories about the reception of media texts, a move that has come to be associated with the Anglo-American field of cultural studies. The failure of cable in providing public access to media production meant that resistance to media power had to be located in the viewer, who was now provided with the cultural and textual skills necessary to an active relation to media texts. Although politically important as a long-due acknowledgement of the complexity of late capitalist cultures, this turn to consumption left the question of alternative models of media production in the dark.

The emergence of the internet in the mid-1990s, however, has re-opened a debate about the possibilities of production through the development of a network of micro-producers having access to audiences and each other through the Net. Beyond the digitisation of established media such as cinema and television, the shift to computers as the central technology of production has spawned novel practices and formats associated with the label 'digital media'. In spite of the massive hype about e-commerce and internet business, a substantial part of the internet is still recognizable as a mutation of media culture throughout its hyperlinked landscape of homepages, art projects, e-commerce, music and film sites, gaming, chats and discussion groups. Digital media thrive on the direct interface between trade and communication and include more conventional entertainment products such as videogames, Web pages, and CD-ROMs but also cultural practices associated with mailing lists, online gaming, and chatlines. What distinguishes digital media as an economic and cultural phenomenon is the multiple possibilities engendered by a machine, the computer, which is used both to access, produce and distribute various types of information in a global *network* mode.

The global network is the fundamental mode of organisation of a digital media culture. The latter, however, is also a central motif in the sociological and economic analyses of contemporary capitalism.[2] Digital media partake of the larger network society, a reorganisation of economic and social relations based on new modes of managing knowledge. The translation of knowledge into the digital code of information is an element in this mutation, but not the only one. What I am more interested in here is not so much the loss of meaning that arguably goes together with the informatisation of knowledge. The management of knowledge through digitisation does not stop at its codification in a binary code. The latter is only a stage in a larger process whereby knowledge is organised through historical principles of efficiency conceptualised according to different scientific, technological and social paradigms. A contemporary cultural politics of digital mediation needs to face up to these modes of organisation as much as to the ideological and hegemonic aspects of governmentality.

I want to look at these developments through the example set by Lyotard in *The Postmodern Condition*. Lyotard argued that the best way to map the current mutations of knowledge was through a pragmatic methodology. Pragmatics looks at the rules governing the production and management of knowledge rather than at their ideological or discursive construction. Lyotard's book, published in the late 1970s, does not refer to a knowledge industry or to a digital media practice. However, it does outline a methodology which allows us to map out the specificities of the power/knowledge nexus in the postmodern condition. Such specificities are here understood in relation to technoscientific modes of management, inspired by cybernetic models, whose logic unfolds differently in the public sector and the more commercially oriented area of digital media.

THE GOVERNANCE OF FRAGMENTS

In academic circles, the cultural politics of digital media have been an object of debate for some time now. They have focussed on different aspects such as the nature of virtual interactions;[3] the transformations of identity facilitated by a disembodying medium;[4] the question of social exclusion;[5] and the ideological nature of cybercultural discourse.[6]

Here, however, I want to focus on knowledge as an essential component of a digital media culture. While critical theory has explored the relation between power and knowledge in terms of a Foucauldian micro-physics of power, it has usually avoided discussing knowledge in relation to its economic value in late capitalism. Much of the work in this area has been conceived as an answer to sociologist Daniel Bell's argument that knowledge has become a central source of value added in contemporary societies, much more so than material goods such as cars or raw materials such as coal and steel. Bell implied that this transformation was going to be extremely beneficial, promising nothing less than the end of the dialectical struggle between labour and capital into a new, much improved synthesis.[7] It is easy to understand the animosity that such claims aroused in Marxist or generally leftist circles, especially since the same argument has been regularly rehashed as the ideological companion to every wave of informatisation.[8]

Some of the questions thrown at Bell's thesis include the issue of the economic quantification of knowledge, the conceptualisation of its exact productivity and even the impossibility of separating knowledge from other types of work (every type of work requires some kind of knowledge).[9] Knowledge however is not simply the raw material of the information society. Knowledge is object and subject of power: in its manifestation as information, knowledge is constituted as flows which must be generated and managed; in its technoscientific mode, knowledge is that which regulates itself as information. In the postmodern condition, the nexus power/knowledge is complicated by a feedback loop that makes its operation pervasive and yet more difficult to analyse.

In *The Postmodern Condition*, Jean-François Lyotard set out to write a 'report on knowledge' and its vicissitudes after the decline of modernity. The most familiar legacy of Lyotard's analysis is his famous assertion that in the postmodern condition the grand narratives of collective emancipation and progress have given way to fragmented, partial and local knowledges. In a certain sense, the very existence of the fragmented, heterogeneous and idiosyncratic universe of the World Wide Web bears witness to the prescience of Lyotard's insights. The disjointed, dizzying collection of sites, opinions, and perspectives on the Web is a visible incarnation of what we thought was referring mainly to the opening of university curricula to the perspectives of race, gender, ethnicity and sexuality.

This emphasis on small narratives is Lyotard's most enduring contribution to the heap of postmodern clichés. What is easily forgotten, however, is that the book's main argument is not about fragmentation but about the management of fragmentation. In order to highlight the underlying restructuring of the rules of knowledge, Lyotard relies on a pragmatics of language games, and a critical evaluation of the function of denotative, prescriptive and performative games in postmodern societies. Lyotard, then, used games as an alternative to a semiotics of signification. Following Wittgenstein, he was interested in the nature of the language games, 'the rules specifying their properties and the uses to which they are put'.[10] Lyotard suggested that the heterogeneity of language games is not the only thing produced by the demise of the grand narratives of modernity: these smaller narratives and heterogeneous games are not left to run rampant across the social body. On the contrary, the fragmented knowledges of the postmodern condition are even more regulated and controlled than the universalistic narratives of the past. The true heir to narratives of emancipation and progress is not fragmentation but what he called a *technological principle of performativity*. Their end has not just left the field free for situated knowledges, but introduced a principle of performativity explicitly modelled on the technological game.

Lyotard distinguishes between different language games such as the 'denotative game (in which what is relevant is the true/false distinction) ... the prescriptive game (in which the just/unjust distinction pertains) [and] ... the technical game (in which the criterion is the efficient/inefficient distinction'.[11] If culture at large is a product of the interaction of all kinds of different language games, in the postmodern condition the most powerful game, the one that organises all the others, is the technical game. Lyotard pointed out how postmodern knowledge has subsumed all the other games to the technical principle of performativity which responds to the criterion 'efficiency/inefficiency'. Underlying all the different uses to which technology is put, the general principle is that it has to work:

> [Technical devices] follow a principle, and it is the principle of optimal performance: maximizing output (the information or modifications obtained) and minimizing input (the energy expended in the process). Technology is therefore a game pertaining not to the true, the just, or the beautiful etc., not to efficiency: a technical 'move' is 'good' when it does better and/or expends less energy than another.[12]

In this sense, Lyotard rightly points out, technology is more closely attached to capital than it is to science. Historically the latter, in fact, is not ruled so much by a principle of efficiency as by a tendency to question its own statements in order to produce new sentences or new paradigms altogether. This does not mean that science is located in some pure speculative domain, outside history and power: on the contrary, the scientific quest is always inextricably pervaded by historical relations of power, but its own dependence on 'paralogy' (a modification of the rules which undermines the solidity of what is known) makes it also susceptible to social change and constitutes its line of flight with relation to the pure exercise of power and control.

Lyotard's approach to technology focuses on what he sees as its core principle, efficiency. In this sense, it starts from an influential tradition of technological critique, from Jacques Ellul to Herbert Marcuse, which identifies technology as a de-humanising principle that submits the wealth of human capacities to a reductivist principle of performativity. Efficiency, however, is at the same time an abstract and concrete force: it drives technological development as a whole but it is always historically articulated. Lyotard's own analysis bears witness to the deep historical contingency of definitions of efficiency. In the late 1970s Lyotard noticed with dismay how knowledge management was completely informed by the technological specificity of a concept such as the 'system'. The systemic principle of performativity observed by Lyotard was based on what today we recognise as an early cybernetic way of looking at machines, institutions, societies and cultures as specific examples of a common techno-scientific principle.

As explained by Katherine N. Hayles, early cybernetics follows on from a first moment identified with the work of Norbert Wiener.[13] An outcome of World War II, the cybernetic system articulated by Wiener conceived of living and mechanical systems as 'islands of order' in a sea of entropy.[14] Entropy was the technoscientific obsession of a pre-cybernetic moment, one associated with the widespread use of thermodynamic machines. Thermodynamic machines such as the steam engine consumed energy and re-released it in the forms of finished products and an unabsorbable, dangerous surplus of heat that nineteenth-century science called entropy. Entropy is the ever-increasing accumulation of disorganised energy/matter that was supposed to bring the universe to the ultimate standstill, the heat death of the universe. Cybernetic systems warded off the disorder outside through a system of feedback loops. The information received from the outside was used to readjust the system internally so that it could actively defend itself against the encroaching chaos.

The cybernetic system thus configured was the ultimate nightmare of post-World War II political thought, and its traces still haunt the paranoid imagination of the 1990s. Fredric Jameson went as far as to argue that conspiracy theories might be a form of degraded cognitive mapping, a rudimentary answer to the need to 'map' a world system of domination which is becoming more and more invisible and codified.[15] Previously, in *The Political Unconscious*, published around the same time as *The Postmodern Condition*, he even blamed Michel Foucault for supporting the idea that power has no outside, only a relentless capacity to modify itself to deal with change. Jameson read Foucault's theories of the microphysics of power as an ally of systemic thought: '...in the political area ... the model of the "total system" would seem slowly and inexorably to eliminate any possibility of the *negative* as such, and to reintegrate the place of an oppositional or even "critical" practice and resistance back into the system as the latter's mere inversion.'[16]

The scariness of these early systemic notions came from the fact that through the operations of feedback mechanisms, established structures of power were capable of exploiting and reabsorbing all types of activity, including oppositional ones. It destroyed the dialecticism of the Hegelian Marx by stating that opposition was not a stage that prepared revolution, but a moment that could be absorbed and maximised through feedback. The system's main purpose is to survive by keeping its own internal relations intact, adjudicating roles and making sure that even opposition is functional. Any deviation from the rules of behaviour which make the system work must either be successfully incorporated or drastically repressed in order to ensure the principle of overall efficiency. Second wave cybernetics, as exemplified by the work of Humberto Maturana and Francisco Varela, introduced an organic feel to the system envisaged by Wiener. It emphasised the interconnectedness and reflexivity of the different elements of the system in the concept of *autopoiesis*, which became a foundational environmentalist concept through James Lovelock's Gaia.

The emphasis on closure as an important attribute of cybernetic systems, however, remained important, and it is this principle that Lyotard sees at work at the beginning of the postmodern condition. This technical management of knowledge is informed by an understanding of institutions, organisations and society at large as semi-closed systems whose performance needs to be monitored and managed. Lyotard, for example, noticed the trend towards the regular production of reports and the collection of statistics as a central principle in the reorganisation of the University.[17] The dissolution of the grand narratives of progress and emancipation, in fact, affected education first, which became conceptualised as a subsystem of a larger social organisation. If modernity came up with the notion that education is a prerequisite of informed political citizenship (and therefore that the right to education is a cornerstone of democracy), the postmodern pragmatics conceive of the latter as a cybernetic subsystem. Education in general is subjected to intense monitoring through the production of tables, reports and statistics to make sure that it does not fail the larger social system whose needs it is its duty to accommodate.

In the early postmodern condition, then, knowledge is regulated through a systemic framework articulated through the principles of the two first moments of cybernetic research. The purpose of management becomes to ensure that all the elements perform their established function correctly. This control is based on a regular monitoring of performance and is just a specific instantiation of a general 'meta-steering' function that has come to define the role of postmodern governments at large. Although Lyotard sees this systemic organisation of knowledge mainly at work in the university, today we can recognise its operation through the scant remains of a public sector – through the welfare system, health, education, the prison system and so on. Indeed the function of governments in the postmodern condition is sketched out more and more as a function of 'meta-steering', an allegedly technical rather than political management of national and international relations based on the overall principle of efficiency and performativity.[18]

This shift to technological meta-steering through policy-making is, of course, strongly associated with the informatisation of government. The notion that technologies neutralise the ideological component of reorganisation is a long standing argument of some strands of science and technology studies. In this case, the introduction of information technologies normalises the notion that governments are there to manage the various sub-systems whose added performance constitutes the overall efficiency of societies. So the correct, more efficient management of public services such as education and health is based on a constant monitoring of performance, whose outcome is the implementation of more efficient organisational structures.

The more visible and frustrating effect of this cybernetization of the State in the postmodern condition is its defusion of ideological critique. It has become almost impossible to contest these changes in terms of a discourse of rights, such as the right to politically informed citizenship, a function which postmodern political rhetoric somehow delegates exclusively to media culture. The means of political citizenship are associated with access to information through the press, television, and the internet, while the question of the formation of the subjects who access this information is left in the dark.

In Lyotard's opinion, however, the notion of performativity and efficiency eagerly applied by postmodern governments is not only ideologically misleading, but is *also* based on an outmoded techno-scientific paradigm, that of thermodynamics. The idea of systemic performance, in fact, implies a highly stable system 'because it is based on the principle of a relation, which is, in theory, always calculable, between heat and work, hot source and cold source, input and output. This idea comes from thermodynamics. It is associated with the notion that the evolution of a system's performance can be predicated if all of the variables are known'.[19]

This quest for precision, the conviction that knowledge of all the variables will inevitably lead to better performance, is a particularly strong obsession of bureaucracies and one which has not disappeared but become exaggerated in a phenomenon such as Blairism. The endless production of reports and statistics is a measure of this general failure to understand that measurement of all the variables is not in itself enough to increase the performativity of a system. It just does not work that way; the more knowledge is generated about a system the more the uncertainty. 'This inconsistency explains the weakness of state and socio-economic bureaucracies: they stifle the systems or subsystems they control and asphyxiate themselves in the process (negative feedback).'[20]

For example, education is subjected both to a destructive process of mechanical monitoring in the forms of regular assessments and exercises, whose principles are derived from an obsolete thermodymanic/cybernetic paradigm; it is *also* tied up in a reactive dependency to an outside which is constituted as an unproblematic source of stimuli which education needs to assess in order to adjust its internal mechanisms. The exhilaration and freedom left behind by the dissolution of grand narratives, the interdisciplinarity and political diversity promised by the latter, must be read in conjunction with the general principles that have governed this dissolution. So we could say that the mutations that made possible the appearance of cultural studies, postcolonial theory, and feminism in university degrees are counteracted by a management strategy that closes them off in a purely performative (in the technical sense underlined by Lyotard) dimension. The public function of educational institutions such as the University, for example, is reduced, and the exhilaration of new fields of knowledge undermined. In Nietzschean terms, we might say that education is turned into a *reactive* force, always awaiting for an outside force to trigger off changes inside. We could then say that the positivist principle of efficiency which operates in the current management of higher education is effectively anti-productive in two ways: it undermines efficiency by trying to control the system too tightly; and it turns education into a passive provider of services rather than an active producer of knowledge.

This threat is all the more serious inasmuch as knowledge is one of the driving forces of late cybernetic capital and therefore more important than ever. A public commitment to the production of and transmission of knowledge, then, should move beyond the obsolete misgivings of 1970s cybernetics and systems theory, and engage different, *active* modalities of production. A pragmatic approach to the postmodern condition is therefore not just about the ideological underpinnings of this orientation towards apparently neutral management. It is also about pointing out that things do not work, and that the notion of government as a meta-steering organ whose function is the optimisation of performance of its various subsystems is obsolete and unworkable *on its own terms*.

NETWORKS OF EMERGENCE

Lyotard was very concerned about the consequences of system theory and early cybernetics taking up the place of the grand narratives of modernity. In his opinion the void left by the decline of the universalist narrative of emancipation threatened to be filled by a positivist principle of efficiency which conceived systems as closed, self-regulating and ultimately repressing apparatuses. In the twenty years since the publication of *The Postmodern Condition* things have taken a further twisted turn. The claustrophobia of system theory has given way to a wild optimism about the possibilities of the network as an anti-hierarchical, infinitely mutating, diffuse environment for the development of a flexible, collective intelligence. Postmodern governments have been mesmerised by the wonders of the digital economy, even as their attempts at intervention have been vehemently dismissed by an essentially libertarian digital media culture. Still, the global fate of nation states, the rhetoric suggests, is to be decided through the development of digital media as sites of trade and communication. What is even better, digital media do not seem to ask for any government intervention, they want to be left alone to proliferate and develop according to pure market logics.

The enthusiasm of postmodern governments for the powers of the market and digital technologies has meant that the public sector has been branded as even more intrinsically unreliable and inefficient. It has become not an island of order in a sea of chaos, but an archipelago of disorder and inefficiency in a sea of blissfully self-regulating market forces. This is true even for those attempts to hybridise public and private in key sectors like transport. Tied-down by its physical responsibility to the welfare of living bodies, the public sector suffers from an earth-boundedness that responds unevenly to the dynamics of the market. The only solution seems to be an intensification of the monitoring processes identified by Lyotard as integral to early system theory. As a result, the inefficiency of the public sector escalates, and does so in direct proportion to the amount of systemic control which postmodern governments deem as the only solution to the endemic inefficiency of publicly-owned assets. Such are the costly ironies of the late postmodern condition.

In its turn, the fast-moving world of digital capitalism has never been merciful in its criticism of 'public', state- or government-run institutions. The cybernetic libertarianism of its American apologists has repeatedly criticised 'bureaucracies' as enemies of innovation and speed. Bureaucracies, including colleges and universities, are slow and boring dinosaurs and nobody who could work for a new exciting start-up would stay there for longer than strictly necessary (indeed Bill Gates dropped out of Harvard the minute he understood Microsoft was going somewhere).

This dynamism of technocultural production associated with digital technologies is obviously controversial: the obsession with innovation worries humanists because it threatens to create a caste of wired up posthumans far removed from the realities of war, violence and starvation which plague most of the world. Indeed, as in late capitalist market conditions, the digital economy is highly selective. Although the aspirations of the digital economy are universalist (everybody should be part of the network), the kind of cultural capital and technological expertise needed to participate is highly concentrated in the Northern hemisphere, and even then it is predominantly found in the urban digital enclaves of areas like Shoreditch in London, Brighton, downtown Manhattan, and Northern California.

In a further development of the post-fordist logic of outsourcing and subcontracting, the digital microbusiness has become the functional unit of the digital economy. Typically composed of three or four employees, linked to bigger companies by occasional contract and to smaller operators through outsourcing, a visualisation of the digital media industry would look pretty much like those scary, spidery maps produced by Mongrel Media's alternative browser, Webstalker. The Webstalker looks under the glittery surfaces of atomised webpages to reveal the peculiar forms of power enacted through the hyperlink. It is not just a matter of being higher up or down in a domain hierarchy, but also of convergence into stronger nodes. It is about outsourcing and subcontracting but also about lateral links and strategic alliances. Most of all, it seems to be about survival in the fiercest of competitive environments where the fortunes of microbusinesses rise and decline in the span of months or even weeks.

The most urgent motivation driving digitisation is the production of the new, because the new has a higher chance of opening up the much coveted new markets. It has become quickly apparent that 'it is not sufficient to just put your information out on a home-page, produce a video or pamphlet etc. and then just wait until something happens. The potential power of mass media has successfully been crippled. Today, reproduction alone is meaningless.'[21] Since access to distribution is not enough anymore – since it is not enough to publish your site on the internet – the tactics of media production go into a mode of '"serial" manufacture fueled by the hope that one of the mixes will turn out to be the Killer App, the Next Big Thing, the Golden Mean, the Ultimate Combination.'[22]

Your financial success is directly proportional (although not ensured) by how quickly you get your product on to the market. You have to produce the first browser, search engine, online bookstore, online auction sites, new concept for a game, most successful internet radio, Web TV and so on. As the history of Microsoft shows, it does not even have to work and, as Microsoft demonstrates again, even if you are bought out by big capital you can still come out with a good deal. You just have to be there first, you must have the imagination and competencies to come up with the newest idea and the best way to implement it first.

It is all very exciting. The brazenness of the digital media industry did come as a breath of fresh air to a technological industry dominated by the mammoth antics of IBM for decades. What the enthusiastic digerati do not mention, however, are the larger rules governing such apparently unfettered production. It is true that the complete exposure of digital knowledge to network conditions has left the concerns of system theory and management behind. In a digital economy characterised by constant innovation, hyperlinkages and fruitful connections the central issue is no longer how you control the variables so as to make the system work. The problem is how to induce innovation, the break-up of paradigms and the establishment of new markets.

The most utopian treatments of the dynamics linking these businesses together show a remarkable optimism. Indeed, digital technologies of communication such as the internet emphasise elements associated by Lyotard with the most inspiring postmodern science: chaos, catastrophe theory and molecular biology. Lyotard's main critique of the management of knowledge based on system theory, in fact, was that the latter had been made obsolete by postmodern science. Postmodern science emphasises the implausibility of closed, regulated systems to which it opposes the unpredictable and yet fertile logic of chaos. In these sciences' emphasis on spontaneous, unpredictable mutation Lyotard saw a refreshing alternative to the asphyxiating world of early cybernetics.

Indeed the digital economy of linked micro- and macro-businesses defined by the convergence of computing, communications and content could not care less about homoeostasis, a technological principle which was concerned mainly with the stability of systems faced by the imminent and continuous threat of entropic disorder. The organisation of the digital economy is pervaded by new technoscientific principles which incorporate the insights of postmodern sciences such as chaos into a new technological paradigm, a new arrangement of the relation of forces and modalities of control which makes the old world of systems look vaguely reassuring. Such a moment incorporates the unpredictability of open systems into a new modality of control, based on proliferation rather than closure. The network, rather than the system, is its technological model. Networks are decentralised, they allow and invite the addition of new links. They are flexible and, as the first netpioneers used to argue, are even capable of self-organisation. In the cybercultural imaginary, the structure of the network evokes the proliferation of difference and even the evolutionary rules of nature.

This development witnesses a move away from modalities of control associated with closed systems towards a more productive engagement with open, unpredictable systems such as those emphasised by chaos theory. In these systems, control is not associated with closure and simple techniques of monitoring through reports. On the contrary, it fully incorporates the dynamism of open systems and their capacity to produce the new and unpredictable through proliferation.

What we have, then, is a further redefinition of efficiency away from the reactive, monitoring-obsessed disfunctionalities of modernist corporations and lean postmodern governments. Within a digital para-digm, efficiency is redefined away from the principle of homoeostasis (stable equilibrium) towards the notion of *emergence*, a key principle of the third wave of cybernetics as exemplified in robotics, network dynamics, catastrophe theory and artificial life. Control operates not through hierarchical organisation, but through selection at the point of emergence.[23] The issue is not so much to keep the system stable but to provide the minimum of control that is necessary to keep systems in a creative middle area, between anarchy and rigidity, where, according to chaos theorists, life evolves. Rather than steering the system from the outside, late cybernetic capital works on the smallest possible rules, the most basic principles: you just need a computer, a modem, the knowl-edge, the energy, and the willingness to work yourself to death. Even as the price of that knowledge is still high in global terms, it is a remarkably accessible set of prerequisites. Third wave cybernetics, the driving technoscientific principle of digital capital, aims to facilitate rather than monitor. The digital economy encourages proliferation and access because it needs the largest numbers of products, ideas, and concepts. The network system does not exclude anybody from the start: every new node is welcomed. However, it does not care whether nodes disappear as long as new ones connect. It acts by selection at the point of emergence, rather than through direct, in-house control of the sources of innovation; it invests and connects rather than pre-struc-tures.

CONCLUSION

My idiosyncratic use of Lyotard's pragmatic methodology in this chapter has revealed the co-existence of different models of cybernetic manage-ment at work in the public sector and in the digital economy. It has not been so much a matter of arguing the superiority of one mode against another as of showing the relative nature of the notion of efficiency and its dependence on different technoscientific paradigms. Late 1990s governments, mostly run by parties with a socialist history, have pursued systemic principles of organisation within, while supporting networked modes of production without. They have not so much set themselves against the digital as operated a bifurcation between the sectors they are immediately responsible for (such as health and education), and those which are seen as crucial to economic development but essentially self-sufficient. The net result has been quite confusing: systemic modes of management in the public sector are undermining their own workings in the name of efficiency, while the neo-Darwinist digital economy of emergence is left to run rampant. In this context the choice between public and private becomes a non-choice, in as much as the opposition is set between the impossibility of an efficient public sector and the brutal vampirism of the commercial world of the digital. This new stage in the relation between the capitalist state and capital itself can be seen as a result of what Gilles Deleuze has called the shift from disciplinary societies to societies of control.[24]

In the passage from the striated space of discipline (which produced the modern state) to the smooth space of control, the digital preys on the analogue, and the private on the public. The digital economy is often *directly* fuelled by the inefficiency of the public sector. The huge amounts of money that inflate the market value of internet start-ups also originate from the expansion of insurance companies in fields traditionally covered by the public sector, such as health. Much venture capital is generated by the private insurance policies which citizens feel the need to take up in order to compensate for the instabilities of the welfare system. The vampirism of the digital economy is therefore double: it preys on the agony of the public sector through venture capital and on the living labour of its producers through the exploitation of emergence.[25]

And still it seems to me that there are lessons to be learned by the digital, lessons that should be incorporated in its own cultural politics and in the larger set-up of postmodern political cultures. The former are being experimented upon in internet circles through the establishment of 'gift economies' of exchange and modes of organisation which use the flexible qualities of the network to political purposes.[26] After all, much of the critique of modern political institutions such as the party came out of a dissatisfaction with its hierarchical and delegational modes of organisation. In June 1999 the transnational protest against global capital organised around major metropolitan centres of the world was organised in a network mode. Advertised and organised through the internet, June 18 was justified both as a way to escape the attention of the police and in terms of a more spontaneously aggregative model of political participation. The network mode has also proven more politically efficient in the establishment of a varied, inclusive debate about international events such as the war in Kosovo. That is, there is an ongoing attempt to engage with the network structure against its neo-Darwinist, vampiric grain, pushing to the surface the self-constituting power of the Negrian multitude.[27] Whether these modes of organisation can be transposed to the more traditional but crucial grounds of the public provision of essential services such as health and education is a much more difficult question, but one that, this chapter suggests, requires urgent political attention.

NOTES

1. Geert Lovink, 'Preface for Bulldozer', posted to *nettime*, 25 November 1997.
2. See Manuel Castells, *The Rise of the Network Society*, Blackwell, Oxford 1996.
3. See Sherry Turkle, *Life on the Screen: Identity in the Age of the Internet*, Phoenix, London 1995.
4. See Rosanne Alluquere Stone, 'Will the Real Body Please Stand Up? Boundary Stories about Virtual Cultures' in M. Benedikt (ed), *Cyberspace First Steps*, MIT Press, Cambridge, Mass. 1991.
5. See Kevin Robins, 'Cyberspace and the World We Live In' in M. Featherstone and R. Burrows (eds), *Cyberspace/Cyberbodies/Cyberpunk*, Sage, London 1995.
6. See Richard Barbrook and Andy Cameron, 'The Californian Ideology', (http://www.hrc.wmin.ac.uk), 1995.
7. See Daniel Bell, *The Coming of Post-Industrial Society: A Venture in Social Forecasting*, Penguin, Harmondsworth 1976.
8. See Kevin Robins and Frank Webster, 'Athens Without Slaves ... Or Slaves Without Athens? The Neurosis of Technology', *Science as Culture* No. 3, pp7-53 (1988).
9. See Frank Webster, *Theories of the Information Society*, Routledge, London and New York 1995.
10. Jean-François Lyotard, *The Postmodern Condition: A Report on Knowledge*, trans Geoff Bennington and Brian Massumi, Foreword by Fredric Jameson, University of Minnesota Press, Minneapolis 1979, p10.
11. *Ibid.*, p46.
12. *Ibid.*, p44.
13. See Katherine N. Hayles, *How We Became Posthuman: Virtual Bodies in*

Cybernetics, Literature, and Informatics, The University of Chicago Press, Chicago and London 1999.

14. See Norbert Wiener, *The Human Use of Human Beings: Cybernetics and Society*, Free Association Books, London 1989.

15. See Fredric Jameson, *Postmodernism Or, the Cultural Logic of Late Capitalism* Verso, London & New York 1991.

16. See Fredric Jameson, *The Political Unconscious*, Cornell University Press, Ithaca 1981, p90.

17. Lyotard noticed how universities were becoming centres of what today we recognise as 'lifelong learning'. Thus 'knowledge will no longer be transmitted *en bloc*, once and for all, to young people before their entry into the work force: rather it is and will be served "à la carte" to adults who are either already working or expect to be, for the purpose of improving their skills and chances of promotion, but also to help them acquire information, languages and language games. Allowing them both to widen their occupational horizons and to articulate their technical and ethical experience' – Lyotard, *op. cit.*, p49. These mutations have been typically understood by more contemporary commentators such as David Noble in terms of a commodification of the traditional functions of the university, the research and educational functions (see David F. Noble 'Digital Diploma Mills: The Automation of Higher Education', posted to *nettime* 16 April 98). The research function of the university becomes commodified when academics enter business partnerships or receive research grants in exchange for commercially viable types of research (see Martin Kenney, *Biotechnology: The University-Industrial Complex*, University of Yale Press, New Haven and London 1986). This early moment of commodification of the research function has been followed by the commodification of the educational function of the university through the establishment of distance learning. Noble is particularly worried about the future of academic staff in a context which is easy to compare to the proletarianisation of the artisans during the industrial revolution. When lecturers are asked to put their courses on the Web while the university keeps the copyright of the material, the door is open to further hierarchical division of labour between researchers, educational experts and proletarianised teachers. The latter are practically expropriated of their imagination via copyright (Noble, *op. cit.*).

18. In his discussion of the virtual state, Paul Frissen notices how, also through the mediation of ICTs (Information and Communication Technologies), 'politics is developing more and more into a sort of 'broker'-politics, in which government plays a more organising and procedural rule.' (See Paul Frissen, 'The virtual state: postmodernisation, informatisation and public

administration' in Brian D. Loader, ed., *The Governance of Cyberspace: Politics, Technology and Global Restructuring*, Routledge, London 1997, p118). And he adds: 'We may witness the development of a political system that is relatively indifferent with respect to policy contents, but normative with regard to the qualities of social steering and the conditions under which this takes place, and this codifies socially crystallised consensus. Politics then becomes a question of style – it can be considered as "a grammar" for societal decision making' (p120).

19. Lyotard, *op. cit.*, p55.

20. *Ibid.*, pp55/56.

21. Geert Lovink, 'Strategies for Media Activism', posted to *nettime*, 2 December 1997.

22. Geert Lovink, 'Current Media Pragmatism', posted to *nettime*, 21 April 1998.

23. Luciana Parisi and Tiziana Terranova, 'The Turbulence of Origins: emergence and control in genetic engineering and artificial life' in *Ctheory: an international journal of theory, technology and culture* (www.ctheory.com), 2000.

24. See Gilles Deleuze, 'Postscript on Control Societies' in *Negotiations*, Columbia University Press, New York 1995.

25. See Tiziana Terranova, 'Free Labor: Producing Culture for the Digital Economy' in *Social Text*, 63, Vol. 18, No. 2 (Summer 2000), pp33-57.

26. See Richard Barbrook, 'The High-Tech Gift Economy' in Josephine Bosma, Pauline Van Mourik Broekman, Ted Byfield, Matthew Fuller, Geert Lovink, Diana McCarty, Pit Schultz, Felix Stalder, McKenzie Wark, and Faith Wilding (eds), *Readme! Filtered by Nettime*: ASCII *Culture and the Revenge of Knowledge*, Autonomedia, New York 1999, pp132-138.

27. Antonio Negri and Michael Hardt draw on Thomas Hobbes's political theory to distinguish between the people and the multitude. Hobbes, one of the fathers of the modern state, was very concerned that the two things should not be confused. In the words of Negri and Hardt, 'The multitude is a multiplicity, a plane of singularities, an open set of relations, which is not homogeneous or identical with itself and bears an indistinct, inclusive relation to those outside of it. The people, in contrast, tends toward identity and homogeneity internally while posing its difference from and excluding what is outside it. Whereas the multitude is an inconclusive constituent relation, the people is a constituted synthesis that is prepared for sovereignity ... Every nation must make the multitude into a people' (Antonio Negri and Michael Hardt, *Empire*, Harvard University Press, Cambridge, Mass.: 2000, p103).

No borders in business: the managerial discourse of organisational holism

KAREN LISA G. SALAMON

'If we want to get somewhere in the future with our enterprises, we need total commitment and a holistic perspective, which quite simply are the basic elements of a religion.'

Lars Funder, CEO of the large chewing gum producer
Dandy, Denmark[1]

To keep employees loyal and corporate identity strong, contemporary management theory speaks of the need to create a general, overall sense of purpose in organisations and of having employees imbibe particular cultural values. Management and its theorists find it problematic that employees' values and references are fluid and often beyond their control. Managers generally acknowledge that the continued creation of economic prosperity depends on their ability to create and maintain particular modes of symbolic production and cultural referentiality. New managerial teachings and practices accordingly focus on methods for creating and maintaining a stable organisational identity and solid loyalty from employees, whilst keeping the workforce flexible and the structures fluid.

Organisational frameworks become transient, and social values and cultural references within those frameworks tend to do likewise.[2] These days, capital transnationalises and 're-engineers' itself for 'lean' production.[3] Companies operate in financial markets where economic value is measured by the expectations and knowledge created, recognised and sold, rather than by production and sale of hardware goods and simple services. When enterprises fail to create and maintain certain impressions in the market and consequently do not achieve the expected value within a certain time, corporate mergers or fissions will follow. These frequent corporate reconfigurations decrease stability in the organisational structures. Consequently, employees of diverse sociocultural backgrounds are brought together under new kinds of contractual conditions. Often teams are formed for short-term projects, after which employees move on to new units.

The contradiction implied in a management ideal of unstable organisational and economic structures (described as 'flexible' or 'prepared for change') that caters for stable organisational identities and loyalties is ostensibly reconciled by rigorously policing the production of meaning within organisations. Since the 1970s, human resource management theorists have been increasingly concerned with the creation and promotion of so-called *corporate identities* and *cultures*.[4] These concepts have been articulated as functional tools and introduced into studies of business organisation, personnel management and strategy.[5] In these studies, successful business presupposes ideological and cultural homogeneity in the organisation and in each individual thereof, often exemplified by a clear and widely recognised 'mission statement'.

A particular section of these studies and policies has appeared under terms such as 'holistic' management, 'spirituality in the workplace' and the 'new tradition in business'. It is concerned with achieving organisational and personal wholeness and harmony at work through the development of spiritual consciousness and humanistic expressivism.[6] To this end, it advocates inducing common recognition of a certain meaning(fulness) in the workforce.

In this chapter, I will present an introduction to the ideological framework of organisational holism.[7] I see it as the product of an influential, albeit relatively small and heterogeneous movement that has radical ambitions and significantly influences contemporary corporate efforts for the reconstruction of workplace realities.[8] I base my analysis on interviews and ethnographic fieldwork conducted between 1998 and 2000, as well as on a number of texts expressing holistic beliefs and spiritual concerns within the field of human resources management.[9] In this essay I shall discuss only a few of the many individual voices advocating holistic spirituality in business. These should be seen as rather radical renderings of more familiar and commonly recognised assumptions adopted by contemporary management theory. Various versions of human resources management theory of the 1990s have subscribed to 'management by values'. Here, it is assumed that individual employees must be influenced into internalising common corporate values.

Influential US and European discourses of corporate personnel management have thus re-articulated the employees as incorporating the organisation, and the organisation as an organic wholeness of its employees. This re-articulation of the relationship between the overall corporate body and the identity of each employee 'den[ies] the analytical distinction between individualism and group life that's been the bedrock of American conservatism *and* American liberalism for a century and a half.'[10] This definition of the relationship between organisation and individual puts new demands on the value-orientation and ideological identification of employees, who 'do not intervene at a distance from their organisation. They *are* their organisation (p48).'

According to this perspective, workplace efficiency must be established via the installation of self-discipline in workers through the creation of commonly shared values and 'corporate culture'. The ideological formation of organisational holism must thus be understood as one particular, influential formation within a broader spectrum of contemporary management ideology sharing a belief in the importance of installing common values in corporate settings. Consequently, I see organisational holism as a social movement that has ramifications for contemporary discourses of leadership and the management of social organisations under capitalist market conditions.

DISHARMONY AND FRAGMENTATION

The Danish professor of management studies, Steen Hildebrandt, has been an influential proponent of a holistic perspective on organisation and of values-driven management in the 1980s and 1990s. His commitment partly grows out of a critique of what he calls the 'fragmentation [that] pervades society, almost as a lifestyle, and which can be found in each single organisation and in each single individual. It leads to a confusion of our thinking, and this confusion creates an endless chain of problems ...'.[11] In an article about developing a holistic perspective in management practice, Hildebrandt argues with reference to an assumed original primordiality of unspoiled holism, which has been destroyed by the human realisation that we are different from and not identical to nature. Hildebrandt acknowledges that this loss of primordial wholeness has led mankind to progress in terms of technical abilities and independence from 'nature's immediate boundaries'. However, he laments that the 'fragmentary process went far beyond the borders of reasonableness'. Hildebrandt advocates a move towards a renewed organisational holism: 'Within the organisational area we can say that each single part obtains its identity through its relations to the entirety. The whole exists by virtue of the contributions of the single parts to the whole.' An organisational system is one of a hierarchy of entities, integrated in each other: 'Each entirety is part of a larger entirety, which in itself is part of a yet larger entirety.' The basic entity is the single employee, who, together with others, makes up subunits within subunits, such as departments, fields of specialisation and separate enterprises. In traditional business management, according to Hildebrandt, these entities do not co-operate sufficiently. They are defined by short-term economic criteria and a myopic focus on individual goals, thereby neglecting the 'processes, paths and movements' involved. 'Specialisation. Standardisation. Synchronisation. Centralisation. Concentration. Maximisation' all add up to a problematic fragmentation of the organisation (pp11, 14, 18).

This development must be refocused by a general introduction of holistic thinking in organisations. Co-operation across specialisations must be encouraged. Previously separate areas such as production and services must be merged. Hildebrandt claims that general industrial trends are already showing signs of this. Enterprises merge and production units and functions unite, something he claims represents a renewed holism. However, a definite end to fragmentation in organisations must be achieved by the invocation of common ideology. A defined common mission, a 'vision', a 'direction', must be formulated and internalised by each employee. According to Hildebrandt, leadership must no longer be placed with individual agents, but rather with the generally embraced ideological holism. Leaders will then be less directorial. Rather than deciding on details, they will rely on 'systems of common rules of the game and cultures which will make the right decisions [by themselves], without the need for management to be [directly] involved. Each employee will, to a larger and larger extent, be his own leader and quality controller'. As common normative patterns and convictions are diffused within the organisation, employees can be trusted to manage themselves in their work and to direct achievements for the benefit of the organisation. The consequence of Hildebrandt's holistic vision seems to be a general implementation of corporate ideology so convincing that each employee will want to discipline her- or himself accordingly, without being directly controlled or managed by superiors. The happy result, according to Hildebrandt, is the disappearance of (Taylorist) 'mass logic and standard-controls' and a 'utilisation of the collective intelligence and creativity of the united group of employees as a source for continual improvement'. Decisions are no longer transmitted hierarchically downwards, but rather 'grow out of the situation and [are] handled with reference to a common consciousness of the mission, vision and culture of the corporation, and from a knowledge of and intimacy with the systems which exist in the integrated firms which each single employee directly refers to'.

Hildebrandt thus seems to predicate a harmonious co-existence of individualism and collectivist consensus in his vision of the holistic organisation. Individuals are assumed to be sufficiently independent from external obligations and ideological beliefs to commit to corporate obligations and identifications. Since at least the early 1980s a number of business consultants, theorists and managers have produced narratives and practices expressing aspects of organisational ideology, based on similar assumptions. These writers and practitioners of management theory share a perspective through which it seems quite logical that a single, authentic, holistic body of 'common consciousness' and shared values should come about in a modern corporate, organisational context involving a heterogeneous group of individuals employed under longer or shorter term contracts.

LEADERSHIP AS MEDIATION OF A COMMON CONSCIOUSNESS

One such practitioner of holistic management and believer in 'common consciousness' as the key to creating a productive working environment is a recently retired managing director, 'E. B'. In the interview I conducted with him in 1998, he described himself as a former rationalist who, after a course in personal development back in 1978, gradually came to the conviction that 'nothing can exist without a consciousness'.

Now in his mid-fifties, E.B. is a board member of the financially successful company that he used to manage on a daily basis. The company sells research, development and production of detergents to the European market. The enterprise is overseas-owned but located in Denmark, and it employs around fifty-five people. A graduate engineer, E. B. was a major figure in the creation of the company. In this capacity, he claims to have made significant corporate decisions based on psychic channelling and clairvoyance. He currently reads publications by – and regularly converses with – a number of mainly North American and British business consultants and theorists. Typically, these are former managers, retired researchers of the natural sciences and human potential experts who, since the late 1970s, have been involved in the spiritual and cultural movement that E. B. calls 'New Worldview'[12] (alternatively known as 'New Age' or 'New Paradigm').[13] Besides being generally inspired by New Age writings in his private life,

E. B. has been particularly interested in those aspects of the movement concerned with – as he sees it – *making work-life more holistic, organic and spiritual*. Through books, e-mail correspondence, mailing lists and international conferences conducted by various groups and individuals in the movement, E. B. gets continued inspiration for his own publications and courses on the issue of *leadership by intuition*. He has also published two books expounding his conviction that all beings – including objects – exist only in terms of their consciousness and are interconnected in an all-encompassing common consciousness.

During his many years as managing director, E. B. claims to have been guided by 'visions received' in the form of dreams during meditation. He described how, in collaboration with his wife and others, he gradually developed a way of 'contacting the consciousness of the firm' and was subsequently able to 'intuit' the right decisions. Responsible for chemical product development in the company, E. B. experienced how his own 'higher consciousness' by meditation connected with the 'higher consciousness' of the company. He claims to have diagnosed and solved problems by this method; for example, he claims to have influenced chemical processes by means of his own consciousness connecting with those of the chemical substances and procedures. To achieve all this, E. B. had to remain *'in total agreement'* with himself: 'Not a single part of me must disagree'. Balance, harmony and spiritual unity were preconditions necessary for success – personal as well as organisational. Doubt and division in a person's mind, or amongst employees in the organisation, would have caused work to fail, E. B. assumes, but 'when one believes, anything can be achieved'.

Here, E. B.'s reasoning follows the New Age conviction that change must begin at the individual level, and that each person involved in the process is responsible for his or her own life situation (following laws of *karma* and reincarnation). Social transformation begins with 'inner', individual transformation at the level of consciousness. Social change only happens when individual beliefs are strong enough. Since existence is assumed to be united both ontologically and monistically, change will gradually spread to involve all of existence.[14] Thus, by common intention and spiritual dedication, 'we are the creators of our own lives. From the inside out.' In the late 1980s, E. B. organised his company according to this individualist and idealist ontology. He was convinced that the company had a 'field of consciousness' of its own, which could be contacted and influenced through meditation. Each employee could partake in the strengthening of the company by entering this field of common consciousness.[15] E. B.'s convictions led him to develop 'an organic circle-structure' with employees working in small circuits that together made up larger units in the overall structure of the entire organisation. Each subcircle had a 'focaliser', who 'summarised the decisions of the group' for the benefit of other units in the organisation. Looking back at the process, E. B. described this 'focalising' as a matter of *mediating common consensus* rather than *leading* or *deciding on behalf of others*. When asked explicitly, E. B. admitted that dissent amongst employees could occur in spite of the 'organic' decision-structures. Individual employees would, at times, disagree with the collective consensus of the organisational 'field of consciousness'. E. B. characterised *'co-workers'* who would persistently fail to come to agreement as radiating 'negative energies'.[16] By their negativity they turned into *'counter-workers'* and would be required to leave the corporate unit. When asked where such people should go, E. B. replied that they must either find another company that suited them better in terms of values, or they must 'work on themselves'. The latter could be done by various kinds of self-analysis and therapy, which could bring these counter-workers back their 'positive energies'. When asked what disadvantaged people who wouldn't be able to improve on themselves in this way should do, E. B. referred to his belief in reincarnation: 'It is probably something they must go through in order to learn.' Negative life-experiences would lead to positive transformations, either in this life or in future lifetimes. Alternatively, they could be *karmic* responses to negative behaviour in past lifetimes.

E. B.'s convictions and practices might seem eccentric, particularly in a management context. However, he is but one of the more explicit, consistently New Age-inspired and rigorous exponents of the holistic formation in personnel management. As is generally the case in contemporary culture- and values-oriented management theory, E. B.'s position addresses workplace organisation, focusing on consensus and beliefs amongst employees. As is also generally known – for example, in the field concerned with 'organisational learning' – contemporary personnel management theory stresses individual responsibility for personal evolution and positive optimism.[17] E. B.'s position differs from those of most mainstream theorists in its cosmological assumptions. Whereas less explicitly New Age-inspired holistic positions, such as that of Hildebrandt, refer to human potentialist views of psychological transformation, cultural evolution and essentialist authenticity, E. B. refers to reincarnation and *karmic* laws. Common to the different holistic positions, however, is the absence of recognised democratic methods, despite the orientation towards consensus. Voting does not seem to be included in their techniques for pinpointing common values and visions adhered to in an organisation. Rather, common goals are found via inspired leaders drawing forth and mediating a common consciousness, consensus or will. Leadership becomes a matter of forming daily practice by incorporating certain values into the 'organisational culture', generally by intuiting a consensus and giving it a name. It is claimed that inspiration actually moves from the bottom-up, but is given voice from the top-down. Intuitive leadership purports to represent the common will of employees and the organic union of the company, without employing a direct representational system.

This ideological perspective on leadership and organisation is generally studied with sympathetic attention, even by management consultants and human resource officers who do not themselves explicitly identify with it. Many of the assumptions entailed in the ideology are gradually becoming adopted as commonsense by contemporary management and organisational theory.[18] This might be the reason why E.B.'s colleagues accepted his organisational practices wholesale. E. B. did not tell employees about his unconventional beliefs and methods until later, when the enterprise had turned out successfully. His methods had by then come to represent an already proven operational management tool. When he finally voiced the alternative procedures and ideological framework behind his organisational changes, he was generally met with sympathy and acceptance, or at least tolerance.[19]

EXCLUSION RE-ARTICULATED AS EXISTENTIAL LEARNING

E. B. and others sharing a holistic ideology thus re-articulate exclusion as a positive chance for individuals and organisations to learn and improve. Exclusion is a natural systemic response to the 'negative' behaviour of certain employees. When it comes to issues of agency and responsibility, it is stated that only those individuals in question can alter their own situation. A change in their existential situation can only happen if they take responsibility for changing themselves. Each soul is thus responsible for its own fate.

E. B.'s views and beliefs must be understood in the context of New Age cosmology, but also as a radical version of broader contemporary understandings of organisation, social causalities and responsibilities. The evolutionary perspective is a commonsense foundation for most discussions of change in modern management.[20] Progressive individual and social evolution is similarly a central New Age dogma. Accordingly, fortune or misfortune can be explained as a consequence of convictions and deeds in a former life. However, spiritual self-development techniques and Human Resources Development serving to unlock spiritually-based human potential can also remedy negative situations in the present lifetime. When E. B. sees exclusion as something which certain people 'must go through in order to learn', he is in line with other New Age-inspired thinkers who argue in terms of cosmic reward and *karmic* dialectics. ('The Universe pays me for being who I am and doing what I love doing.'[21]) The exclusion of employees who do not fit positively and organically into the organisation is not perceived as discrimination or exclusion from a working community, but as a holistic response. Removing negativity from the company is a necessity for keeping the organisation sound and harmonious. However, similar understandings of exclusion in terms of holism, health and purity are common amongst managers and consultants who are not explicitly New Age-oriented.[22]

Descriptions of organisations as (anthropomorphic) biological organisms that can move out of balance, attract viruses or grow overweight are commonly used in management literature. Writers might not speak in terms of 'negative' and 'positive energies', but may use organic, medical metaphors such as 'ushering out viruses' from the organisational body (for example, dismissing employees who will not adapt to new forms of production). Whether in E. B.'s New Age variant or in other versions, arguments for institutional exclusion play on images of the well-functioning organisation as a unified, healthy, moving, evolving, positively energised body-machine or transforming organic body. Problematic employees are described as individual cells of negativity, viral infection or stagnation, that need to be transformed or removed when they disrupt the functioning of the overall organism. Thus, the organisation is being construed as a unity with no space for internal disagreements. In its New Age-inspired form, it has its own consciousness, and a leader who is the voice representing the organisation, mediating inspiration from its 'collective consciousness' (and from otherworldly realms). Each of its employees carries full responsibility for her/his own fate, achievements and ability to learn and progress. Each individual takes independent responsibility for interacting harmoniously with all others involved in work processes which are assumed to grow organically out of their unity. Thus, E. B.'s views on leadership and organisation combine a radical individualism[23] with claims of collective, holistic monism and a lack of specific personified agencies of leadership.

INTUITING COLLECTIVE VISION

In an article on intuition in business, the American journalist Nancy Rosanoff connects contemporary premises for strategic planning with the importance of building collective visions and having intuition in business: 'Every business person knows the importance of good timing. Strategic planning in the current corporate environment is becoming less focused on the details of a three- to five-year plan and more focused on building collective vision and mission. This allows intuition to play a more important role in both planning and implementing'.[24] As was the case in E. B.'s presentation of his holistic organisation, no particular agency is mentioned in Rosanoff's discussion of organisational strategy by intuited, collective vision. Readers are left to wonder where this intuition – or collective vision – comes from and who intuits it. The visions and decisions for business planning in Rosanoff's presentation appear as agency-free organic growth, similar to the 'collective consciousness' of E. B.'s enterprise. However, Rosanoff seems implicitly to have placed the work of intuiting visions – or collecting those visions – with the formal leadership of the company, as this is where authority in strategic planning is generally held. This implied understanding of strategy and leadership in terms of mediation is parallel to E. B.'s description of his own work as a leader getting into contact with the 'collective consciousness' of the organisation and intuiting the next steps to take for the organisation as a whole.

Management researcher R. Daniels represents a more explicitly holistic advocacy of intuitive leadership in his discussion of information technology management functions. He argues that chief executive officers must begin to see the organisational system as larger and different from the sum of its parts. 'Synthesis, adopting a general manager's perspective and strategic skills, all involve [a] holistic view of the world and the relationship of parts to a greater whole,' he claims. 'Rather than seeing organisations as comprised of parts of a machine, those who hold to this perspective see elements like strings on a harp.'[25] As in E. B.'s references to the 'common consciousness' of the enterprise, Daniels defines the organisation as a unity greater than the sum of its parts. To do this, he employs a metaphor drawn from musical harmony. With the introduction of this metaphor, the issue of agency calls for attention again. Readers are left to wonder whose hands strike the chords on the organisational harp and according to which musical scores or organisational programmes. The implication is that the harmonious interplay of sounds comes about by inherent mechanisms in the musical instrument itself. As in E.B.'s company, this would imply that values and goals are produced in the corporate organism as such, by consensus and 'collective consciousness', rather than through independent decisions by management. Harp-strings vibrate at the inspired touch of the musician's hand. Similarly, the intuitive organisation manager is moved to act by some extra-human, metaphysical factor of unknown inspiration.

THE PRIORITY OF A WHOLE OVER ITS PARTS

Contemporary holism as a management ideology can be related to Romanticism and later German language writings of organicist, vitalist and biologist systems thinking in the late nineteenth and early twentieth centuries, partly associated with cultural and political totalitarian thinking and anti-democratic movements.[26] The contemporary definition of holism, such as that used in the management writings of Hildebrandt and Daniels, seems to have been first formulated in these terms by the Viennese *Gestalt* philosopher Christian von Ehrenfels, who lived from 1859 to 1932. Ehrenfels defined wholeness as 'the priority of a whole over its parts'. The concept became influential in the English-speaking world with the institutionalisation of the human potential movement in the United States in the 1970s.

The many versions of holistic theory that have appeared since the 1890s share the proposition that an entity or part can only be identified in terms of its relations with all other parts. This carries metaphysical implications, since the whole is defined as ontologically different from, and of a more primordial and authentic nature than, the mere sum of its parts. Consequently, holistic theory implies a history of origins, an evolution and a teleology. Furthermore, when taken as a fundamental ontological proposition and cosmology, its logic implies a systemic inclusion of all existence into a single, organic, monistic unity. Achieved wholeness implies (sacred) completion, harmony, transcendence and a surpassing of any kind of lack and contradiction. It is seen as original authenticity that implies complete identity, where all parts fit homogeneously together to the extent of *being one*, and where fragmentation and dissent no longer exist. When holism is complete or undisturbed, there is interconnection of all phenomena in one single, all-inclusive, monistic system. Any tiny occurrence is believed to have systemic effects, such as in the popular version of chaos and complexity theory called the Butterfly Effect – the notion that a butterfly stirring the air today in Peking can transform storm systems next month in New York. By this mechanism, destructive or 'negative' occurrences can easily bring the whole out of 'balance' and 'harmony', but creative or 'positive' energies and acts can strengthen and balance the whole. Accordingly, amongst activists such as E.B. professing New Age holistic beliefs, it is generally accepted that single positive thoughts or acts can trigger a process gradually leading to a progressive transformation of whole organisations and societies, for example, by influencing the overall 'common consciousness' via meditation.

Thus, holistic positions on organisation and management imply that all employees are equally incorporated into the body of the organisation, and that the totality of the workplace has priority over its parts. To achieve an authentic holistic organisation, fragmentation and dissent must be removed. Each employee must give priority to the collective. The role of holistic leadership is to give a voice to the consensus and thus to determine which values to follow. However, since the organisation including its leadership is perceived as a single body, consensus is defined as a collective will or consciousness. The leader is accordingly seen as the embodiment of the collective will, or the voice of the collective consciousness. Leadership thus has the privilege of intuiting and voicing the values and aims of the organisation, but it is not the primary agency in the decision-making of a company. That agency rests beyond any single part, but entails the whole.

'CORPORATE RELIGION'

Managers using holistic concepts are often more explicit about agency and less concerned with metaphysics than the voices quoted above. One such manager is the Danish advertising agent, Jesper Kunde. He uses holistic and religious concepts for explicitly operational purposes. In his 1997 marketing manual, *Corporate Religion: The Path to a Strong Business*, he writes: 'The main goal of a Corporate Religion is to strengthen and regiment the efforts of the enterprise, no matter at which market it attempts to sell its brands. This makes a Corporate Religion into a holistic outlook, and an ideological outlook.'[27]

Contrary to many holistic texts on management, Kunde seems less inspired by New Age thinking than by aggressive advertising and marketing in his highly conscious use of symbolic constructions. His manual advocates the centrality of 'vision' and 'mission' to a management strategy that claims to be holistic. His presentation is explicit in introducing the collective visions of the company as an ideological construction created by top management and set in motion by particular, identifiable agents. What E.B. designated an organically grown 'collective consciousness', Kunde identifies as a common 'set of values' developed and orchestrated by central management. Traditional industry had certain products as its focal point. Kunde's managers must have a particular brand of ideology as the central product to define all other products. Each organisation must become homogenised and united in order to carry out its mission. Thus 'employees become missionaries, figuratively speaking, and there is room only for co-workers, not for counter-workers ... In the future, the most important qualification of an employee will be that he is a true believer. Only when that is ascertained can the corporation spend time on estimating individual abilities (pp134, 129, 16ff).'

We see here the same discourse of polarities and exclusion that we saw in E. B's discussion of 'negatively-charged' employees. Like those, Kunde's counter-workers 'must leave and find another place to go'. Despite such similarities, the approaches of Kunde and E.B. differ on the issue of agency. Their respective positions can be seen as conspicuous examples of the differences existing within the field of contemporary management theory over the merits of values-based, holistic organisation. While they agree on the importance of creating and maintaining a strong, common, ideological focus amongst employees, they seem to have different understandings of the origins of this ideological focus. Where Kunde's model operates with a 'religious leader' – a strategic and hegemonic agent of ideological production – in E.B's model, this agency is implicit and collective. E. B. articulates the corporate ideology as an organic growth, naturally evolving out of the (rather diffuse) collective consciousness and mediated by the prophetic leader. The primary force moving the 'common consciousness' and speaking through the organisational leader is one of supernatural origins. E. B. does not use the word 'religion', which implies dogma and inflexibility; he prefers the term 'spirituality', as do most other voices of holistic management. Kunde seems not to mind dogma, so long as it can be used to build up a successful organisation and maintain a strong corporate identity. His use of holistic values is a highly pragmatic operationalisation of cultural and ideological phenomena and social trends. According to Kunde's position, religion is an operational ideology created by people. The term 'religion' is mainly a rhetorical move to stress the all-encompassing qualities of the ideal corporate ideology. Kunde does not state whether any metaphysical powers are at work in the creation of such an ideology or in the selection of leadership. His 'corporate religion' is not an organic growth out of the corporate organism or the product of a higher common consciousness, but a willed ideological creation by management: 'The strong religion has a self-reinforcing effect and keeps all employees in place – even in the remotest corner of the corporation (p41).'[43] Furthermore, the 'corporate religion' inside the organisation carries over into a strong, external 'brand-religion' with customers, as has been the case for Coca-Cola, Harley-Davidson and The Body Shop.

A COMMUNITY OF BELIEVERS DIRECTED BY ONE UNIFYING FORCE

Other managers agree with Kunde, as he places the power (usually termed *responsibility*) of creating the collective ideology with top management. Lars Kolind is the retired CEO of the successful electronic hearing-aid enterprise Oticon in Denmark (see note 22). He is a politically influential voice, speaking in various media in favour of management by values. He reconstructed the Oticon enterprise according to these beliefs and concerns. Kolind states that the top manager must act as a spiritual leader.[28] He must take the first step in defining the values that employees must identify with. Kolind is an active participant in the Danish Lutheran Church community, and has drawn his inspiration from the Bible in the formulation of such core values. He does not claim any direct contact with the divine in this process. His understanding of agency in the creation of organisational core values remains closer to Kunde than to E. B.'s prophetic, New Age-inspired understanding of leadership. However, E. B. is not the only holistic manager who sees himself as a leader governed by a higher force. Executive Director James F. McMichael of the Wisconsin State Commission on Ageing has a similar vision of intuited, holistic management:

> The vision I have is of an organisation which resembles a community of believers directed by one unifying force which the members both individually and collectively intuit. As a manager, I am nothing more (or less) than a conduit through which that power can work. And that power works not only through me but through each and every employee in that organisation. As a manager, my role, as compared with others, is more in articulating and focusing the direction that power seems to be giving us ... And while this style of management may sound more difficult than the top down, 'Tell'em what they need to know and make sure they do it' approach, you will find in the long run it is much easier, more productive, and vastly more creative and successful because the organisation is no longer limited to your personal power but expanded to an infinite power, a power which cares about you and will miraculously provide if you will just listen.[29]

As I read the different positions on holistic leadership discussed above, they all share an erasure of identity-differentiation between management, enterprise and employees. Management, employees and the enterprise relate as a totality to the same single source, which is ultimately given voice by management. The executive director is but a conduit, channelling and focalising the will of an infinite power. Depending on which version of holistic management we look at, this force is taken to represent either the intuited will of the collective consciousness of employees (the sum total of all entities in the organisation) or an infinite power moving beyond the realm of the employees. With a few exceptions, such as that of Kunde's, these organisational representations do not include any individual strategic agencies responsible for the re-articulation of ideology. Ideological and cultural change is introduced as collective will or supernatural inspiration. This articulation of leadership carries implications for the nature of management, explicitly and self-reflexively portrayed as a mediation of ultimate power and truth to a working community of homogeneous believers.

AUTHENTIC CORPORATE IDENTITY THROUGH COMMON VALUES

A manager can thus create a strong position for him- or herself as a representative of the generalised collective by referring to a collective subconscious will or a miraculously providing power, whilst downplaying his or her role as the primary and responsible decision-maker. The kind of agency that is evoked therefore exerts a strong claim on authenticity in leadership and policy that cannot be mustered by any old autocratic manager. Peter Pruzan, a management theorist at the Copenhagen Business School and a consultant to several commercial organisations, has described a similar construction of leadership in terms of integrity and authenticity as an 'agreement between private, personal values and the corporate values of management'.[46] Pruzan finds that organisations lack integrity when the 'private values' of the manager are detached from those of the corporation. Young, qualified, creative, loyal and responsible employees in particular will not accept such a detachment. They want to work in corporations with strong, convincing and consistent value foundations. The contemporary demand for qualified young people in the work-market thus becomes yet another reason for constructing a convincing (symbolic, A=A) relation of identification between management, organisation, employees and products/brand.

Pruzan, Kolind, Kunde, McMichael, Hildebrandt and E. B. all argue that an actual identificational unity can be achieved through a common set of values, however differently they define the qualities of this unity. As I understand these ideological positions, they assume that an authentic identity between management, firm and employees is not only possible, but also a prerequisite for the creation of any successful enterprise. These management theorists and practitioners believe, furthermore, that a commonality of ideological values will make it possible to avoid the mechanistic, Tayloristic instrumentalisation and objectification of employees. By implication, an organisational 'holism' founded on common ideology may *subjectify* employees (my phrase, not theirs).[31] Such organisation, it is claimed, is in marked contrast to that of traditional industrial organisations. These tend to treat employees structurally as exchangeable tools in the production process, and to manipulate structures to serve the profit gains of managers and shareholders. With the introduction of holistic management it is believed that employees will no longer be instrumentalised. Rather, they will be drawn into the collective identity of the entire corporation, and symbolically subsumed into the organisational whole.

However, I would claim that in these approaches employees enter a different kind of objectification. According to holistic management theory, employees of the holistic unity must identify with and be part of the collective consciousness of the organisation. They must formally, or symbolically, situate themselves on the same level as the leading agency of the production management. By this re-identification they become *subjectified*, part of the single 'acting ego' of the organisational body. Seen through the holistic management lens, this results in the liberating and empowering of employees. However, I wish to draw attention to the consequences of this re-articulation in terms of what it means to be an employee and part of a corporate organisation. The models presented by the management theorists and practitioners quoted above leave no room for private dissent, individuation or counter-ideology. Employees become part of the organisational whole, acting agency and collective consciousness, but not in the capacity of their own individuated, private selves. As shown in the positions represented, employees and managers alike must stake their private identities and show a complete self-investment. Membership of the corporate community implies sharing its visions and common sense of purpose. There is no room for employees who do not completely identify with the project. The alienated 'wage-earner' approach is no longer acceptable. No longer can employees rely on correctly and instrumentally carrying out tasks and orders.[32] As the corporate body is maintained via the collective production of marketable meaning, ideological foundations *(common values)* are more important than simple production capacity for the identity and long-term competitiveness of an enterprise. Alienated workers, investing some manpower but neither mind nor soul, therefore risk becoming excluded as 'counter-workers'.

EMPLOYMENT – BODY, MIND AND SOUL

The re-articulation of the workplace as an authentic value-based community and fountain of collectively meaningful ideology appears incompatible with the radically individualistic demands on each employee to carry sole responsibility for remaining a positively charged co-worker, harmoniously fitting into the organisational whole. It also seems out of place in the new structures of short-term employment via subcontractors and the general mobility that characterise contemporary work markets. However, the underlying threat of exclusion from the organic whole, as represented in the talk about counter-workers and negative energies, corresponds to those concrete work contracts that even middle-class, specialised, white-collar employees face today. Employees generally have little job security (also defined as 'having more freedom'), and are not necessarily guaranteed long-term employment, or pensions, or capacity building possibilities.

The contemporary work market presents employees with a combination of individual responsibility for personal success, general mobility, insecurity in jobs and demands for total ideological and identificational investments in the workplace. Each new workplace represents the claim of (yet another) collective identity, community and mission statement. Thus, employees must become travelling, individualistic consumers of disposable authenticity, who will eagerly prepare themselves to adopt the 'corporate religion' of their next new workplace.

Unwittingly or explicitly, holistic theories of management operate with an ideology of homogeneity, uniform consent and totality. In practice, this is probably never fully achieved; still, it is a widespread and non-problematised ideal. In spite of its claims of having left the fragmented and mechanistic paradigms of modernity behind, it still resembles a modernist purification project.[33] The re-articulation of the enterprise that ontologically constitutes more than the sum of its human, technical and financial parts becomes a process of totalisation. The redefinition of leadership and employees into one social body is a negation of individuation and real social and cultural differences.

Workers are no longer physically controlled, nor do managers need to exert direct control, as their share in the collective ideological consciousness will have made them self-disciplining and part of the same body of interest. The principal assumptions of holistic management imply that there are no single localisable foci, nor independent agents of power. Everyone is in power, or no one (no one present in the world, that is). Accordingly, positions and dispositions of power are impossible to address with any directness, as everybody is implicated through the collective consciousness of communally-shared values. Besides its claims of promoting individual and collective liberation and self-realisation, the holistic vision represents a new strategy of disciplinisation. Panoptic measures are replaced by attempts at installing self-regulating ideology into employees and managers, who are expected to transform themselves into 'self-managing' holistic systems. Having identified with the ideology of the organisational body, the ideal co-worker becomes reconstructed as radically individualistic and communally holistic at the same time.

The holistic model presented by the voices discussed above presents a paradox, as I see it. With the exception of perhaps its most essentialist versions, such as E. B.'s explicitly New Age re-articulation of work-reality, it presents itself as a radical break with instrumentalist management ideologies and theories, whilst marketing itself as yet another operational management model. It claims authenticity and ideological stringency in its attacks on the alienation and hypocrisy of 'traditional' organisational models. In the less essentialist versions, such as Kunde's 'corporate religion', it claims to have an ontological status, but simultaneously plays at being simply a representation.

WHERE 'COMMON CONSCIOUSNESS' AND AUTHENTICITY DWELL

These days, management theory re-articulates corporate existence as a holistic project of authenticity, community and totality. At the same time, employees live radically individualistic lives of hypermobility and flexible timing, with disposable and commodified identities in short-term work communities. This re-articulation of the meaning of work, workplaces and corporate leadership is a conspicuous, self-consciously cultural part of the contemporary transformations of what Lawrence Grossberg has referred to as 'popular mattering maps',[34] and the nature and sites of authority in present-day lives. By its claims to authenticity and harmony, holistic management ideology operates simultaneously on cultural identifications, affect and ideological 'common sense', and thus can be seen as a conscious cultural strategy of change in the contemporary, global, corporate landscape. Its politics are articulated in terms of culture and spirituality, but its logic of exclusion is nonetheless politically real. The harmonious 'co-worker' is part of the company's body and soul, and vice versa. But the 'counter-worker' must carry individual responsibility for not fitting in. Problematic, inflexible and negative workers remain isolated from the 'community of corporate believers' until they achieve the personal transformation needed to integrate into a collective consciousness again or leave the company. Work is thus transformed from a site of interest-struggles, materialism, hierarchy and alienation to that of a community where 'common consciousness', spirituality and authenticity dwell, and all within the Oneness of a homogeneous cultural policy.

NOTES

1. From a jacket endorsement of Jesper Kunde's book, *Corporate Religion: Vejen til en staerk virksomhed*, Boersen, Copenhagen 1996. As here, all translations from the Danish are my own. Versions of this paper were given at the conferences, 'Crossroads in Cultural Studies', Tampere, Finland 1998 and 'Cultural Politics/Political Cultures', University of Sussex, September 1998. I want to thank Lawrence Grossberg for insightful discussions all along, and Niels Aakerstroem Andersen, Bettina Mogensen, Poul Poder Pedersen and Inger Sjoerslev for their constructive comments to various versions of the paper.

2. I do not claim any single, particular causality to be at work here. As I see it, cultural and ideological changes induce organisational change and vice versa, in an unstable, multifaceted and multidimensional interaction.

3. 'The term 'lean' designates the need for institutions to keep costs low, organisation simple and production times short.

4. *Harvard Business Review* timeline showing central concepts of management science since 1922. David Sibbet wrote of 'vision' as the most recent core concept for 'leadership'. See *75 Years of Management: Ideas and Practice 1922-1997*, *Harvard Business Review*, Boston 1997.

5. See, for examples of this, Mats Alvesson and Per Olof Berg, *Corporate Culture and Organizational Symbolism: An Overview*, Walter de Gruyter, Berlin 1992; Barbara Czarniawska and Guje Sevón (eds), *Translating Organizational Change*, Walter de Gruyter, Berlin 1996; Geert Hofstede, *Cultures and Organizations: Software of the Mind*, McGraw Hill, New York 1995; Edgar H. Schein, *Organization Culture and Leadership*, Jossey-Bass, 1985; Fons Trompenaars, *Riding the Waves of Culture: Understanding Cultural Diversity in Business*, Nicholas Brealey

Publishing, London 1993. For an ethnographic approach, see George E. Marcus (ed.), *Corporate Futures: The Diffusion of the Culturally Sensitive Corporate Form,* University of Chicago Press, Chicago 1998.

6. See Paul Heelas, *The New Age Movement,* Blackwell, Oxford 1996, p115.

7. My use of the term 'ideology' here refers to a conceptual scheme providing a foundation for programmes of social and political action. To qualify as an ideology, such a scheme must be explicit enough to be meaningfully presented to (and formulated by) a group of people. It will never have a singular meaning, but depend on individual interpretations in given contexts.

8. My discussion of these texts and narratives will seek to demonstrate that individual expressions are identifiable as aspects of a single ideological formation. I base this claim partly on their mutual quoting from each other and from other common sources of reference, and partly on their similar specialised vocabulary. Some of the authors and proponents of these texts belong to a common social network communicating regularly via the Internet and at conferences. Several of these authors agree that they belong to a common 'paradigm', 'world-view' or 'movement'. The individualisation of spirituality and cultural interpretation is part of the explicit claims of the movement: it is believed that each individual must develop her or his own sense of meaningfulness in life and at work. Often, however, authors also express differences in their various interpretations. See, for example, the discussion between Keshavan Nair and Michael Toms (Michael Toms (ed), *The Soul of Business,* Hay House, Carlsbad, CA 1997, pp123ff). Toms has a North American background, and refers to various forms of self-affirmation and naturalness in terms of authenticity and idealism. Nair has his origins in India, and refers to Gandhi and material detachment in his articulation of business ideals.

9. Since the early 1980s, academics and managers have written about personnel management in terms of 'resources'. Common to human resources management perspectives is 'that human resources policies should be integrated with strategic business planning and used to reinforce an appropriate ... organisational culture, that human resources are valuable and a source of competitive advantage, that they may be tapped most effectively by ... policies that promote commitment and which ... foster a willingness in employees to act flexibly in the interests of the "adaptive organisation's pursuit of excellence" ' (Karen Legge, *Human Resource Management: Rhetorics and Realities,* Macmillan Business, London 1995, p66).

10. Christopher Newfield, 'Corporate culture wars', in George E. Marcus (ed) *Corporate Futures: The Diffusion of the Culturally Sensitive Corporate Form,* University of Chicago Press, Chicago 1998, p47.

11. Steen Hildebrandt, 'Fragmentering contra helhedssyn – På vej mod helhedssyn i ledelsespraksis', in Hildebrandt and Alken (eds) *På vej mod*

CULTURAL CAPITALISM

helhedssyn i ledelse.... billeder fra praksis, Forlaget Ankerhus, Hinnerup 1992, p9.

12. *Verdensbillede* – literally 'worldpicture' in Danish.

13. The Findhorn movement in particular had influenced E.B. See W. I. Thompson, *The Findhorn Garden*, Harper and Row, New York 1975. For other influential books arguing for neo-spirituality inspirations in business, see Barrie Dolnick, *The Executive Mystic: Intuitive tools for cultivating the winning edge in business*, HarperCollins, New York 1998; John Renesch (ed.) *New Traditions in Business: Spirit and Leadership in the 21st Century*, Berrett-Koehler, San Francisco 1992; Margaret J. Wheatley, *Leadership and the New Science: Learning about Organization from an Orderly Universe*, Berrett-Koehler, San Francisco 1992. For discussions written from 'outside', see Melton, Clark and Kelly, *New Age Almanac*, Visible Ink Press, Detroit, MI 1991; Paul Heelas, *op. cit.*; and Michael F. Brown, *The Channelling Zone: American Spirituality in an Anxious Age*, Harvard University Press, Mass. 1997.

14. Monism ultimately refers all existence to a single category. In neo-spiritual traditions this position is a central part of the cosmology. The widely read Indian-American author and speaker, Deepak Chopra, writes: 'The *Law of Pure Potentiality* could also be called the *Law of Unity*, because underlying the infinite diversity of life is the *unity* of one all-pervasive spirit. There is no separation between you and this field of energy. The field of pure potentiality is your own Self' (Deepak Chopra, *The Seven Spiritual Laws of Success: A Practical Guide to the Fulfillment of your Dreams*, Amber-Allen Publishing/New World Library, San Rafael, CA 1994, p10).

15. As can be seen in other metaphors below, such as 'improve on themselves', these figures of speech imply a division of each individual into several psychological agents. The individual accordingly is an object for her/himself, to be ever improved upon by her/himself. I will not discuss the psychological theories that must be operating for these kinds of formulations to be perceived as true and possible statements, merely observe that such formulations represent a culture of self-objectivation. Here, multiple agents are contained in the same personality, and it is believed that they operate on each other. The issue of being truly identical to oneself – and having all these agents behave in accordance with one central position – thus becomes pressing in the constitution of the subject.

16. Rather than the Danish term for employee, *ansatte*, E. B. consistently used another common term *medarbejder*, 'co-worker'. When speaking about problematic employees, he used a newly-coined word, *mod-arbejder*, 'counter-worker'.

17. A dominant management-ideal is that of the Learning Organisation, which

154

focuses on employees' continuous individual learning as a route to organisational adaptability and success. For a recent version of the LO ideal, see Mike Pedler and Kath Aspinwall, *A Concise Guide to the Learning Organization*, Lemos & Crane, London 1998.

18. In the late 1990s, holistic and values-driven management attracted significant attention in business papers, seminars arranged in industrial organisations and in networks of personnel managers. Several influential professorships at business schools in Europe and North America are occupied by management researchers who subscribe to holistic and values-driven management and who publish extensively besides being interviewed regularly on the issue.

Highly influential management consultants play down distinctions between individual and organisation, and advocate consensus, common visions and values and speak in terms of existing 'corporate culture' (for example, James M. Kouzes and Barry Z. Posner, *The Leadership Challenge: How to Keep Getting Extraordinary Things Done in Organizations*, Jossey Bass, San Francisco 1995; Tom Peters, *Liberation Management: Necessary Disorganization for the Nano-second Nineties*, Knopf, New York 1992).

19. Perhaps E.B.'s introduction of intuitive management really did alter the organisation in the ways he believes it did. But maybe similar alterations would have happened anyway or by other methods as well. Perhaps the introduction of such methods would produce similar transformations in other organisations, perhaps not. There is no way we can get to validate this, as each situation will be unique and unrepeatable. However, business education is built on designing success from copying and adapting known cases of success. It is assumed that the preconditions for creating a successful business organisation can be described and distilled into systemic form. This might work for highly quantifiable aspects of business, such as finance, industrial ergonomics and transport logistics, but I want to argue that management science has problems when applying similar assumptions to issues of product strategy, personnel psychology and cultural issues. I find it necessary to state this position explicitly, since I tend to get questions from colleagues in management studies and management consulting who make a living from giving advice based on past experiences!

20. The general strongly evolutionist perspective can be illustrated by a quotation from a Danish manual for managers which claims to 'illustrate the way to renewal usually shown by capitalist competition and animal life' ... 'it isn't the change-over of old units, but rather new units growing forth that work according to completely different and more functionally able principles. You'd better learn from that, otherwise Darwin will have your

arse.' See Larsen and Lützhoeft (eds), *Slank og Raa. Business Process Reengineering & andre drastiske rationaliseringsmetoder i praksis,* Forlaget Sporskiftet, Charlottenlund (Denmark) 1995, p4.

21. This quote comes from the prominent North American New Age author and publisher Shakti Gawain. It is quoted regularly on a website called Spirit at Work (www.spiritatwork.com). This version of *karma* represents a syncretistic, western, individualistic rendering of eastern traditions.

22. The following view exemplifies this trend. The quote is from a radio interview with a politically influential former CEO Lars Kolind:

> Interviewer: 'If you are a cleaning-assistant because you need to make some money but otherwise do not wish to invest much creative or emotional competence in the job; if you'd like to leave at 4 p.m., when your duty is done, then can't you be part of this thing that you call the *great competence leap*?' Kolind: 'No, you can't. And I believe that the number of people who just don't care about what they do for a living and just want to pass time – I'm convinced that that number is but a tiny percentage of the population, and that we must remain firm and state that those of the population who actually don't care what they do will not have any place in the competence-society of the future. These people will have to accept that this is what they have chosen themselves, and there just isn't anything to do about that' (Danish National Radio Channel 1, courtesy of the journalist Ane Saalbach, *Mandat/DR*, April 1999).

23. Radical individualism is a project of self-construction and identity-formation where the individual refuses to identify with larger identity-formations such as those founded on kinship, ethnicity, nationality or religious background, or with collectivist, universalist positions such as socialism. It is an essentialist, particularistic position of self-referential identification, as far as this is possible, and it relates to other possible identifications in terms of negations of 'what I am not'.

24. See Nancy Rosanoff, 'Tapping the Intuitive Power in Your Workplace' (www.speaking.com/articles_html/NancyRosanoff_207.html). The phenomenon discussed here is transnational, and continually changing and developing by cross-national communication across Europe and America; thus I do not make a strong point out of stating the nationality of the various sources and interviewees in this article.

25. R. Daniels, 'CEO's look at the IT function: expectations of impact and what to do differently', www.ese.scu.edu/rdaniels/html/research/ceos.html. Musical metaphors and the image of the symphonic orchestra playing with or without a musical director are images often used in holistically inspired texts on organisation.

26. See Anne Harrington, *Re-enchanted Science: Holism in German Culture from Wilhelm II to Hitler,* Princeton University Press, New Jersey 1996,

for an in-depth discussion of the origins of holism in the German intellectual tradition.

27. Jesper Kunde, *Corporate Religion: Vejen til en staerk virksomhed*, Boersen, Copenhagen 1997, p13. All translations from this book, including the subtitle, are mine. However, the author has given his book, otherwise written in Danish, an English main title, and he uses American English versions of other central terms.

28. Lars Kolind, lecture and conversation with the author at Copenhagen Business School, 27 April 1998.

29. James F. McMichael, *The Spiritual Style of Management: Who Is Running This Show Anyway?* Spirit Filled Press Inc., Havana, FL1998. McMichael is currently a Senior Management Trainer for the Center for Public Management at Florida State University. He has formerly served as executive director and president in various corporations, such as the Wisconsin State Commission on Aging. He describes himself as 'a transformed person' (www.sampleassociates.com/jim.html).

30. Peter Pruzan, lecture at the Copenhagen Business School, 28 April 1998. See his 'The question of organizational consciousness: can organizations have values, virtues and visions?' (paper presented at the World Philosophers' Meet 1998: Second Parliament of Science, Religion and Philosophy, Geneva, August 1998; and 'The trajectory of power: from control to self-control' (unpublished paper).

31. These texts never talk about 'subjectification' or 'objectification', but use expressions such as 'soul in the workplace', 'passion' and 'integrity' (e.g. Toms, *op. cit.*).

32. Reality is somewhat different from this ideological position. Even in a so-called value-based company, such as that of Lars Kolind, it is mainly white-collar/information and knowledge-workers who are touched by the demands for a full identification with values. Blue-collar workers, who are still working along Tayloristic lines in separate quarters of the company, are not expected to represent company values to the same extent. This probably touches upon the nature of their work (still based on physical working abilities rather than knowledge and specialisation) and their general lack of influence. This complex demands a separate analysis and will not be further discussed here.

33. See Zygmunt Bauman, *Modernity and the Holocaust*, Polity, Cambridge 1991.

34. For a broader discussion of the transformations of 'popular mattering maps', see Lawrence Grossberg, *We Gotta Get Out of This Place: Popular conservatism and postmodern culture*, Routledge, New York 1992.

Truth and appearance in politics: the mythology of spin

TIMOTHY BEWES

SUBJECTIVITY AND OBJECTIVITY IN POLITICS

At the height of its investigation into the 'cash-for-contacts' scandal in the summer of 1998, the *Observer* newspaper discovered a sales pamphlet of Lawson Lucas Mendelsohn (LLM), a lobbying firm whose three partners had all at some time been advisers to the three most prominent Labour Party politicians.[1] The pamphlet included a page with two columns headed 'The Passing World' and 'The Emerging World': 'To the Passing World belongs "ideology", to be displaced by "pragmatism",' reported the *Observer*. '"Conviction" will be replaced by "consumers"'. 'Interestingly,' the report continued, 'these committed Blairites tell us that "politicians who lead" will be replaced by "politicians who listen".'[2]

It is difficult to imagine that this table ever informed potential clients of LLM of anything they didn't already know, since its themes are some of the most over-rehearsed in contemporary political commentary. Modern politics, it is often claimed (in the name of analysis), is obsessed with image to the exclusion of ideology; spin has triumphed over substance. An alternative, almost equally commonplace rendering of the same tendency is found in the observation that the Labour Party represents the 'feminisation' of politics; the values being pursued are those 'womanly' virtues – listening, contingency, lack of ideology, consumerism, passivity – which in the nineteenth century went largely unrepresented in the public sphere. The political rhetoric of the Labour Party increasingly seems to recognise the domain of personal existence. 'Interior' values such as sincerity, honesty, ethics, traditionally associated with the private sphere, are mobilised – some would say manhandled – into the public sphere; Blair's willingness to speak about family life and about his Christian faith, to present himself (as in his pre-election conference speech in October 1996) as a figure asking to be *trusted*, all denote a highly ambiguous combination of 'subjective' and 'objective' values jostling together on the political stage. None of this is information that one should have to pay a lobbyist for; it is part of the overt cultural agenda of the Labour Government itself to render anachronistic any talk of ideological principles and publicly defended 'positions'. Such things are characteristic values of the classical liberal conception of the political sphere; they constitute objective (as opposed to subjective) phenomena, since they inspire action from *without* rather than motivate it from *within* the self.[3]

In sociological theories of modernity, subjective and objective culture constitute two poles of a dynamic which determines the course of modernisation itself. This dynamic is expressed most concisely in Georg Simmel's early twentieth-century writings on metropolitan life: subjective culture denotes 'values which the soul derives from the instincts of its own inspiration or by acting upon itself' – the examples he gives are religious enthusiasm, moral sacrifices, and other such 'developments which perfect the soul purely internally, or which involve it in an immediate ethical, erotic, suggestive relation to other persons ...'[4] Objective culture designates 'cultural formations in which the perfection of the individual is routed through real and ideal spheres outside of the self' – examples being the refinement of taste as it is expressed in aesthetic judgements, the forms of comportment and tact, according to which an individual becomes 'a delightful member of society', etc.[5] It is of the nature of modernity, says Simmel, that subjective culture comes increasingly to be threatened, undermined, or colonised by the domain of objective culture. Modern techniques of production, writes Simmel, in which the relationship between producer and consumer is infinitely mediated, mean that subjectivity itself is 'destroyed and transposed into cool reserve and anonymous objectivity', since 'so many intermediate stages are introduced between the producer and the customer that they lose sight of each other.'[6] There is no escape from this for Simmel; the loss of subjectivity and autonomy is simply the pay-off of the modernising process. Spaces for the subject emerge in modernity – the work of art is one such space, which as Simmel says, 'requires only one single person, [and] requires him totally, right down to his innermost core.'[7] Yet increasingly, such spaces are compartmentalised and therefore *administered* by objective culture – in the cultural institutionalisation of art as a weekend pleasure, for example. In the academic world philosophy, as opposed to the sciences, is a space in which objectivity plays a secondary role, while its product is considerably unmediated and undetachable from its subjective origin; yet, in the institutional forms of Philosophy or Art, such subjective expression is parcelled off from the social world, which is rendered progressively less susceptible to its influence.

Honesty is a characteristic of subjective culture therefore; the emphasis on *appearing* honest belongs to objective culture. The crudest manner in which the Labour Party is said to have a commitment to objective culture is in its much-discerned obsession with 'spin', presentation and image, to the exclusion of ideology (or 'socialist principles'). The LLM pamphlet represents an apparent schizophrenia characterising contemporary politics, which attempts simultaneously to embody an ethics of subjective integrity, whilst enacting the objective criteria of political exigency. When Jack Straw declared on Radio 4, in the middle of the cash-for-contacts affair, that 'We have not only to be above suspicion, but to appear to be above suspicion',[8] the emphasis, for all its apparent reasonableness, is on *appearing* to be above suspicion; *being* above suspicion, one assumes, would make appearing to be above suspicion entirely redundant.

Both cultural and political theory are highly unsatisfactory in explaining, or offering any solution to this situation – primarily because each, in a different way, capitulates to a certain situation of stasis. For cultural theory, this stasis is of a diachronic character, in the form of *inevitability*, and it pertains to the nature of modernity; for political theory, the stasis is synchronic, denoting a condition of conceptual fixity, and it refers to the transhistorical, transcultural relation between politics and morals. Let's take these one at a time.

1. The objectification of culture, for Simmel at least, is not merely a side-effect but the essence of modernity. To attempt a definitive bisection of the realms of private and public reason, of subjective and objective culture – to ascribe certain activities as appropriate to each – is deeply misguided, since such sentiments fly in the face of the reifying processes of modernity, which cannot be reversed.

In a column in *The Times* on the cash-for-contacts affair, Michael Gove wrote the following, in a passage which recalls Simmel's analysis of modern mental life: 'The increasing reach, and complexity, of government, allied to the growing specialisation of professional life, the sophistication of modern communications and the money politics demands, has led to the emergence of a new class. The gentlemen in politics have been replaced by players.'[9] The opposition 'gentle-men'/'players', like the opposition subjective/objective culture, is ascribed an inevitability by Gove in his article; from this point of view it is difficult to see how the present climate of political life, charac-terised by the predominance of image over substance and the disproportionate power attaching to press spokesmen, could be any different than it is. Gove's article, which assimilates politics to a 'cultural' model of modernity, indicates that the link between the democratisation of power and the loss of political integrity is a struc-tural, pre-ordained one. Who would want to go back to a pre-modern society in which a disfranchised majority enjoy a more intimate rela-tionship to their labour, for example, at the expense of their democratic rights?

2. On the other hand, classical political theory – since Machiavelli anyway – presents politics as entirely concerned with utility and objec-tivity, rather than subjective intentions and motivations, which belong to the private sphere. Thus for political science, all talk of a progressive confusion between the spheres of subjective and objective culture misses the point. Isn't the distinction, and the confusion, simply a trans-historical condition of all political societies? Hasn't the political always been understood as a realm of appearances? 'To those seeing and hearing him,' writes Machiavelli in his classic manual on statecraft, the prince 'should appear a man of compassion, a man of good faith, a man of integrity, a kind and a religious man. And there is nothing so impor-tant as to seem to have this last quality.'[10]

This basic 'truth' of politics renders any critique of government spin and image-mongering focused upon the current climate utterly innocu-ous. The point of the *Observer* investigation into cash-for-contacts was obscure, and remained so even at its conclusion, since no clear instance of wrongdoing, besides a bit of unpalatable boasting by Derek Draper, the lobbyist at the centre of the affair, was uncovered. The row over 'cash-for-contacts', as the editor of the *Observer* Will Hutton was forced to admit, was a row over nothing more tangible than a 'culture' of New Labour in which 'cronyism', networking and informal contacts were the primary mechanisms of political influence. The most im-mediate conclusion to draw from the episode was that there was nothing *substantially* insidious about New Labour. This was no controversy over policy, for example, but rather a mood, a perception – an *image*. It is not wrongdoing, any longer, but the *appearance* of wrongdoing that has become impeachable. 'We are not sleazy people', insisted a New Labour spokesman at the time; the party merely has the image of something tainted – and this, it turned out, was the only point the *Observer* had to make in its 'exposé'.

From the point of view of political theory, the cash-for-contacts scandal is the effect of an increasing and confusing slippage between politics and morals. Was the *Observer* seriously suggesting that politics should function without 'circles of influence', or meetings arranged between business and government? Is there any difference at all between what Labour calls 'vested interests' and mere interests, without which politics is a game without substance? What would a politician without interests look like? Who, or what, would he or she represent? The scandal of cash-for-contacts is that there was no scandal; as in the Clinton revelations, no political imprudence was uncovered, only a widespread level of 'contact' between ministers and lobbyists that was deemed 'morally inappropriate'.

If the press campaign over cash-for-contacts, and the eruption in recent years of the issue of 'sleaze', signify the 'inappropriate' intrusion of moral concerns onto the classical terrain of politics, this intrusion is both irreversible and originary, constitutive of the political sphere itself. Morality has already – one could say *always already* – entered the political sphere, in the form of the *distinction* between politics and morals.

On a television programme filmed before the cash-for-contacts affair was 'exposed' in the *Observer*, but broadcast after it, Derek Draper made a curious statement which revealed the split between subjective and objective culture to be necessary, even intrinsic to the modern political consciousness. On the programme, called *Hypotheticals*, a panel of politicians, journalists and lobbyists, including Draper, considered the 'hypothetical' case of a Treasury minister who, having made a tax decision in favour of a pharmaceutical company, was subsequently revealed to be having an adulterous affair with the company Chairman's daughter. Draper's intervention was made in the context of a debate over whether or not the minister should be obliged to leave his post:

> What if he refused to resign? What if he felt he'd done nothing wrong? What if indeed he had done nothing wrong and he just said to the whips and the Prime Minister, 'I'm not resigning'? ... This guy hasn't done anything wrong ... He fell in love with someone else who was a bit embarrassing unfortunately; so, totally hypocritically, to save their majority, the whips and the Prime Minister forced him out, and [the *Guardian*] totally hypocritically, in order to sell copies, [has] taken it all

and bunged it all together and hyped it up ... – but the guy has done nothing wrong![11]

A week before the broadcast, Draper had been held up by the *Observer* newspaper as the most monstrous embodiment of New Labour's image-led agenda; here, he puts himself on the other side of the equation, the side of subjective and moral integrity which, by his implication, exists at a radical remove from the false world of appearances. The claim to subjective integrity may always, as here, be mobilised on behalf of the political sphere (as it was by Bill Clinton during the Lewinsky affair). 'You have to trust us,' implored Tony Blair in 1996. During a television interview over the Bernie Ecclestone Formula One funding controversy in 1998, he reiterated, 'I'm a pretty straight kind of guy';[12] while in the same week an exasperated Downing Street spokesman was quoted insisting, 'Look we're not sleazy people – but this is the world we live in.'[13] The classical political-theoretical understanding of politics as the realm of appearances offers no rationale whatever for legislating over what is or isn't proper to the concerns of politics. In conducting its campaign against the *appearance* of Labour sleaze, the *Observer* revealed its own implication in the increasing predominance of appearance over truth in the matter of politics. The distinction between truth and appearance is a dominant 'mytheme' of our culture; it determines the relation between the public sphere and the private, and between politics and morals, and it informs another widespread contemporary perception: the threat currently posed to politics itself by the incursions of subjective culture.

CULTURAL ANXIETY (1): THE END OF POLITICS

The 'end of politics' is a chimera that haunts political commentators both on the left and the right; it is the product of this essentially static conception of the relation between politics and morality. The 'end of politics' imagines a scenario in which public life is perpetually on the point of being invaded and debased by the concerns of the private sphere. When New Yorkers aver that their President's 'personal life' should be left personal, this liberal distinction between subjective and objective culture, between private and public life, is invoked and further cemented into place. When Bill Clinton insisted that his relationship with Monica Lewinsky was a private matter between himself, his wife and daughter and 'our God', or when Tony Blair maintains that the New Labour government will not legislate over people's private morality, the endurance of the subject-object distinction, and its centrality to prevailing models of the political sphere, is clearly demonstrated.

The relation between politics and morals, conceived as a structural one, is derived from Machiavelli. Benedetto Croce, formulating the classical liberal position, writes that 'A man blessed with genius or real capacity will take liberties with everything but not what constitutes his passion, his love, his glory, the fundamental justification and purpose of his being' – i.e. his role as a public man.[14] A person's 'private' morality, in other words, is irrelevant to his or her suitability for public office. In a sense, 'unethical' behaviour is *constitutive* of public life; for Croce, the demand for honesty in politics is a simple category mistake. 'Men loved and revered for their spotless probity and for their intellect and learning are occasionally made heads of States. But they are at once put out of office again, with a doctorate in ineptitude added to their other titles.'[15] Hannah Arendt has written frequently of the inverse correlation between politics and truth. Goodness, she writes, 'as a consistent way of life, is not only impossible within the confines of public life, it is even destructive of it.' Goodness cannot come out of hiding and assume a public role without becoming corrupt in its own terms. Values such as sincerity by their nature cannot be transferred to the public realm of appearance without losing what is specific to them. The political theory that informs these remarks is Machiavelli's, in which glory – that is to say, the recognition of one's peers – that is to say, *appearance* – is the criterion for all political action.[16]

The predominant response on the left to the Blair/Clinton phenomenon has been remarkably close to this classical liberal distaste for the mingling of the private and public spheres. Chantal Mouffe, writing in *Soundings*, finds the Americans' obsession with Clinton's sex life 'deplorable', a symptom of the 'degeneration of the democratic public sphere' and the 'trivialisation of political discourse'.[17] The focus on Clinton's sexual history was a consequence, she says, of a new kind of 'bland, homogenised political world' in which the search for consensus has replaced democratic debate. For Mouffe, 'antagonism' is the 'stuff' of democratic politics; consensus may be necessary, but 'it must be accompanied by dissent'. New Labour's consensual, apolitical rhetoric, she argues, seeks to remove its enemies rather than 'make room for' them; in so doing, it prevents 'a vibrant clash of democratic political positions'.

Mouffe acknowledges the inability of political theory to comprehend what is happening; yet she reproduces that failure of comprehension in her own diagnosis. To demand that New Labour 'make room' for 'dissenting' opinion is to value not the 'vibrant clash' of democratic argument, but its opposite: consensus. In his 'Idea for a Universal History with a Cosmopolitan Purpose', Kant writes that 'Man wishes concord, but nature, knowing better what is good for his species, wishes discord.' He illustrates this as follows:

> In the same way, trees in a forest, *by seeking to deprive each other of air and sunlight*, compel each other to find these by upward growth, so that they grow beautiful and straight – whereas those which put out branches at will, in freedom and isolation from others, grow stunted, bent and twisted. All the culture and art which adorn mankind and the finest social order man creates are fruits of his unsociability.[18]

This is a formula that does not work in reverse; discord, 'unsociability', cannot be sustained as a political objective, or even as the *means* to a political objective. Mouffe radically underestimates the extent to which the New Labour project is a well-developed ideological implementation, one that has no precious attachment to the abstract 'democracy' she champions. She calls New Labour's 'Third Way' the 'desperate strategy' of a left which has been out-manoeuvred ideologically.[19] This is a hopelessly belated judgement; the 'Third Way' is an ideological vehicle for an already existing adversary – the neo-liberal hegemony, and its contemporary political embodiment, the British Labour government. The 'end of politics' is not a 'cause for concern', as Mouffe insists;[20] the 'end of politics' is the ideological vehicle for a specific political agenda which it is the task of her 'oppositional' position to confront and oppose. Conceding the possibility of the end of politics is, in some sense, to beckon that possibility into existence.

What is at issue here is a certain anxiety over what politics *should* be about. The liberal common sense which holds that politics is 'by definition' a realm of antagonism, or appearance, or extrinsic values – a domain of 'objective culture' in other words – in opposition to the morality, consensuality, femininity and integrity of the subjective sphere, for example, is as much a piece of romanticism as Jacob Burckhardt's nostalgia for the grandeur of the Renaissance despots.[21] This distinction between subjective and objective culture is mobilised every time someone accuses modern politicians of being more concerned with 'image' than 'substance', or of placing a higher value upon the work of its spin doctors than that of its junior ministers. The concept of spin is worth discussing in some detail here, since it embodies in microcosm these anxieties concerning what politics is and what it 'should be' in the context of the relation between truth and appearance.

CULTURAL ANXIETY (2): THE CONCEPT OF SPIN

Very soon after one starts thinking about spin, it begins to lose its coherence. To talk about 'spin' is to talk about two things: firstly, public opinion, and the excessive attention which politicians are nowadays thought to pay to it; and secondly, ideology and false consciousness – the concept of spin presupposes a distinction between a 'spun' and an 'unspun' world, between our contemporary, 'medialed' reality and an earlier, more 'believable' version. In this respect, spin is a version of the Fall of Man narrative, a myth that, like all such metaphors, is riven with political and philosophical contradiction. We only become aware of our existence in Paradise at the moment we are cast out of it. Similarly, an earlier world of 'unspun' politics can never be enjoyed except retrospectively. We never experience an era of political 'honesty'; we only ever remember it, and regret it as something lost.

Conversely, the moment when we become aware of the existence of spin is the moment of its evaporation. Effective spin, one presumes, requires a general unawareness of its existence. The contemporary visibility of spin and spin doctors must, logically, inhibit their operation. 'Soundbites' are today immediately recognisable as soundbites. In the same way that the expulsion of Adam and Eve from the Garden of Eden is the moment of their birth as individuals and 'subjects', so, perhaps, the appearance of the concept of spin represents our graduation to adulthood as political subjects. Spin is an inherently paradoxical concept – yet it structures the representation of our political reality like no other.

There are several versions of the spin hypothesis, as it is entertained on the left. The first is the most straightforward: the government has no substantial ideological agenda; it is like a leaf blown in the winds of public opinion. Thus, hawkish, warmongering Blair is a man whose ambition is both to scotch public opinion of Labour as a party of closet pacifists, and to assume Margaret Thatcher's title of the resolute, unswayable leader who is 'not for turning'. Blairite politics plays to the gallery; Blair's speech after the death of Diana was an astute act of politicking, effectively capturing the mood of the country and securing a mandate as the politician who understood the will of the people. His condemnation of the payments of sums unknown to Mary Bell by Gitta Sereny, after the publication of *Cries Unheard*, as 'inherently repugnant' was an intervention similarly calculated to gratify the hounds of public opinion. Like no other politician since Thatcher, Blair has an instinct for seizing the moment and turning it to rhetorical gold.

New Labour ministers are professional politicians, interested in holding onto power only, not in changing the world; hence their reluctance to make the case forcefully for policies (such as the repeal of Section 28 of the Local Government law, or Britain's entry into the European single currency) which it perceives to be unpopular. New Labour is the ultimate in postmodern politics: substance-less, supremely pragmatic, 'ideologically footloose'.[22] Like the aspirational petit bourgeoisie analysed in Bourdieu's *Distinction*, New Labour represents a political identity stunted by the commitment to appearance:

> Torn by all the contradictions between an objectively dominated condition and would-be participation in the dominant values, the petit bourgeois is haunted by the appearance he offers to others and the judgement they make of it. He constantly overshoots the mark for fear of falling short, betraying his uncertainty and anxiety about belonging in his anxiety to show or give the impression that he belongs. He is bound to be seen – both by the working classes, who do not have this concern with their being-for-others, and by the privileged classes, who, being sure of what they are, do not care what they seem – as the man of appearances, haunted by the look of others and endlessly occupied with being seen in a good light.[23]

Individually and collectively, high-profile Labour ministers are easily caricatured in this way. Lord Snowdon's widely reproduced photograph of Peter Mandelson reclining in his own £1800 Eames chair is a beautiful illustration of the fact that New Labour as a whole gives a higher priority to the image it presents (to the business community, say) than to the task of redefining and remaking Britain after the years of Thatcherism, according to a certain vision of its own.[24] New Labour is a narrowly aspirational party, engaged in discarding its origins in class and socialist politics for the hearts and the votes of conservative Middle England.

The second version of the spin hypothesis is a critique of the first: of course the Labour government has an ideological agenda, the most immediate task of which, like all ideological operations, is to appear not to be ideological. Labour is committed to the medium (rather than the message) because it recognises the emphasis which today's world attaches to presentation and appearance. Labour is dealing with the reality of the modern world. It is highly competent in its manipulation of the media since, despite the 'cynicism' of the old left, it has maintained a consistently high level of popularity in the opinion polls. It is precisely the supporters of the first hypothesis who fail to understand the power of the media in a technological age, who cherish an idealistic, thoroughly naive attachment to a truthful political ethos which has long vanished, or which never existed at all, or which, when it did, had no relation to political or social reality. The Labour Party is engaged in a moderately progressive agenda – as progressive as possible, given the competitive global market and the post-Thatcherite political climate – which it covers up for fear of alienating its new voters in Middle England ('redistribution by stealth'). Beneath the spin, therefore, lies the truth of an ideological agenda waiting to be laid bare. Unfortunately, a policy of giving 'words to the right and deeds to the left' makes heavy demands on the interpretative abilities of party members. Blair's 1999 conference speech on the 'forces of conservatism' was his most explicit appeal yet to a left that has failed to appreciate that a changing world demands new strategies of political intervention.

The third position proposes a radicalisation of the above, and – on the basis of the perceptions described at the beginning of this section – refuses to attach any *legitimacy* to the concept at all. 'Spin' lends support to the idea of an existing domain of politics outside 'vested interests'; the concept of spin is itself ideological. Thus the *critique* of government spin, and the attempt to penetrate through it, bolsters the hypothesis of a sphere free from the operation of ideology. *The Guardian*, according to this analysis, fulfills an ideological role that is necessary for the survival of the concept; its campaigning attacks on the government, its refusal to attend Downing Street briefings, and its personalisation of the spin issue by focusing on 'spin doctors', perform the task of containing the enormity of the 'image over substance' issue. 'Which of these men runs Britain?' asked a *Guardian* headline under a photograph of Tony Blair and Alastair Campbell, immediately polarising the issue into the legitimate politician, on one hand, and the media manipulator on the other.[25] The idea is conveyed that, if Mandelson were picked off by the journalists or Campbell sacked, then the current political 'malaise' would begin to be solved: this is the explanation for the hilarity on the left when Mandelson lost his job over the Geoffrey Robinson affair. The concept of spin maintains a spatial model of politics and politicking – like the base and superstructure model of ideology: beneath the spin-mongering there exist the rudiments of 'authentic' politics and politicians. The concept itself is part of the ideological work of the government; spin is a *line* that we are being spun, and the media are complicit in spinning it. This is the intellectual left approach, theoretically informed, and convinced most forcefully that it, at least, has not been spun a line about spin.

Such remarks notwithstanding, it is this version of the spin hypothesis that I shall be arguing for in the rest of this essay, although its nuances need careful delineation if it is to avoid succumbing to the ideological complacency which characterises the first two versions. It differs from them, however, in a crucial respect. For the first two, spin is the *mediation* of reality, a veil to be penetrated in order to arrive at the truth. The 'intellectual left' approach is the reverse of this: the concept of spin removes all awareness of the fact of the *always*-mediated nature of empirical reality. 'Spin' is the latest version of a mechanism by which, in Lukács's words, bourgeois thought 'enter[s] into an unmediated relationship with reality as it [is] given'.[26] Spin is a reified form of mediation; spin effects the disposal of mediation itself, and thus a reversion to immediacy.

In a passage in *Minima Moralia*, Adorno interrogates the opposition of truth and appearance in the context of the classical Marxist theory of ideology. For the theoretically-informed consciousness familiar with the base and superstructure model, the discrepancy between the 'economic framework' of late capitalism and its 'political façade' is slight: 'Everywhere the sham character of supposed public opinion, the primacy of the economy in real decisions, can be demonstrated.' This doesn't alter the fact that the façade is real for the majority of people. 'For countless individuals ... the thin, ephemeral veil is the basis of their entire existence. Precisely those on whose thought and action *change*, alone essential, depends, are indebted for their existence to the inessential, illusion ....' He concludes the paragraph by saying that the essence of the world 'is abomination; but its appearance, the lie by the virtue of which it persists, is a stand-in for truth.'[27]

Adorno's perspective here is deliberately paradoxical and implicitly Hegelian. He is writing about the base and superstructure metaphor at a time when the 'simple' version of the metaphor still had plenty of advocates; thus his remarks now appear essentially unremarkable. Yet the concept of spin proposes the same spatial relation between truth and appearance that is implied in the base and superstructure metaphor, and which suggests the former's *mediation* by the latter. It is a model that is incompatible with the Hegelian notion of culture that I have argued for elsewhere in this volume, which understands dialectical mediation as the *vehicle* of truth, rather than its interruption.[28] In *History and Class Consciousness*, Lukács quotes from Hegel's *Lectures on the Philosophy of Religion*, as follows: 'There is no immediate knowledge. Immediate knowledge is where we have no *consciousness* of mediation; but it is mediated for all that.'[29] The concept of spin is a false promise of immediate knowledge. The transparency of 'spin' as a cultural phenomenon is, after all, its essential component. Its effect must therefore be the precise opposite of what it claims – must be, in its own terms, an increase in the degree of mediation, rather than its removal, which is impossible. Yet the real effect of the cultural manifestation of the phenomenon of spin is to throw into question the legitimacy of these terms themselves. Any 'immediacy' it achieves is done so only in the Hegelian sense described above: an absence of the *consciousness* of mediation, amounting therefore to a real regression in freedom and democracy.

At one level then, Peter Mandelson, the 'master spinner', functions symbolically in the same way as the Hollywood movie *The Truman Show*. Just as the film buoys up our sense of contemporary reality by producing the fiction of an entirely constructed world – one that, as the conclusion of the film shows, the hero is able ultimately to step out of – so Mandelson buoys up the legitimacy of the political institution, and the political enfranchisement of the individual. At another level, the implications of the concept of 'spin' are much more profound, since they concern the prevailing conceptualisation of reality itself. Spin reinforces the belief in modernity as the progressive mediation of truth by 'appearances', by 'objective culture'. It is a scenario that necessarily leads to political impasse. Its corollary is the 'tragedy' of modern life, which Simmel calls the tragedy of culture: that what Kant calls 'concord', ideality, the unity of the spheres, retreats faster than we can pursue it, yet we are incapable of abandoning the pursuit. The rupture between subject and object is widened in proportion to the level of determination we exert in order to bring them together.

CONCLUSION: MEDIATISATION VS. MEDIATION
The logical end of this diagnosis is a society of hyper-individualism, founded upon a fetishistic relation to authenticity and individuality that in no way challenges the hegemony of consumer capitalism, or its dominant ideology of instrumental rationality. For Simmel, modern life increasingly demands the retreat of individuals into a 'non-reifiable' selfhood:

> If modern man can, under favourable circumstances, secure an island of
> subjectivity, a secret, closed-off sphere of privacy – not in the social but

in a deeper metaphysical sense – for his most personal existence, which
to some extent compensates for the religious style of life of former times,
then this is due to the fact that money relieves us to an ever-increasing
extent of direct contact with things, while at the same time making it
infinitely easier for us to dominate them and select from them what we
require.[30]

One consequence of Simmel's model of the irreversible and acceler-
ating 'objectification' of culture is a conception of political radicalism
predicated upon the intransigence of the refractory, unpliant individual. Such a conception is illustrated, perhaps, by a Manchester United
Football Club supporter and shareholder who appeared on Channel 4
News around the time of the Murdoch takeover of the club: 'Mr
Murdoch,' he said unreasonably, 'cannot buy me as an individual
shareholder.'[31] Or, as Armando Iannucci wrote in a column in the
Guardian about his own refusal to subscribe to cable television, 'I'm
not distressed by the modern world. I just think Rupert Murdoch's a
shit.'[32] As political sentiments go these are profoundly subjective; they
seem unencumbered by ulterior motives, impervious to logic and politically indomitable. They bespeak the appearance of a political
consciousness boasting the autocratic disposition of the medieval
despot, though with a sphere of influence no wider than its own interiority.

'I just think Rupert Murdoch's a shit', directed against a universally
recognisable symbol of 'mediatisation', looks like the most compre-
hensible response to a world where constructive political critique has
become perfectly homogeneous with the objective world it once
opposed; where political scandals are no more heinous than the investigations which expose them; where the most rigorous critical stance
finds itself eventually howling against the objective world *tout court*;
and where the subjective guilt of politicians no longer exists, merely the
regrettable fact of 'the world we live in'. Each of these assumptions,
however, is fundamentally erroneous: 'constructive' political critique,
in a climate of political regression, is a *failure* of political critique; the
Observer investigation into cash-for-contacts was not structural or
inevitable, simply inadequate; the subjective howl is as mediated a
response as the objective world it howls against, and entirely ordained
within an ethos of unlicensed consumerism; the 'world we live in' is the
result of an absence of mediation, not an excess of it.

Each of those false assumptions is founded upon a cultural theory of
modernity as the progressive alienation of the subjective and objective

worlds. Simmel describes its logical consequence: 'These counter-tendencies,' he writes, 'once started, may press forward to an idea of completely pure separation in which all the material concerns of life become increasingly objective and impersonal, so that the remainder that cannot be reified becomes all the more personal, all the more the indisputable property of the self.'[33] Commenting upon this passage, Lukács observes that Simmel brings to a halt his theory of modernity at the very point at which a political intervention is demanded. The progressive alienation of subjective from objective culture – a thesis which is implied in and ratified by the concept of spin – is a privileged moment in Simmel's thought, as is the category of the individual itself. 'In this way the very thing that should be understood and deduced with the aid of mediation becomes the accepted principle by which to explain all phenomena and is even elevated to the status of a value: namely the unexplained and inexplicable facticity of bourgeois existence as it is here and now acquires the patina of an eternal law of nature or a cultural value enduring for all time.'[34]

Belief in the concept of spin, in the predominance of 'appearance' over 'reality' in contemporary politics, implies the following collective pathology: a fetishistic attachment to immediacy and individuality which has no politically progressive significance – in fact, quite the contrary. As Chantal Mouffe points out, this same complex has led to the recent successes of certain fascist or quasi-fascist parties in Europe, who have been able to pose as the embodiment of a 'spin-free' popular politics.[35] The theory of a gradual divergence of 'individuality' from 'politics' through modern history is the route to an anxiety which sees the latter as progressively corrosive of the former; at the same time, it crystallises the notion of the realm of politics as distinguished from the subjective sphere on the basis of its inferiority to it.

The truth is closer to the statement found in Hegel's *Philosophy of Religion*: that 'immediacy itself is essentially mediated.'[36] Immediacy is a construction and a product of mediation; concomitantly, mediation is the route to real immediacy, which is the truth *of* mediation. The alternative model – that immediacy and mediation stand at opposite poles of an irreconcilable and ever lengthening axis – is a recipe for political powerlessness, as modernity is conceived as a dynamic of increasing autonomy and unmanageability. Capitalism represents this polarity as the progressive mediation and 'autonomisation' of social reality, on the one hand, and the subjective regression of individuals to a condition of 'immediacy' on the other. Contemporary political discourse has responded to and reiterates this ideology by interpellating individuals motivated by nothing other than the immediate 'truths' of self-interest. Thus 'appearance', in the form of 'spin', is inversely or 'negatively' fetishised, while substance or truth – what Georg Simmel calls 'subjective culture' – is (positively) fetishised. It is the duty of any progressive political orientation to mediate this double fetishism. Mediation is the truth of all politics, insofar as it refuses 'things as they are'. Progressive politics is a practice of constantly mediating an unacceptable immediacy; with the concept of spin, in other words, political intervention itself is stigmatised.

Armando Iannucci's refusal to buy cable TV is not a rejection of the *mediated* world, therefore, but of an *unmediated* one. 'In the thousand-year Murdoch Reich that so many media commentators warn us is about to commence,' he writes, 'the sad truth is it'll be us who'll be the Waffen SS. Murdoch himself will only be following orders.' The logic of capitalism is the boundless gratification of demand, insidious and benevolent at the same time; consumerism interpellates individuals existing at a level of pure immediacy, 'tyrants over [their] own destiny', motivated by nothing other than self-interest. Murdoch, says Iannucci, is no leader but 'the most successful follower in history', his philosophy none other than the commercial profitability of 'lobbing as much of what the people want back in their transcontinental faces'. 'Mediatisation' is not mediation but its opposite; and the same is true of the concept of spin. *'I just think Rupert Murdoch's a shit'* is not a retreat into subjective immediacy but a refusal of it – along with the polarising tendencies that posit individualisation at the same time as they assert an ever-greater administration of people's reality. Capitalism not only demands but compels, indeed presupposes subjective withdrawal, the very process by which it subjects those subjects to the increasing autonomisation and anonymisation of the 'objective' world.

This preservation of an interior, sanctified space is underwritten by the agenda of contemporary politics. The present government has an explicit commitment not only to the 'objective' domain, but also to the 'subjective' one; to the distinction between the two, and to the domain of 'culture' which affirms each in its respective place. Politics becomes 'merely' administration at the same time that private life is reduced to a domain of free, unrestricted, atomised, alienated and politically irrelevant action.

Real immediacy, of course, is perpetually elusive, its attainability in inverse proportion to the determination upon it. When senior Labour figures insist on the need to counter the accusation that New Labour is more concerned with image than substance, they outline an objective which is self-defeating. Tony Blair and Gordon Brown say not that we have to get back to real policies, but that we have to *convince the electorate* that we are more interested in substance than image; we have to *refocus attention* on our achievements rather than our appearance.[37] As Adorno observed, 'naivety' and 'sophistication' are concepts which are 'endlessly intertwined' in our reflective age. Certainly, they can no longer be played off against each other. 'Mediately to affirm immediacy, instead of comprehending it as mediated within itself, is to pervert thought into an apologia of its antithesis, into the immediate lie.'[38] Spin, which implies the clean separation of such oppositions as naivety and sophistication, immediacy and mediation, subjective and objective culture, is an apologia for the antitheses of thought – immediacy, the play of interests, the material logic of capitalism itself. The close relation between truth and mediation is explained most concisely and eloquently in Hegel's Preface to the *Phenomenology of Spirit*: 'Of the Absolute it must be said that it is essentially a *result*, that only in the *end* is it what it truly is; and that precisely in this consists its nature, viz. to be actual, subject, the spontaneous becoming of itself.'[39] Politics is an activity in which, of necessity, the 'veneer', appearance, *is* the truth; in which subjective and objective culture are unified in the attempt to remake the world; in which individuality demands and attains an objective visibility.

With its simultaneous affirmation and disaffirmation of the realm of appearances, New Labour excludes all engagement except that on the most alienated, objective, calculating level, on the one hand, or that which is content to affirm the truth of a restricted sphere no wider than the subjective boundaries of the individual, on the other. These 'extremes' are in fact identical, as I have tried to show in this essay, yet their polarity is implied in the concept of spin. They are both false and discountable, yet their inevitability is implied in the concept of spin. They presuppose a rigid distinction between truth and appearance, a distinction which is deconstructed by the activity of politics itself, but reconstructed in the concept of spin. Predicated on the opposition of mediation and immediacy, 'spin' is *for that reason* a non-political concept; it has no utility for a politics of resistance; indeed, its disposal is a precondition for any re-articulation of a progressive critical politics in the present.

NOTES

1. Neal Lawson had worked for Gordon Brown before the 1997 general election, Ben Lucas for Jack Straw and Jon Mendelsohn for Tony Blair. The 'cash-for-contacts' scandal blew up around the activities of such suppos-

edly independent 'lobbyists' who, according to the *Observer* investigation, were emblematic of a 'culture of cronyism' within New Labour. The most prominent among them was Derek Draper, a flamboyant former aide to Peter Mandelson, whom the *Observer* reported having boasted to its undercover reporter of wanting nothing other than to 'stuff [his] bank account at £250 an hour'. See *Observer*, 5 July 1998.

2. Greg Palast and Antony Barnett, 'Chilling extracts from the New Age lobbyists', *Observer*, 12 July 1998, p7.

3. See Hannah Arendt, 'What is freedom?' in *Between Past and Future: Eight Exercises in Political Thought*, Penguin, New York 1977, p152. Appearance, as Arendt notes, is essential to such political concerns; their value (Machiavelli's *virtù*) lies in their performance: 'For, unlike the judgement of the intellect which precedes action, and unlike the command of the will which initiates it, the inspiring principle becomes fully manifest only in the performing act itself ...'

4. 'Subjective culture' in *On Individuality and Social Forms*, ed. Donald N. Levine, University of Chicago Press, London and Chicago 1971, p230.

5. *Ibid.*

6. Georg Simmel, *The Philosophy of Money*, trans. Tom Bottomore and David Frisby, Routledge, London 1990, p457.

7. *Ibid.*, p455.

8. Jack Straw on *The World This Weekend*, BBC Radio 4, 12 July 1998.

9. *The Times*, 7 July 1998. Gove alludes to a book by Peter Riddell, *Honest Opportunism: The Rise of the Career Politician*, Hamish Hamilton, London 1993, which makes a similar point at greater length, and with conclusions which evince a similar neutrality: 'Has the career politician become more ideological, or, alternatively, more opportunistic?' asks Riddell, characteristically, in his final chapter. 'A good case can be made for either view ...' (p270).

10. Niccolò Machiavelli, *The Prince*, trans. George Bull, Penguin, Harmondsworth 1961, p101.

11. *Hypotheticals: Caught in the Act*, BBC2, 11 July 1998.

12. Quoted by Jonathan Freedland, 'How Labour gambled on Diana image', *Guardian*, 28 August 1998.

13. A Downing Street spokesman, quoted by Jonathan Freedland, 'Suddenly the red rose doesn't smell so sweet', *Guardian*, 12 November 1997.

14. Benedetto Croce, 'Political honesty', in *The Conduct of Life*, trans. Arthur Livingston, George G. Harrap, London 1925, pp253-4.

15. *Ibid.*, p250.

16. Hannah Arendt, *The Human Condition*, University of Chicago Press, London and Chicago 1958, p77; see also 'Truth and politics' in *Between*

Past and Future: Eight Exercises in Political Thought, op. cit.

17. Chantal Mouffe, 'The radical centre: A politics without adversary', *Soundings* Issue 9 (Summer 1998), pp14, 15.

18. Immanuel Kant, *Political Writings* (second enlarged edition), trans. H.B. Nisbet, Cambridge University Press, Cambridge 1991, pp45-6.

19. Chantal Mouffe, 'The radical centre: A politics without adversary', *op. cit.*, p18.

20. *Ibid.*, p17.

21. See Timothy Bewes, 'Cultural politics/political culture', in this volume.

22. This phrase is Roy Hattersley's; see his article 'Pragmatism must not still conscience', *Guardian*, 14 May 1997.

23. Pierre Bourdieu, *Distinction: A Social Critique of the Judgement of Taste*, trans. Richard Nice, Routledge & Kegan Paul, London 1984, p253.

24. Snowdon's picture of Peter Mandelson was commissioned by Vogue and appeared in no. 2399 of the magazine (June 1998), pp128-9.

25. *Guardian*, 26 January 1999.

26. Georg Lukács, *History and Class Consciousness: Studies in Marxist Dialectics,* trans. Rodney Livingstone, Merlin, London 1971, p156.

27. Theodor W. Adorno, *Minima Moralia: Reflections from Damaged Life*, trans. E.F.N. Jephcott, Verso, London 1978, pp112-13.

28. See Timothy Bewes, 'Cultural politics/political culture' in this volume, especially the concluding pages.

29. Georg Lukács, *History and Class Consciousness: Studies in Marxist Dialectics*, trans. Rodney Livingstone, Merlin, London 1971, p218, n. 20 (see G. W. F. Hegel, *Lectures on the Philosophy of Religion, One-volume edition: the Lectures of 1827*, trans. R.F. Brown, P.C. Hodgson, J.M. Stewart, University of California Press, Berkeley, Los Angeles and London 1988, p158).

30. Georg Simmel, *The Philosophy of Money, op. cit.*, p469.

31. Channel 4 News, 9 September 1998.

32. Armando Iannucci, 'Rupert the bare', *Guardian*, 31 December 1996.

33. Georg Simmel, *The Philosophy of Money, op. cit.,* p469.

34. Georg Lukács, *History and Class Consciousness, op. cit.*, p157.

35. Chantal Mouffe, *op. cit.*, p15.

36. G. W. F. Hegel, *Lectures on the Philosophy of Religion, op. cit.,* p157.

37. See, for example, Michael White's report 'Labour goes back to basics', *Guardian*, 12 January 1999.

38. Theodor W. Adorno, *Minima Moralia, op. cit.*, p73.

39. G. W. F. Hegel, *Phenomenology of Spirit*, trans. A.V. Miller, Oxford University Press, Oxford 1977, §20, p11.

New Labour: the culture of government and the government of culture

ALAN FINLAYSON

INTRODUCTION

Over the few years of its existence both critics and enthusiasts have advanced various themes or ideas as central to the 'project' of New Labour. Some have focused on constitutional reform and the possibilities for an enhanced democracy,[1] others on the illiberal nature of the government's social authoritarianism.[2] Where some see a radical and bold agenda others find only vacuity and sloganeering. Still others point to a perceived capitulation to the exigencies of the global capitalist market,[3] the abandonment of substantive commitments to equality,[4] and the extent to which the government emulates Thatcherism in its refusal to take on corporations and force them to be more responsible in the long-term.[5] Theorists have pointed up the affinities between New Labour and the New Liberalism of the turn of the century, something to which Blair has made explicit his allegiance,[6] or the ways in which New Labour ideology involves a fusion and re-articulation of elements of the liberal, socialist and conservative traditions.[7]

This list of interpretations could proliferate – probably endlessly. Perhaps each of them grasps some part of the overall phenomenon. But the extent and variety of such interpretations is indicative of both the generally fluid nature of contemporary politics and the specific character of New Labour. The 'project' of the government is in development, some of its contours are clear but much has yet to be made concrete. This makes it difficult to pin down what exactly is going on if the focus is restricted to the government and the Labour Party. To understand in more depth what is going on we have to take note of a larger context.

This chapter tries to place New Labour in that wider context and to

look at the way in which it is redefining the modes by which government takes place. Specifically the concern is with the increasing salience
of 'culture' as a mode of government, but it is important to realise that
this occurs along with (to some extent because of but it is also a
contributory factor in its own right) wider developments in British
economy and society – developments of which Blairism is just a part,
as was Thatcherism, and as will be every future political project. It
begins by briefly summarising some of the changes underway in the
organisation and management of the British state. Then we will exca-
vate some of the immediate intellectual sources of New Labour,
focusing on those theorisations that have emphasised the need for a
new kind of politics and a new kind of state as a response to structural
transformations in the economic and social spheres. We will then
consider what has been termed the 'Schumpeterian Workfare Regime'
before, finally, offering some points about the way in which culture has
become a key mode of governance and a site for the fostering of legitimacy.

Such an analysis requires us to begin by taking New Labour seriously and accepting that it is interested in politics for a purpose. We
cannot simply dismiss it as fabrication, 'mere' spin or simply an inane
'focus-group' style of politics. For Blairism the point of being in
government is to stay there and to stay popular but only so that the
historic mission of creating what Blair has called, on several occasions,
a 'twenty-first-century model nation'[8] can continue. Blairism is
concerned to transform the British state and the British economy in
order to meet perceived challenges brought about by much wider
transformations. New Labour's distinctiveness lies not so much in its
attempts to change British politics or society, as their predecessors tried
to do, but in its greater potential for bringing about such change while
maintaining the legitimacy of the social order. Perhaps this will turn
out to be New Labour's 'historic' role.

STATING THE CHANGE
Throughout the 1980s Thatcherite reforms of the institutions of
government (scaling down the civil service, privatising industries,
introducing new forms of regulation and 'rolling back' the state) began
to reduce the function of government to that of central co-ordination
within a network of institutions; government was replaced by governance. For example, the Department of Heritage, formed in 1992,
managed a number of policy sectors and networks, inducing them to
follow ministerial strategy rather than taking direct control.[9] Using

financial incentives and the power that comes from holding purse strings, institutions and organisations (in this case relating to Heritage, Broadcasting, Media, Arts, Sport, National Lottery, Libraries, Museums and Galleries) could be run at arm's length through demands for business plans and the imposition of methods of performance assessment. The Department of Culture, Media and Sport has continued this pattern. It does not directly interfere in the running of cultural institutions yet is clearly in a position to act in ways that manifestly do alter them. As core funder it can demand that policy actors behave in circumscribed ways. Government becomes like a head office, franchising out its standardised operations allowing individual units to operate independently but subject to rules and procedures formulated from above.

This is an increasingly widespread pattern of 'governance' – 'governing without government' as Rhodes has put it.[10] Instead of monolithic structures the state manages through a range of institutions, exercising control rather than command, steering without hierarchy. This is a sound hegemonic strategy for a state in flux, entailing relational processes of contracting and the building of strategic alliances. It combines with the dissipation of the power of national governments to control the flow of trade or regulate the practices of commercial companies that transcend borders, and the growth of international and supra-national state institutions, leaving us with what Jessop has described as the 'hollowing out' of the nation-state.[11]

The new discourse of public management, NHS reorganisation, the creation of grant maintained schools and the Next Steps Agency (to list but a few 'innovations') built on these trends and transformed key organisations of the state. New Labour has inherited this 'hollowed out' state model, and in this sense undeniably operates on a terrain set by Thatcherism, even if it has not become comprehensively Thatcherite.[12] But Thatcherism did not entirely succeed in securing its neo-liberal project of state 'withdrawal'. Its mistrust of collective or state institutions and its hostility to the notion of society prevented it from understanding the communal and cultural underpinnings of market relations. By contrast, New Labour believes in the need to generate relations of mutual obligation and trust that underpin the contract society, and in a new kind of role for the state in their production.

The legacy of the Thatcherite reforms is a set of state institutions that cannot expect automatic approval on the basis of deference to authority or the belief that 'they' know what they are doing. They must justify themselves through their 'market' performance – their efficiency, value-for-money, quality of service and so forth, and are made accountable through the publication of their achievements and failures. New Labour's 'modernisation' entails an extension of this logic. Schools are encouraged to diversify more and to reach their attainment targets or face direct intervention. Universities, perhaps, will eventually set differential rates for fees leading to a premier league of super-funded institutions and a range of competitive options for students.[13] Performance-related pay, pledges and quality commitments will form the framework of accountability.

But there is a contradiction in a government committing itself to this consumerist logic. Although there is competition for the contract to govern us, the rules of that competition are quite different to those of the market. Only the very rich or multi-national corporations can exercise a meaningful choice as to which kind of state they are to live under. Certainly governments now market themselves as attractive regimes, and their countries as territories ripe for good investment, but this does not constitute much of a basis for the relationship between the state and its citizens. If we are reduced to mere consumers of the state and democracy then social relations remain anomic and privatised, undermining the very things – the shared framework of values and mutual responsibilities – which make even the most liberal of free markets function.

As a result, in order to pursue a substantial market-based reform of the state-society relationship it becomes necessary to find new ways of building consensus and legitimacy for the state and society. But the specific benefits of the state or of a commitment to sociality can no longer be the source of this legitimacy, for they are exactly what has been hived off to bodies judged on the grounds of pure efficacy. Thus it is the state *as such* and sociality *as such* that must find a new ground on which to stand. That they are failing to do so is clear from the fact that political criticism has become increasingly pre-occupied with finding reasons to question the honesty or propriety of politicians, their managerial competence or the quality of their hairdressing rather than their political and economic ideas.

New Labour in office clearly does believe in a role for the state and for a public political life, but it does not conceive them in terms of blunt intervention. Instead it is prone to exhortation and the employment of policies that function to exhort – this is most obviously the case in those areas where state institutions are most entangled with the lives of citizens: health, social security and education. Here, while individual agencies are released from direct control they are more intensely encouraged (and induced) to behave in particular ways. Meanwhile, citizens are instructed to care for their health, to develop within themselves the skills necessary to find work and to take more of an interest in the education of their children rather than expect the state to do it all for them. They are to recognise their responsibilities as well as exercise their rights. Simultaneously it is quite logical for government to develop a deep interest in its media representation. The people need to be reminded of what government does for (or to) them and informed (through advertising for example) about what they can get from it.

Thus, slowly, a new sort of relationship between government and people evolves, one in which the state pretends that it regards its citizens as separated, individuated units, not to be represented by sectional institutions. For New Labour the individual is an ever changing, self-creating, reflexive entity. Society can no longer be conceived as any sort of homogenous mass or bloc best analysed along one axis such as class. Rather, notions of plurality are emphasised. But this plurality is not seen as emerging from forms of difference embedded in the varied historical and cultural experiences of different groups of people. Plurality for New Labour goes all the way down and becomes the difference of individuation. The task of government is to enhance and increase that individuation, to introduce the conditions for the structural competitiveness of the state and to encourage the autonomisation of lifestyle which is both cause and effect of the former.

As a consequence it becomes suspicious of institutions that perpetuate 'out-dated' forms of identity and organisation. Sectional institutions are understood to hinder the simultaneous development of a coherent collective united by constitutional aspirations and a society made up of differentiated individuals. People need to be freed to have an unmediated relationship with the whole of society or the state. There must be a direct relationship, for example, between party and membership, one not mediated by intermediate political structures like internal party organisations. Similarly trade unions, LEAs and so forth mediate the relationship of individual to service provider and should be limited or re-shaped to fit the reflexive individual.

This entails a levelling down, a form of decentralisation, and the placing of control in the hands of individuals. But that control takes the form of a kind of market choice (One-Member-One-Vote in the party, direct management of schools accompanied by free choice and league tables, doctors who don't intervene between 'customer' and 'service provider', mayors directly elected without boroughs getting in the way and so on). Its necessary corollary is a simplification of that which is chosen – parties narrow down the choice of candidates for election, schools are restricted in what they can teach and when. But the state must compensate for the destabilising effects of markets by training a modernised high-tech workforce and consumers. Government must speak directly to the people through the media and it must attempt to embody the values and aspirations which we now lack.

But this process does not occur in a vacuum, as if produced out of the whims of political leaders. It occurs against a background of social and economic change, and the interpretation of that change. It is to this we now turn.

THE SOURCES OF NEW LABOUR

New Labour does not formulate political ideas on the basis of a substantial moral claim about the nature of society and the distribution of its resources so much as on the basis of a 'sociological' claim about the novel condition of contemporary society; a belief that the world has been transformed, while our political ideas have not kept pace.[14] As Blair puts it in his explanation of the Third Way: 'Just as economic and social change were critical to sweeping the Right to power, so they were critical to its undoing. The challenge for the Third Way is to engage fully with the implications of that change.' The changes are: global markets and culture; technological advance and the information industries; transformation in the role of women; disaffection with distant political institutions. The Third Way response is to aim for a 'dynamic knowledge-based economy founded on individual empowerment and opportunity, where governments enable, not command, and the power of the market is harnessed to serve the public interest': the reinvigoration of civil society, partnership government and international co-operation.[15] Policy is thus derived from the truth of certain social facts – this is the nature of New Labour's 'pragmatism'.

The basis of such thinking can be found in many places but it boils down to a set of arguments concerning 'post-fordism', some of which were initiated under the banner of 'New Times' as waved by the Communist Party of Great Britain in the 1980s and disseminated through *Marxism Today*. New Times was about appropriating and 'grasping the future'.[16] It was predicated on the assessment of social forces and the nature of social organisation, from which strategies for political intervention could be developed. This took the form of an overwhelming concern with 'the knowledge economy' and the impact of information technologies on industrial organisation and consumer lifestyle. In *The Manifesto for New Times* (MFNT) it was argued that:

at the heart of the new times will be production based on a shift to information technology and microelectronics. New technology allows more
intensive automation and its extension from large to smaller companies,
pulling together the shop-floor and the office, the design loft and the
showroom. It allows production to be both more flexible, automated
and integrated.[17]

Under post-fordism, it argued, the nature of work has been transformed and the division of blue and white collar blurred. Service
industries become the main source of employment, with women's part-
time employment increasingly important, while traditional union
organisation is undermined.[18] Along with the internationalisation of
finance and the globalisation of the firm this was believed to have led to a
transformation in competitive pressures, the undermining of policies for
full-employment and the rise of 'an assertive individualistic consumerism'.
'Post-fordism' was not only the end of the massification of industry
but of massification as such. As *Marxism Today* put it: 'Mass production, the mass consumer, the big city, big-brother state, the sprawling
housing estate, and the nation-state are in decline: flexibility, diversity,
differentiation, mobility, communication, decentralisation and internationalisation are in the ascendant ... Our own identities, our sense of
self, our own subjectivities are being transformed.'[19] Fordism was not
merely an industrial arrangement. It was an overarching social formation, defining a relationship between state, individual and society. Its
passing was taken to mean that social interests have fragmented such
that no state could effectively and legitimately represent them.
There have been many arguments concerning the accuracy and veracity of such an account of post-fordism. It is not possible to assess and
evaluate them here.[20] But whatever one thinks about this it is necessary to
realise that the arguments of a publication such as MT and others with
related perspectives on social change have deeply affected New Labour.
In the 1980s claims about the decentralisation of the firm, the need for
new kinds of team management and new forms of independent work
spread throughout the study of business, management, economics and
political studies. And this sort of interpretation of changing capitalist
economics also shapes New Labour's attitudes to the economy and public
policy. It influences the Third Way critique of traditional social democracy and politics and leads to the guiding idea that the state must be
structured in a way that enables people and companies to participate
within the new economy. For the Third Way, post-fordism or the knowledge economy is the analytical key to understanding Thatcherism, the

eclipse of Keynesianism and to answering the question of what is to be done. A recent Demos collection on the Third Way speaks of 'the profound forces of globalisation, which have sharply altered the operating environment for government. Governments can no longer easily erect barriers to the exchange of money, regulate precisely what media their citizens consume, insulate their economies from global business cycles or pursue autonomous defence strategies.' One of the core challenges is that of 'achieving the transition to an economy based on intensive application and development of knowledge'.[21] The importance of such 'change' is asserted throughout contemporary government publications and speeches. Addressing the TUC in September 1999 Blair claimed that the transition to the knowledge economy was 'the fundamental issue' of our time. Changes to welfare policy are predicated on the belief that:

> 'The structure of the economy has changed, industrial patterns and working conditions are very different and the labour market has needed to adapt accordingly. People's lives and their expectations have been transformed ... There have been profound economic and social changes since 1948. But the welfare state has failed to keep pace. Reform is therefore essential.[22]

When he was Shadow Employment Spokesperson, Tony Blair wrote in MT of 'a new political settlement between the individual and society' which determines both their 'rights and obligations', a notion of citizenship understood as embedded in community and 'a new approach – neither old style collectivism nor new style individualism', a policy debate no longer dominated 'by a battle between state and market'.[23] Blair's 'new agenda' was 'fundamentally different from the issues that dominated debate in the past'. It entailed constitutional reform and devolution, and a 'non-ideological' recognition that 'the market is essential for individual choice.' Collective action was no longer about 'war for supremacy between management and labour' but enhancing 'the power of individual employees, not just to protect their position from abuse, but also to grant them the capability to use or exploit capital'. It was about the application of technology and the better education of workers, the liberation of 'untapped potential'.

All these claims are still fundamental to Blairism. Post-fordist flexibility, or what Blair has called the 'fast-forward future', creates and requires a new individualism and autonomy that should be enabled, not interfered with, by the state. It is not the job of the government to protect workers from capital nor to defend capital from the workers. It is the job of government to assist and encourage the development of various forms of investment and the flexibility necessary to compete in a rapid and expanding global economy and to 'unleash their potential'.

Such a position, based on sociological convictions about the direction of society and economy, can easily cease being a *political* claim and become a *managerial* one about how to run things better; about how to correctly understand the shape of present day capitalism and how best to organise a population to respond to it. Out of this – what we might call 'the Demos tendency' – has developed a kind of vanguardist futurism where the purpose of politics is 'to resolve the big conflicts of interest and lend direction to complex societies'. It is 'a way to solve problems and a means of providing security and a stable sense of belonging'.[24] This is a vision of a new politics for the administration of a world of change. A politics that takes place across spheres of society and that cannot proceed through the traditional channels of hierarchical, civil service-run government; the simple issuing of commands and passing of laws.

The recent political analysis of Anthony Giddens shares with the general drift of post-fordist thinking, and with 'New Times' in particular, the conviction that we face 'a world that has taken us by surprise' in which old ideas of socialism and Keynesianism are obsolete; that our concepts of knowledge and control need to be re-thought to fit a society too complex, fluid and diverse to be managed by a central state. For Giddens the new politics must be a 'life politics', concerned with the emancipation of lifestyle, identity and choice. Individuals must have the tools, and live under conditions, that enable them to be the reflexive actors of late modernity. The concentration of power and the attempt to dominate social life from one centre is both undesirable and impossible. Instead the capacity of social agents to act must be increased and the state must therefore cease being directive and become 'generative'. Giddens calls for a 'social investment state' that develops an entrepreneurial culture, offering protection in a way that encourages risk and opens possibilities.[25]

'Third Way' theorists explicitly emphasise the social conditions for sustaining stability and security in the new environment. This allows them to critique Thatcherism and to relate the project of securing state legitimacy to that of generally securing social order and cohesion. For Giddens, Thatcherism undermined social relationships, failing to understand the context of the new world or to see the necessary cultural and moral underpinnings of a market society (a point strongly made by John Gray).[26] The new politics must be concerned with redeveloping or repairing social cohesion and solidarity – a 'philosophic conservatism'.[27] The normative and moral character of traditions has been lost to a 'de-traditionalising' world. In an increasingly interdependent international order, our local actions have global consequences and make us increasingly exposed to new forms of risk. This globalisation and 'radicalisation' of modernity have begun to uproot even deeply held traditional assumptions about personal areas such as the family or sexual intimacy.[28]

For Giddens, equality matters because inequality leads to disaffection and conflict, undermining social cohesion. Equality of opportunity is not enough since 'a radically meritocratic society would create deep inequalities of outcome, which would threaten social cohesion.'[29] In this way the ethics of equality are not derived from its being a principle as such but because the effects of its absence are an offence against the constitution of a cohesive society. We have seen this trend across New Labour for several years now, for example in the report from the Commission on Social Justice.[30] It is part of what Ruth Levitas deprecatingly terms 'the new Durkheimian hegemony'.[31] Equality is recast as inclusion and its opposite as the enemy of social harmony. Inclusion becomes a concept applied across policy areas – education, pensions, culture and so on. Inclusion is important since it is the only way to bring security to people in the new society. It is part of the logic of the new economy which must draw on all the talents and creativity of people. It means, at heart, bringing people into the knowledge economy and enabling them to be the kinds of well educated and technologically literate individuals both made possible by 'New Times' and made necessary – since without them there will be nobody to produce or consume.

This is all a little bit along the way from Thatcherism. Where dogma driven neo-liberals sought to liberate the market from the state, New Labour seeks to deploy that state in the name of the market because it sees that the market itself has changed. To facilitate that change only the state, with its virtual monopoly of education and its key role in social security, can assist. Where Thatcherism foundered because it could not see the contradiction between valorising tradition at the same time as advocating an economy that, by its very nature, destroys tradition, New Labour seeks out ways to ground a new kind of social and economic order, developing a political ethic of open ended democracy and of governance oriented towards encouraging risk and the entrepreneurialism of life-style. It is a programme based on the necessity of managing the completion of a transition from one mode of capital accumulation to another. Such a programme requires more than policies that alter the way governments interfere with the economy. It requires a restructuring of the relationship between the state, the economy and citizens. But states must act not only to reproduce the economic conditions essential to continued capital accumulation. They must also secure the conditions for its social and ideological reproduction.

THE 'SCHUMPETERIAN WORKFARE REGIME'

In response to the post-fordist perspective and the enthusiasm of the present government for all things high-tech and knowledge-led one may simply choose to dispute the facts and figures querying the extent to which any of it is actually happening.[32] But one could also accept that something is occurring without granting it quite the autonomy sometimes imputed to economic change by the vanguard army of modernisation. Social and economic transformations may be born out of underlying trends and forces but they are always brought to fruition and directed by political actors.[33] Recognising this is essential to understanding what is happening. The long term decline of the British economy does not have a single neatly applicable solution – responses to it can and have varied. Thatcherism was one such attempt at completing the 'blocked' modernisation of the nation. New Labour offers another – one that employs the state to foster new kinds of social and economic subject capable of taking their place in the brave new world. Furthermore there is a sense in which states and governments, even with their reduced power base, can bring about some of the things they thought were already there. Acting on sets of deeply held assumptions about what the future holds, New Labour will bring that future into being.

Whatever the arguments it is clear that New Labour does not primarily understand state power in traditional behavioural, institutional or constitutional terms but works on the basis of multi-dimensional assumptions.[34] It sees political and governmental power in far broader terms, at the same time as believing that capacity to be heavily circumscribed. This is part of the reason for conflict between New Labour and those Tories who repeatedly accuse them of ignoring parliamentary protocol and procedure. New Labour does not understand the state simply in terms of governmental practices and does not recognise itself as limited by the Palace of Westminster. Instead, as we have seen, government is conceived as an enabling institution and as the centre of a variety of networks of policy formulation and implementation. This affords it the indirect form of power that sets agendas and leads policy by inducement rather than direct intervention. More than this, Labour recognises the overall power of government to shape perceptions and set frames for all those working within state based institutions and potentially those beyond it. This perspective underpins attitudes to the reform of education and welfare where the direction is increasingly that of setting targets, defining expectations and focusing the options of both service employees and those who receive that service.

Here the emphasis is on exposing not only the welfare system to cold winds but the claimant as well. The options by which the claimant can shelter from such blasts are then set by government-enforced procedures. As the House of Commons select committee has recognised, 'the notion of a service-wide system appropriate to everyone is becoming increasingly a fiction'.[35] Hence the system is reoriented towards more nuanced forms of relationship with 'clients', shifting from the imposition of certain kinds of state support to the inducement of certain kinds of choice. From a monolithic fordist system where pay-outs and treatment are uniform we move to a post-fordist one where standardised packages are given a gloss of pseudo-individuation with tailored 'care-packages' and a focus not on keeping citizens or claimants in their place, but on re-shaping their place and their perceptions of their place.

Welfare-to-work is not a new policy. It builds on various training schemes developed in the 1970s and re-worked by the Tories in the 1980s into programmes such as the Youth Training Scheme and Youth Opportunities Programme. It also has precursors in schemes developed by the 'new' Democrats in the United States.[36] What is interestingly new about welfare-to-work is the way in which it combines options for employment with work in the voluntary sector, with the environmental task force, or involvement in education or training. Furthermore it seems also to involve an explicit role for government in employment creation – something of a novelty after such a long period of neo-liberal rule. Employers are given a subsidy to give full-time work to the long-term unemployed and there are national insurance exemptions for those employing the low-paid. This combines with the rhetoric of a new contract between the state and citizens in which the return for being flexible enough to take work where it is available is the guarantee of state assistance in finding it and the assurance that work will pay.

The Tories did make use of some subsidies, and to some extent welfare-to-work is a continuation of policies that were incipient in the Major government.[37] What is most novel about the present developments is the aspect of compulsion. While there is a choice between forms of work and forms of training, for the long-term unemployed and for 18-24 year olds out of work for more than six months staying on benefit is not an option. Where Conservative governments moved towards various schemes in order to reduce the statistics of unemployment New Labour is committed to this version of 'workfare' as a way of actually reducing unemployment and thus, by extension, as a way of providing particular sorts of workers for the new economy. While the rhetoric is that of active government intervening to achieve full employment, the practice, with its orientation towards training and flexibility, is clearly supply-side. Social inclusion requires the willingness to be fit for the labour market and hence allows the combination of compulsion with claims about social justice. It is clearly not the government's intention to tackle employment policy through Keynesian procedures of macro-economic management. Its role is to facilitate the individual in becoming ready to face an unmanaged and unmanageable economy. Thus: 'the government is determined to build an active welfare system which helps people to help themselves and ensures a proper level of support in times of need'.[38] Such an approach emerges in part out of a communitarian interpretation of the causes of decline in which they are found to reside in inappropriate moral attitudes. The response is to try and foster a sense of individual responsibility and duty balanced by an acknowledgement of the responsibilities of the government and of society.[39] But it also emerges from the desire to generate new kinds of active welfare recipients who are clear that ultimate responsibility for their self-improvement rests on obtaining the right skills and capacities for entering the flexible labour market. Underlying such proposals is a clear moralisation, but one that can be understood as feeding into a strategy of governance aiming to change the culture and outlook of those it touches. Similar motivations can be seen in the way the government is developing a generalisable discourse of community and partnership to displace that of market and contract.

This is an intriguing strategy of governance. Where that term is usually used to describe the relationship between government and the agencies with which, or through which, it operates, one can see a form of governance behind welfare to work that aims at the individual claimant. A 'work ethic' is encouraged and the claimant individualised so as to regard him or herself less as an object of state policy and more as a subject who must take on the responsibility for change and development. A number of analysts have opted to describe the sort of state/society relationship in development here (and that is emerging in Europe out of post-fordism) as a 'Schumpeterian Workfare Regime'.[40] The aims of the Keynesian Welfare State were to secure full employment through policies formulated on the basis of managing a national economy. Given that the mode of mass production was somewhat inflexible, the emphasis of economic policy could be on the demand side and achieved through the alliance of the state with the key social and economic corporations. This involved a degree of collectivism and the provision of a large-scale system of welfare support. But we are now witnessing the shift from welfare to workfare. For the Tories the motivation behind such policy shifts had more to do with cutting welfare expenditure than reforming the nature of the labour market itself.[41] New Labour, as we have seen, has furthered Thatcherite reforms to the state and has entered into the wholesale reform of the social security system through the development of welfare-to-work schemes. It has rejected ideologically-driven neo-liberalism while endorsing the supposedly 'pragmatic' aspects of Thatcherite change. It is thus developing a version of the 'Schumpeterian' state.

The Austrian economist Joseph Schumpeter was concerned to develop a theory of economic development as opposed to the static models of idealised economic processes that tended to dominate neo-classical economic theory. Schumpeter placed special emphasis on the role of entrepreneurs and described economic transformation in terms of endogenous factors as opposed to the effects of external 'contingencies' (among which he counted population change). He focused on the question of how 'the economic system generates the force which incessantly transforms it ... a source of energy within the economic system which would, of itself, disrupt any equilibrium that might be attained',[42] arguing that:

> the essence of economic development lies in the fact that the means of production, which hitherto have been put to certain static uses, are being deflected from this course and are devoted to new purposes ... These new combinations are not carried through on their own accord ... but for their realisation are in need of a kind of intelligence and energy which inhere only in a minority of economic agents. The intrinsic function of the entrepreneur consists in carrying out these new combinations.[43]

From this perspective economic growth occurs because of changes in the supply side as opposed to that of demand. It is driven by entrepreneurial innovation such as the creation of new goods, or their better deployment, new techniques of production or marketing, the establishment of new markets or new sources of supply and so forth. Inventions may make possible new developments but require entrepreneurial innovation to be deployed. This means that the availability of investment capital (through banks and other credit sources for example) is crucial to economic development. Where neo-classicists had sought for the way towards a state of economic equilibrium, Schumpeter pronounced 'stationary capitalism' a contradiction in terms and found the core characteristic of capitalism to be its change-ability, its 'creative destruction'.[44] Thus economic management is not about steering the economy towards a notional point of stability so much as managing change and promoting it.

Innovation comes from knowledge. Economic processes cannot be understood in terms of the rational calculation of essentially utilitarian agents. Rationality proceeds on the basis of fixed routines whereas innovation consists in departing from the tried and tested ways of making economic decisions. Factors such as consumer taste or want are thus not external to the economy but are endogenous: 'It is the producer who as a rule initiates economic change, and consumers are educated by him if necessary; they are, as it were, taught to want new things, or things which differ in some respect or other from those which they have been in the habit of using.'[45]

In sum this is a supply side approach, but one that limits the capacities for rationally predicting what will happen in the future, since innovation, by definition, is not explicable from within the confines of the present routines. It follows that the way to manage an economy is to ensure the flexibility to take up new innovations and to encourage their development; that governments can't plan ahead but can create conditions for the circulation of knowledge and the continued supply of entrepreneurs to innovate. One could extend this logic into other areas of social organisation, such as the public service, and – combined with the interpretations of 'New Times' and 'reflexive modernity' – one has a vision of a permanently evolving social order, the enemy of which is any kind of conservatism since the future depends on our 'permanent revision' and open embrace of change.

The 'Schumpeterian Workfare Regime' thus represents an attempt to promote a kind of permanent innovation as the way to enhance structural competitiveness. The role of the state is greater than with a neo-liberal system since it must work to move the national economy into the international arena and prepare it by ensuring that the conditions are there for permanent innovation. It is a supply-side strategy where it seeks to ensure a sufficient skills-base in the workforce and can encourage investment in, for example, research and development, and in small firms with innovative strategy. The state arenas of social security and education thus become central since both can be used to enhance the competitiveness of the supply side.

Jessop summarises the role of such a state, in terms of economic and social reproduction, as:

> to promote product, process, organisational and market innovation in open economies in order to strengthen as far as possible the structural competitiveness of the national economy by intervening on the supply side; and to subordinate social policy to the needs of labour market flexibility and/or to the constraints of international competition'.[46]

As Torfing points out, and as we have seen, this is more appropriately termed a regime than a state as such, since, while 'the state may retain the overall responsibility for the formulation, legitimisation and outcome of different policies' ... 'the responsibility for operationalising and implementing these policies is to an increasing extent shared with different non-state actors with self-organised policy networks.'[47]

As Torfing also argues, the forms taken by any particular SWR will vary in different countries depending on the strategies employed. He identifies neo-liberal, neo-statist and neo-corporatist versions. The neo-liberal version seeks to reduce the role of the state and to privilege the market, though it may use the state in order to secure that freedom for markets. The neo-statist version employs the state to re-organise the economy and society through developing competitive management in the public sector; for example, new forms of multi-faceted governance. Within the neo-corporatist strategy there is greater integration but in a more open framework of policy networks. He further distinguishes between offensive and defensive strategies. The offensive aims to be pro-active, perhaps utilising workfare schemes to offer empowering education and training within a universalist system, while the defensive strategy prioritises punitive policies towards the unemployed.[48]

Torfing argues that reforms to the Danish welfare state have proceeded on the basis of an offensive neo-statist strategy. They have been able to do so because of specific features of Danish society such as a strong tradition of universalist welfare provision, a labour movement that has been closely involved in active labour market policies and their regional implementation, and the separation of the benefits system from the offering of employment. By contrast, he argues, in Britain there is not such a strong commitment to universalism; the union movement is fragmented and confrontational, while the linking of the benefits payments system and the job centres intensifies claimants' hostility to the finding of work.[49] As a result Britain has tended to pursue more neo-liberal strategies operating on a defensive, punitive, basis.

But these 'deficiencies' of the British system are not simply inherent in British life, though their embeddedness in social and state institutions makes change difficult. They are also the result of many years of Conservative hegemony. The task of a government committed to a 'post-fordist' kind of analysis and to developing a welfare system involved in the active creation of workers and employment is to break these habits and 'traditions'. Thus the task is fundamentally as political as it is managerial. It is inherently one that must encourage people to embrace change, to alter their outlook on what work means, on how work is to be found and to shift their perceptions of what they can expect out of life for themselves and their children. Much New Labour and Third Way discussion is, as a consequence, explicitly concerned with how to tell what Charles Leadbeater calls an 'economy story'; to 'show why it is uniquely well-placed to tap the knowledge economy's potential for growth, innovation and productivity'; ' a story about how the economy will develop, that will help people to make sense of how they and their children will make their living, what sort of companies they will be working for, making what sorts of products and using what sorts of skills.'[50] In short, the dilemma for New Labour is that of finding ways to justify change to politics, work-life and social life in a situation where people in their public, private and financial lives are dispersed and suspicious of state action. Thus it has to extend the practice of governance into larger and larger areas of life. It does so via discourses that are populist and 'community' oriented.

CULTURE AS STRATEGY OF GOVERNANCE

In a recent article Ralf Dahrendorf has addressed the relative absence of the idea of liberty in Third Way thinking.[51] He points out that this political philosophy seems to reject traditional democratic institutions, seeking to supplant parliaments with referenda and focus groups. It makes saving for pensions compulsory and insists that we must work regardless of family commitments. It advocates a state that 'will no longer pay for things, but tells people what to do'. This argument begs questions as to what being 'liberal' actually entails, and particularly of what liberty means for us at this point in our history. For the advocates of New Labour the charge of illiberalism would no doubt be rejected on the basis that they are enabling people to be free by educating, training and exhorting them while keeping those pesky kids off the streets at night.

For Foucault liberty and liberalism were never to be understood through such straightforward claims about the presence or absence of freedom. Rather liberalism is a 'rationality of government' concerned with the ways in which government is actually possible. In analysing the developments of nineteenth-century political economy and the growth of the modern state he argues that liberty comes to be seen 'not only as the right of individuals legitimately to oppose the power, the abuses and usurpations of the sovereign, but also now as an indispensable element of governmental rationality itself.'[52] Security and cohesion are maintained through liberty and not despite it. The activity of government is oriented towards a kind of continual preoccupation with how it is possible to govern a society and an economy, to relate them to each other and to maintain security within the social itself through developing forms of liberty.

Thus far we have been concerned with changes in institutional structure and procedure, but the underlying theme has been the question of how New Labour can maintain legitimacy and coherence within the conditions it identifies as characterising our present. In short, we need to think specifically about its practice of government or governance. New Labour's economic and welfare policies are both oriented towards the reproduction and regulation of a particularly paradoxical economic subject – one that is ever more immersed in the sphere of productive consumption, in order to forge an identity that is separate from it. For the state this presents problems, since it wants and needs people to engage in the activity that keeps the weightless economy floating, but at the same time must manage a society which is opening itself up to a proliferation of activities that cut across the very social and moral structures that constitute it. The enabling state thus becomes an 'exhortatory state', seeking to change 'identities' and 'govern by culture' instead of direct regulation. Just as the knowledge economy needs new kinds of individual, so it requires a new kind of state to manage and mould the new citizens – though the reverse is also true: the knowledge economy presents a strategic opportunity by which government can maintain and extend itself. We are not just being governed for the knowledge economy, it is also a mechanism by which we are governed, demanding a new order of ceaseless movement and innovation. As Stephen Byers suggests:

> The answer must lie in the modernisation of all our social and political institutions. We must look at everything afresh, from the detail of indi-

vidual policies down to how we develop policy, communicate and deliver
it ... The more creative you are, the more dynamic and enterprising, the
more you stand to benefit.[53]

Foucault concentrated attention on excavating the functioning of the
disciplinary society – the structures of order and control embodied in the
prison, hospital, asylum, school, barracks and so forth. But, as Deleuze
points out, he also suggested that the disciplinary society is becoming
supplanted by a society of control that 'no longer operate[s] by confining
people but through continuous control and instant communication.'[54] In
such an environment there is continual monitoring of performance and
procedure. This, for Deleuze, is related to a form of capitalism that no
longer directs itself towards production but to the sale of services, the
opening of markets and the practice of selling. The organisation of society
shifts onto finding new forms of custody as opposed to old forms of
confinement; the introduction of business methods into education and
permanent techniques of student assessment; forms of medicine that,
rather than seek patients, seek to identify the subjects at risk. 'In disciplinary societies', he writes, 'you were always starting all over again (as you
went from school to barracks, from barracks to factory), while in control
societies you never finish anything – business, training, and military
service being coexisting metastable states of a single modulation, a sort of
universal transmutation.'[55] Or as Blair puts it, 'There will be no slowing
down in the pace of change ... The speed of our modernisation
programme will be accelerated. By definition modernisation has to be a
continuous process ... Modernisation and improvement have to be a
permanent drive to ensure that things really are getting better.'[56]

Where once the state had to intervene to make society and its citizens fit for the new industrial economy (by forcing people off land and
into cities, by developing disciplinary education systems to begin training them), now the state must intervene to bring about the people of
the knowledge economy – the true reflexive individuals, possessing a
kind of permanently revisionist self, an empowered and mobile subject
(geographically, economically and psychically) who is his or her own
entrepreneur of selfhood. The state will cease to be a tool of direct
intervention but will become merely an enabler, while those individuals and the associations of which they may be part move in to fill the
space left by the state. This is 'a double movement of autonomization
and responsibilization'. People and organisations are set free, yet they
must also take on the burden of establishing moral direction and exercising responsibility.[57]

In New Labour-speak this mutates into attempts to govern through exhortations to community and responsibility. Community becomes for the government both a problem and a solution, something it must revitalise, through which it can reach individuals and re-orient them, but into which it cannot fully go. As Nikolas Rose points out, 'community, rather than society, is the new territorialisation of political thought, the new way in which conduct is collectivised.'[58] In New Labour's discourse of community, questions of moralisation, individualism, citizenship, responsibility and adaptability all cohere. The management and refinement of communities becomes the procedure by which security and legitimacy can be attained in the 'fast-forward future'. 'Community' or 'civic' life are taken to be intrinsic to human life, even spontaneous formations that are merely suffering disruption or blockage.

For Blair, the construction of the new nation will require 'drawing deep into the richness of the British character', [59] for 'change is in the blood and bones of the British – we are by our nature and tradition innovators, adventurers, pioneers'.[60] He thus attempts to define the collective of Britain as one which always has been and wanted to be developing and changing, but which has been held back by the 'forces of conservatism'. The only opposition to wealth creation and economic expansion becomes these forces of reaction. Our national economy rests on people being encouraged to fulfil and manifest their potential. This of course fits into the new language of human and social capital, the notion that everyday interactions, relations and deeds can be something which we account for, foster, develop and invest wisely. Citizens' rights, roles and responsibilities all cohere (economically, morally, politically and psychically) around this commitment to what Jack Straw calls 'active community', a strategy of 'social intervention' rather than 'social engineering'. Straw claims that the Third Way involves extending 'the idea and practice of volunteering – of people doing something for each other rather than having the state do it for them and so diminishing them.' Voluntary activity is 'the essential act of citizenship'. Clearly there is a paradox behind a state acting so as to encourage voluntary activity because the state itself can't take any such role. Citizenship, a 'political' category, consists in part of our volunteering to do certain things, expressing our essential communality, a 'natural' category. In order to be the kinds of people we are supposed to be, responsible for ourselves and not mediated by the state, that very same state has to act to make it so.

Thus this new mode of governance cannot operate through the supposedly 'old' ways – through government intervention, legislation or anything so crude as taxing people. For Perri 6,

> Culture is now the centre of the agenda for government reform, because we now know from the findings of a wide range of recent research that culture is perhaps the most important determinant of a combination of long-run economic success and social cohesion. The mistake of both statist left and laissez-faire right was to ignore this fact.

Educational achievement cannot be enhanced without 'a shift in the mentalities of parents and children towards valuing education and investing time and energy into it'; law and order requires changing the cultures of the people who live in areas with high crime rates; environmental improvement rests on changing attitudes to energy efficiency, and unemployment requires addressing not only economic barriers to the long-term unemployed 'but also their own cultural and attitudinal handicaps'.[61] This is, in Nikolas Rose's phrase, an 'etho-politics' which 'seeks to act upon conduct by acting upon the forces thought to shape the values, beliefs, moralities that themselves are thought to determine the everyday mundane choices that human beings make as to how they lead their lives. In etho-politics, life itself, as it is lived in its everyday manifestations, is the object of adjudication'.[62] Threats made to, or penalties imposed upon, the welfare recipient, for example, are attempts to induce certain forms of behaviour, to change the outlook and culture of the people concerned.[63]

Through this 'technology' of governmentality we are to become self-regulating, our progress and direction monitored through the setting of parameters of action assessed through the agencies of state governance. This individual-oriented strategy combines with the general re-structuring of state and government, such that 'joined-up government' demands an internal reflection by agencies upon their own efficiency, measured by their ability to generate and draw on the resources of contemporary social scientific research and knowledge. Government becomes an information hub. We access our welfare rights through kiosk technology and paying attention to television advertisements; school-teachers are updated on the latest findings; 'best practice' is disseminated throughout the medical profession. This feeds back into the process of legitimation since it finds and forges a new role for government. No longer will it have the pretence of being able to intervene directly to halt the disruptive actions of capitalist enterprises, nor will it find cash to inject into failing public services. But it will act as a kind of management consultancy, gathering and circulating 'evidence based research'.[64] Government too must put itself up for continual reinvention, receiving validation through continually grounding itself in the effectiveness of its outcomes as assessed by us, the consumers of the governance state. The practice of Total Quality Management in the firm extends into government and out into the management of communities. Just as personnel managers have been encouraged to see their working environments as active communities, so the community becomes a kind of firm that will cohere only if the patterns and flows of control and participation are correctly administered. By happy coincidence, for the discourse of Blairism, the old divisions of society, economy and state are gone. The management of the economy, the protection and development of communities, the freedom and security of individuals all become part of one overall process of setting things free to thrive in the ever changing world of global financial transfer.

CONCLUSION

New Labour is not a weak, ephemeral, fraudulent or phony political movement. Alleged personality clashes between members of the government, the creation of a new elite of lobbyists, media correspondents and youthful advisers are all largely irrelevant to understanding what it is up to. It is not an imitation of Thatcherism and it is not simply 'business as usual' for the state in a capitalist society, acting only to secure the best return on investments for the businesspeople who fund the party.

New Labour's is a political project that emerges from quite definite intellectual and political trends within western capitalist economies. It takes these trends and makes them into the foundation of a programme for the continued transformation of the practices of political, economic and personal existence. As such it can be understood best by reference to the debates and discussions that centre on explicating the nature of current transformations and by appreciating the specific ways (specific to the UK, specific to the context of the Labour Party) in which it constructs a response. Crucial to this is the underlying desire to govern through changing the culture of people, firms, government and communities in order to develop a way in which wealth creation and moral cohesion can be combined. In fact these two are found now to be as one – a historic opportunity thrown up for 'socialists' and which New Labour believes it has grasped. The lines then become drawn between the 'conservatives' who resist change and those who embrace 'modernity and justice' with 'the courage to change'. Ultimately this means that the object of New Labour's state practice is different to the object of state practice under previous UK governments. Where some have tried to manage economies, to organise and mediate the interests of trade unions and employers, to administer state-wide systems of delivery, New Labour's object is quite explicitly different. The twenty-first-century nation needs a knowledge economy and strong civic ties. How is it to obtain these? 'The answer is people. The future is people.'[65] They will lead us into the future in which we will be free to do anything we want. Except stop.

NOTES

1. See for example Stewart Wood, 'Constitutional Reform – living with the consequences', *Renewal*, Vol. 7, No. 3 (1999), pp1-10.

2. E.g. Ralf Dahrendorf, 'Whatever Happened to Liberty', *New Statesman*, 6 September 1999, pp25-27.

3. See for example, David Held, 'The Timid Tendency', *Marxism Today* (November/December 1998), pp24-27; Doreen Massey, 'Editorial: Problems with globalisation', *Soundings* 7 (Autumn 1997).

4. E.g. Roy Hattersely, 'Why I'm no Longer Loyal to Labour', *The Guardian*, 26 July 1997.

5. Amongst others see Colin Hay, *The Political Economy of New Labour*, Manchester University Press, Manchester 1999.

6. Andrew Vincent, 'New Ideologies for Old?', *Political Quarterly*, Vol. 69, No. 1 (January 1998), pp48-58. See also Tony Blair, *Let Us Face the Future*, Fabian Society, London 1995.

7. Michael Freeden, 'The Ideology of New Labour', *Political Quarterly*, Vol. 69, No. 2 (1999).

8. See Tony Blair, *Speech to Labour Party Conference*, 29 September 1998; *Speech to Labour Party Conference*, 28 September 1999.

9. See Andrew Taylor, ' "Arm's Length But Hands On". Mapping the New Governance: The Department of National Heritage and Cultural Politics in Britain', *Public Administration* 75 (1998), pp441-466.

10. R.A.W. Rhodes, 'The New Governance: Governing Without Government', *Political Studies* 44 (1996), pp652-67.

11. See Bob Jessop, 'The transition to Post-Fordism and the Schumpeterian Workfare State' in Brian Loader and Roger Burrows (eds), *Towards a Post-Fordist Welfare State?*, Routledge, London 1994.

12. See Stephen Driver and Luke Martell, *New Labour: The Politics of Post-Thatcherism*, Polity, Cambridge 1997.

13. See Elspeth Johnson and Rana Mitter, *Students as Citizens: Focusing and Widening Access to Higher Education*, The Fabian Society, London 1998.

14. See also Alan Finlayson, 'Third Way Theory', *Political Quarterly*, Vol. 70, No.3 (1999), pp271-279.

15. Tony Blair, *The Third Way: New Politics for a New Century*, The Fabian Society, London 1998, pp6-7.
16. *Marxism Today* (MT), October 1988, p3.
17. *Manifesto For New Times* (MNFT), 1989, pp6-7.
18. MFNT, 1989, p.7.
19. MT, October 1988, p3.
20. See for example a special issue of *Economy and Society* edited by Colin Hay and Bob Jessop in 1995.
21. Ian Hargreaves and Ian Christie (eds), *Tomorrow's Politics: The Third Way and Beyond*, Demos, London 1998, pp1-10.
22. Speech by Alastair Darling (Secretary of State for Social security) to the IPPR, 23 September 1998.
23. Tony Blair, 'Forging a New Agenda', *Marxism Today*, October 1991, p32.
24. Geoff Mulgan (ed), *Life After Politics*, Fontana, London 1997, ppx, xii.
25. Anthony Giddens, *The Third Way*, Polity, Cambridge 1998, pp99-101.
26. See John Gray 'After Social Democracy' in Geoff Mulgan (ed.), *Life After Politics*, Fontana, London 1997.
27. See Anthony Giddens, *Beyond Left and Right*, Polity, Cambridge 1994, pp247-8.
28. See Anthony Giddens, *The Consequences of Modernity*, Polity, Cambridge 1990; Anthony Giddens, *In Defence of Sociology*, Polity, Cambridge 1996; Anthony Giddens, *The transformation of intimacy: sexuality, love and eroticism in modern societies*, Polity, Cambridge 1992.
29. *Ibid.*, p101.
30. The Commission on Social Justice/Institute of Public Policy Research, *Social Justice: Strategies for National Renewal*, Vintage, London 1994.
31. Ruth Levitas, 'The Concept of Social Exclusion and the New Durkheimian Hegemony', *Critical Social Policy*, Vol. 16, 1996, pp5-20.
32. Amongst others see Paul Hirst and Grahame Thompson, *Globalization in question: the international economy and the possibilities of governance*, Polity, Cambridge 1996; David Held, 'The Timid Tendency', *Marxism Today* (*November/December* 1998), pp24-27.
33. See the points made by Doreen Massey, 'Editorial: I'm not an economist but ...', *Soundings* 10 (Autumn 1998).
34. See Martin Smith, 'Reconceptualizing the British State: Theoretical and Empirical Challenges to Central Government', *Public Administration*, 76 (Spring 1998), pp45-72.
35. Cited in *ibid.*, p62.
36. See Desmond King and Mark Wickham-Jones, 'From Clinton to Blair: The Democratic (Party) Origins of Welfare to Work', *Political Quarterly*, Vol. 70, No. 1, pp62-74.

37. On this question of continuity see Jonathon Tonge, 'New Packaging, old deal? New Labour and employment policy innovation', *Critical Social Policy*, Vol. 19, No. 2, pp217-232.

38. DSS, *New Ambitions for Our Country: A new Contract for welfare* (summary), 1998, p16.

39. On the influence of communitarianism see Stephen Driver and Luke Martell (1997), 'New Labour's Communitarianisms', *Critical Social Policy*, pp27-46. On communitarianism and stakeholding in welfare see Emma Heron and Peter Dwyer, 'Doing the Right Thing: Labour's attempt to forge a new welfare deal between the individual and the state', *Social Policy and Administration*, Vol. 33, No. 11, pp91-104.

40. See Bob Jessop, 'The Transition to post-fordism and the Schumpeterian workfare state', *op. cit.*; Jacob Torfing, 'Workfare with Welfare: Recent Reforms of the Danish Welfare State', *Journal of European Social Policy*, Vol. 9, No. 1 (1999), pp5-28.

41. See Colin Hay, *Re-Stating Social and Political Change*, Open University Press, Buckingham 1996.

42. Joseph Schumpeter, 'Preface to Japanese edition of The Theory of Economic Development', cited in Nathan Rosenberg, *The Emergence of Economic Ideas*, Edward Elgar, London 1994, p156.

43. Joseph Schumpeter, 'On the Nature of Economic Crises', cited in Erich Schneider, *Joseph Schumpeter: Life and Work of a Great Social Scientist*, Bureau of Business Research, University of Nebraska, 1975.

44. Joseph Schumpeter, *Capitalism, Socialism and Democracy*, Routledge, London 1992.

45. Joseph Schumpeter, *The theory of economic development*, Oxford University Press, Oxford 1961.

46. Bob Jessop, 'The Transition to post-fordism and the Schumpeterian workfare state' in Roger Burrows and Brian Loader, *Towards a Post-Fordist Welfare State?*, Routledge, London 1994.

47. Jacob Torfing, 'Workfare with Welfare: recent reforms of the Danish Welfare State', in *Journal of European Social Policy*, Vol. 9, 1 (1999), pp5-28.

48. *Ibid.*, p9.

49. *Ibid.*, pp24-5.

50. Charles Leadbeater, 'Welcome to the Knowledge Economy' in Ian Hargreaves and Ian Christie, *Tomorrow's Politics: The Third Way and Beyond*, Demos, London 1998, pp12-13.

51. Ralf Dahrendorf, 'Whatever happened to liberty', *New Statesman*, 6 September 1999, pp25-27.

52. Cited in Colin Gordon, 'Governmental Rationality: An introduction' in Graham Burchell, Colin Gordon, Peter Miller (eds) (1991), *The Foucault*

effect: studies in governmentality, Harvester Wheatsheaf, London 1991.

53. Stephen Byers, 'People and Knowledge: towards a new industrial policy for the 21st century', in *Is Labour Working*, Fabian Society, London 1999, p45.

54. See 'Control and Becoming' in Gilles Deleuze, *Negotiations, 1972-1990*, trans. Martin Joughin, Columbia University Press, New York 1995, pp169-176.

55. Gilles Deleuze, 'Postscript on Control Societies', in *ibid*., p179.

56. Tony Blair, 'Foreword' in *Is Labour Working*, Fabian Society, London 1999.

57. Nikolas Rose, 'Inventiveness in Politics', *Economy and Society*, Vol. 28, No. 3 (1999), p476.

58. *Ibid*., p475.

59. Tony Blair, *Speech to Labour Party Conference*, 30 September 1997.

60. *Ibid*.

61. Perri 6, 'Governance by Culture', in Geoff Mulgan (ed), *Life After Politics*, *op. cit.*, p273.

62. Nikolas Rose, 'Inventiveness in Politics', *Economy and Society*, Vol. 28, No. 3 (1999), p477-8.

63. Frank Field, 'Re-Inventing Welfare: A response to Lawrence Mead' in Alan Deacon (ed.), *From Welfare to Work: Lessons from America*, London Institute for Economic Affairs, 1997, cited in King and Whickham-Jones, *op. cit.*, p71.

64. See John Lloyd, 'A New Style of Governing', *New Statesman*, 4 October 1999, pp12-13.

65. Tony Blair, *Speech to Labour Party Conference*, 28 September 1999.

Creative accounting: consumer culture, the 'creative economy' and the cultural policies of New Labour

JO LITTLER

In Stephen Bayley's book *Labour Camp: The Failure of Style Over Substance,* the former creative director of the New Millennium Experience shares his views on New Labour's cultural policies and practices. As the title suggests, Bayley's opinion is not exactly favourable; and this in itself is not particularly surprising, given Bayley's dramatic resignation as creative director of the Dome and the general reputation of the 'style guru' for designer tantrums and waspish comment. What *Labour Camp* does, firstly, is to argue, through anecdote and invective, that from Cool Britannia to Lord Irvine's wallpaper, from the Dome to the 'branding Britain' debates, New Labour manifests the triumph of 'style' over 'substance', and has offered a cultural regime consumed by the superficial aspects of image. Moreover, this is not just any old 'shallow' image either, but an exceptionally *dull and debased* one: the second charge of the book is that cultural standards are being lowered. As proof, Bayley shudders, we now have in charge of the Arts Council former Granada chairman Gerry Robinson, the 'caterer to Nescafé society'.[1]

Bayley's account is structured by the belief that design or art should not be 'political' and that it can somehow exist in a zone 'outside' politics. Similarly, the critique rests (somewhat incongruously, coming from the former director of the Design Museum) on the idea of 'style' and 'substance' as mutually exclusive entities, on the idea of a binary opposition between 'image' and 'reality'. Consequently, the title *Labour Camp* figures in the text as if it were an obvious enough insult in itself, and the verdict of a 'shallow' style is formulated through a thinly-veiled homophobia, directed in particular towards Peter Mandelson and Chris Smith.

Why should the account of a residually Thatcherite critic and the theoretically moribund usage of 'style' and 'substance' as mutually exclusive entities be of interest here? I would suggest that the terms employed in *Labour Camp* are worth noting precisely because of their *familiarity*, because of the extent to which such commentaries on Labour's cultural policies had, by 1998 if not earlier, become hegemonic within certain sections of the media. In this respect, the book was echoing, as well as eliciting, many other media reports about Labour's concern with 'style' over 'substance'.[2]

Let us take another example which focuses on the cultural policies and discourses being promoted by New Labour. In an extended feature article in *Guardian Weekend* in November 1998, similar terms were differently mobilised by Jonathan Glancey, who bemoaned the current state of 'dumbed-down' British culture, arguing that it merely offered a watered-down culture packaged in the wrapping of free enterprise. This has been caused, he argued, primarily by well-educated, well-meaning liberals who have unwittingly betrayed the populace. Their pursuit of 'democratic' art has necessarily produced a populist culture in which second-rate art is encouraged at the expense of that which could have been great.[3]

What both these arguments have in common is not only a shared distaste for Labour's cultural policies, but an identification of the fact that the cultural policies introduced since the government came into office in 1997 have consistently articulated and promoted a connection between 'culture' and 'industry'. Whilst it is easy to sympathise with the issues that prompt Glancey's critique, the danger in this article is similar to that in *Labour Camp*, namely the tendency to throw out the notion of democratic art, to revive the idea of 'the great', and to mix these discourses with one recommending expanded access. To look at this from another angle, both accounts, whilst pinpointing that something is rotten in the cultural state of Labour, are problematic precisely because of the way they *interpret* this newly manifested connection between discourses of 'consumerism' and the 'culture' which causes them so much displeasure.

Historically, the intersection between 'culture' and 'industry' has been a theoretical space in which distinctly undemocratic prejudices have crept in, often unannounced ('high culture' was a phenomenon constructed not only through an opposition to mass culture and consumption, but to their synonyms, the lower-class and the feminine) and this is certainly the case here, in Bayley's snobbery about 'Nescafé society' and Glancey's return to 'the great'.[4] The issue therefore becomes how to understand and find a suitable language in which to identify New Labour's cultural policies without collapsing into the pitfalls of either idealising 'culture' as a space separate from the rest of the social world or, conversely, of celebrating any linkage between culture and industry as necessarily emancipatory by virtue of cultural diffusion, a position only too compatible with neo-liberal economics. It is helpful, I suggest, to locate an analysis of this particular conjunction between culture and industry in relation to an understanding of the history of British cultural policy and the politics of discourses of consumerism. To these ends, this chapter will look at policies on culture alongside the more diffusive, *discursive* effects of New Labour's allegiances.

CULTURE, SOCIETY AND THE STATE

To analyse the relationship between cultural policy and commerce under New Labour it is instructive to return to and reassess some of the ways in which the relationship between culture, cultural policy and commerce has been historicised and theorised by the left. As Raymond Williams demonstrated so persuasively and eloquently all those years ago in *Culture and Society*, the separation off of 'culture' as a relatively autonomous space can be historically located in the transformations of industrial modernity. The construction of a sphere which was formulated as beyond the material, political, social and economic, emerged as part and parcel of a system of industrialised labour organised around the pursuit of capital. The meaning of culture changed from the tending of crops, animals and, by extension, people, to become an independent noun meaning a system of objects and attitudes which were cordoned off from, and which were thought of as transcending, society. Infused in Romantic thought, packaged through individuated authorship, 'Culture' gradually came to function as both a sanitising disclaimer of this system and as a marketable product unto 'itself'.[5]

In their recent book *Culture and the State*, David Lloyd and Paul Thomas revisit *Culture and Society*. Like many other recent commentaries they argue that Williams's work contains a strain of romanticism, noting that in his writing what 'remains as a powerful presence is a vestigial conception of culture representing the possibility of "the whole man" against the division of labour'.[6] They argue that in his idea of culture as 'a whole way of life', Williams retains the idea of culture as a possibly utopian site but wants to give this a socialist inflection; he implicitly pursues a project of 'saving culture by making it socialist'.

This text is not alone in locating a streak of Romanticism in Williams's work.[7] Where it differs from some other critical re-evaluations, however, is that its outcome is neither the recommendation of positivist empirical scrutiny as the only legitimate mode of cultural analysis (the idea that 'truth' can be found in the details), nor the wholesale dismissal of Williams. Rather, acknowledging its own relationship to the founding text, it sympathetically traces and critiques Williams's conceptual trajectories and suggests that his schema can be re-theorised by drawing from Gramscian and post-structuralist theory as well as from occluded Chartist narratives. I want to summarise their analysis here, as it provides a useful frame for understanding Labour's cultural policies and affiliations, as well as providing suggestions for a more progressive politics.

Lloyd and Thomas emphasise that not only was culture established to compensate and function as a substitution for the alienation of labour, but that 'aesthetic culture becomes the ground or condition of possibility both for thinking and forging the human subject'.[8] They suggest that the notion of 'culture' was developed not in opposition to society so much as to provide the *principle* through which individuals became citizens for the state (p67). To some extent this echoes – as well as Williams's and E.P. Thompson's work – Foucauldian-inflected commentaries which have astutely elaborated upon how 'culture' was deployed throughout the nineteenth century as a mechanism for dispelling 'anarchy' (to use Matthew Arnold's terms) and disseminated through a range of institutions and practices to induce the formation of a civil and docile populace.[9] (To take but one frequently cited example, a key reason why London's National Gallery was built in Trafalgar Square was because it was a popular site for public demonstrations – it was explicitly hoped that the gallery would have 'a softening effect'.[10]) But where Lloyd and Thomas offer a new and useful perspective is to link this usage of 'culture' to the *politicality* of the modern state. Highlighting how the process by which aesthetic culture became separated as a distinct sphere paralleled the rise of representative democracy, they argue that culture and the modern state are coeval: that they bring each other's terms into being.

Foregrounding the extent to which having a representative system – that is, having someone to speak *for* a constituency – was resisted and eloquently argued against, of how it 'was not easy to gain acceptance for the notion that being represented was the normative mode of one's relation to political life',[11] *Culture and the State* argues that the 'representative' mode came to shape both cultural institutions and aesthetic ideals. This discourse around 'culture' provided the terms of what being a citizen and being a state meant. As the state came to mean 'the best self' rather than a conjoined whole, so too 'the function of culture' became 'to cultivate the identity between the ideal or ethical man in every object and the state which is its representative' (pp46-53). This ideology of *being represented* was therefore echoed and facilitated by an expanded and idealised notion of culture; and likewise by cultural institutions which were becoming increasingly 'sectioned-off' from other processes and realms, particularly that of work.

For instance, examples of the former include how the poet becomes a representative of all men, speaking *to* rather than amongst them; and how schools became a mode in which a teacher, representing the state and knowledge, imparted wisdom unto their pupils (pp20, 79). And as culture became a space which functioned to educe a citizen from a human being, it could of course be used as a space in which a struggle towards an endlessly deferred process of becoming 'fully human' could take place. In this way, culture as a separate sphere was explicitly used as the basis to delay further enfranchisement. Whereas the (proto-Gramscian) Chartist position argued that working produced relevant knowledge, the classic Victorian liberal position argued that disinterested education must precede the vote (pp83-4). Education in this formulation explicitly meant *distance* from labour. The sectioning out of spheres was, therefore, crucial in dismantling the opposition to mutual democratic forms of cultural politics, and in particular, Lloyd and Thomas argue that the extent of the *struggle* over this terrain, and the degree of critical consciousness of this by the Chartists and others, has been totally obscured.[12]

I cite *Culture and the State* at length here for two reasons. Firstly, its account is important because it exhaustively demolishes any remaining strands of credibility for the still entrenched idea that 'culture' can function as a utopian space outside of, or acting as consolation for, social conditions. The left has a long history of investing in a notion of that reified by-product of industrial capitalism, high culture. As Alan Sinfield, terming this phenomenon 'left-culturism', puts it, 'the idea that culture transcends material conditions has a strong socialist lineage'.[13] *Culture and the State* implicitly poses as its alternative a range of sites which offer mutual, democratic participation beyond that of the *representative* model – not a theoretical model which is new on the left, but one whose legacy in terms of recent cultural policy has tended to become obscured.[14] Secondly, its focus on the politics of the relationship between governments, cultural institutions and the uses of 'culture' provides us with both a historical perspective with which to think through New Labour's cultural policies and with a political frame with which to trace their connections to previous governmental formulations of culture. If we look at *Creative Britain*, the 1998 collection of official speeches and pieces by the Minister for Culture Chris Smith, for example, a glaringly obvious and pervasive motif which remains, alongside the (sporadic) strategies for 'inclusion', is that 'culture' is in many ways fundamentally a separate sphere.

PRIVATE LIVES

Creative Britain has a clear investment, and I use the term deliberately, in the notion of 'culture' as a realm of individualised creativity. We are told that 'individual creativity is where it starts'; and the notion of culture which is being mobilised owes a great deal to a Romantic notion of high culture, with Smith informing us that it can 'lead us into a deeper world than that which exists on the surface'.[15] The extent of the stake in this notion is apparent even as he is exhorting us to embrace what might previously have been described as 'low' cultural forms:

> The deepest cultural experiences will frequently come, for all of us, from the heights of fine opera or the sweeping sounds of a classical orchestra or the emotional torment of high drama. But we shouldn't ignore the rest of cultural activity at the same time (p4).

The assumption here is clearly that the aesthetic of the sublime, of a romantic excess of feeling, is what fundamentally counts, and this is why he is trying hard not to ignore other cultural models (for which read 'the low'). The most important type of 'culture' functions as the 'fully human', a utopian site, a space for experiencing 'deep' emotions, to be encountered individually. In this respect, the separation of culture as a realm unto itself, the notion which emerged from liberal modernity and the gradual introduction of representative democracy, is still firmly in place.

But at the same time, this discourse has been accompanied by a multitude of actions which clearly do *not* mark the entrenchment of a notion of 'culture' as a separate sphere. To start with, Labour's renaming the Department of Heritage the Department of 'Culture, Media and Sport' (DCMS), and the concomitant widening of its remit, necessarily involved an expansion of the meaning of 'culture' deployed by the government. Drawn away from a notion of 'heritage', which was often regarded as reactionary, anachronistic and nostalgic (particularly, but not exclusively, by critics on the left), the Department now encompasses a far broader field, one in which for the first time culture is brought 'down' to the same discursive level as sport and the media.

Secondly, there has been the encouragement of areas which would once have been regarded as 'low' culture, despite Smith's occasional need to cordon off particular areas with the velvet rope of true cultural worth: *Creative Britain* is stacked with references to popular music, cinema and design. Certainly, the fact that the distinctions between 'high' and 'low' culture are collapsing does not go unnoticed. High and low cultural forms are to be linked, however, through the idea that they should be disseminated and conjoined with industry.

The value accorded to the individual and to individualism is a central motif of *Creative Britain* and of policies like NESTA, the National Endowment for Science, Technology and the Arts. This was primarily conceived to 'help talented individuals develop their full potential'; secondly to 'turn creativity into products and services which we can exploit in the global market'; and thirdly to convince the public and business of this agenda (p30). The key link being made is between *individualised* creativity and the market:

> The Creative Industries as a whole are big business. They are the fields in which jobs have been created and will be created, into the next century. And they all depend ultimately in the talent of an individual or the intellectual property that is created in order to succeed. That is why I welcome all moves to increase exchanges between the cultural and business world (p51).

What this rhetoric does is retain the ideology of high culture in the sense of individualised creativity and genius, and to disseminate this into an increasingly expansive cultural field – one which now includes 'high' and 'low' culture – with the primary aim of financial profit. We might say that the ideology of the 'separate spheres' as discussed in *Culture and the State* is present *qualitatively*, in that 'culture' is still an individually nurtured or private quality which is created in a space distinct from the rest of social life.

And so the entrepreneurial creative subject addressed by *Creative Britain* is a descendent of Enlightenment man who pursues his private self-defined interests, autonomously constructs his own identity and products, and to whom the State's rightful role is one of facilitation.[16] In its current form, this is part of a larger project: Sylvia Bashevkin has identified as a key third way theme the increasing role of political leaders to operate as facilitators between individuals and corporations, in which individuals are encouraged to take what corporations offer. She adds that it is a project which goes hand in hand with the treatment of NGOs as less important than business-achieving individuals, and an increasing moral agenda of personal responsibility.[17] Similarly, in *Creative Britain* – while 'social inclusion' is nominally on the agenda, and social regeneration gets an occasional mention – the primary term is *individualism*, either backed up by, or as a means of achieving, economic growth.

ENTREPRENEURIAL LEGACIES

We can understand more about this cultural policy discourse by locating it in the history of post-war cultural provision, in relation to what Jim McGuigan has termed the slow movement from traditional social democratic arts funding to one based around 'economistic' principles.[18] I want to discuss this by focusing on how other historical models have negotiated the conjunction between commerce and culture.

Creative Britain, as already mentioned, relentlessly pushes to centre stage the relationship between culture and industry. Whether discussing art galleries, music, heritage sites or contemporary films, Smith has continually been at pains to point out the economic benefits of the arts, of the financial profitability of culture. '[W]e have recognized' he states at the beginning of the book, 'the importance of this whole new industrial sector that no-one hitherto has even conceived of as an industry' (p26). However, this fashioning of areas in 'the arts' as industries is deeply indebted to, on the one hand, Thatcherism – prior to which mentioning the arts and money in a shared cultural breath was by and large anathema – and on the other, left models of cultural provision, most significantly developed in the practice of the Greater London Council during the 1980s.

Thatcherism attempted to fashion state arts bodies in the image of corporate business practice. The previous 'gentlemanly' agreements of cross-party appointments were by and large abolished; the lines of privilege and institutions previously dominated by the 'snobbocracy' (the Old-Boy white aristocratic network) were infiltrated and snipped by the entrepreneurial New Boys (the white, self-made businessman network). Cuts in state subsidies, demands for accountability and efficiency savings, and the refashioning of institutions in managerial terms were accompanied by a welter of attempts to encourage business sponsorship in the arts. The extensive use of public money to privilege and support the private sector took place through mechanisms such as Office of Arts and Libraries leaflets proclaiming that *The Arts are Your*

Business, through the extension of such bodies as The Association for Business Sponsorship in the Arts (ABSA), and by the 1984 formation of the Business Sponsorship Incentive Scheme (BSIS).[19]

An alternative model explicitly connecting cultural policy to consumer culture was produced by the Greater London Council, in which the agenda was to politicise mass cultural forms and develop pleasure, skills and social cohesion in local communities.[20] Alongside the Greater London Enterprise Board, the GLC established community recording studios, non-commercial video distribution in public libraries, and independent and radical book distribution co-ops and publishing houses. This 'progressive cultural industries approach' emanated from the GLC's Economic Policy Group rather than its Arts and Recreation Committee. Producing reports and a major conference, *Cultural Industries and Cultural Policy in London*, the Economic Policy Group 'showed how important the cultural sector is to London's economy [and] concluded that public policy should treat the cultural sector as a co-ordinated whole'.[21] Whilst it was not, as Franco Bianchini has pointed out, the most highly financed of the GLC's cultural policies, it had significant impact as a new idea. In a radical departure from the policy-making tradition of the left, it involved working *through* rather than *against* the market.

Both of these projects linked explicit signifiers of consumer culture to cultural production in different ways. Thatcherism dismantled the previous social democratic/liberal consensus to create policies which effectively extended a High Art discourse through – and into – wider corporate use, thereby compounding the undemocratic tendencies pre-existing within the state 'arts' sector. The GLC enabled co-operative community groups and organisations to deploy technologies more readily associated with mass production and consumption in order to develop useful skills and redistribute cultural power. It attempted to fashion *alternative cultural markets*.

The very enthusiasm of the DCMS for the cultural industries has been a key part of its new identity. Like the old GLC activities, it attempts to influence the sites producing cultural products or services, but unlike those practices, it has tended not to do this for an end goal of cultural democracy or community integration. At one moment in New Labour's pre-history, attention was actually given to this type of cultural politics. In 1986 Geoff Mulgan and Ken Worpole published their *Saturday Night or Sunday Morning?*, a book doubling as a historical excavation of left cultural policies and polemical manifesto, urging Labour to adopt more of the culturally populist strategies of the

GLC.[22] Now the senior figure at the No. 10 Policy Unit, however, Mulgan seems to have done little to prevent the wholesale marginalisation of this agenda.

Instead, the cultural policies and affiliations of New Labour draw significantly from those established under Thatcherism in their emphasis on economic growth or profit. The rhetoric of individualistic Romanticism is entirely compatible with Thatcherite entrepreneurialism, and the renaming and widening of the remit of the Department of Heritage now looks at least as much due to the governmental 'recognition' of the economic potential of the cultural industries as to an anti-elitist agenda. It is noticeable that the only 'shape-up' speech in *Creative Britain* is delivered to libraries. Indeed the sponsorship initiatives of the Thatcher years are not merely praised but encouraged and extended into an approach which asks not merely what business can do for the arts, but what the arts can do for business:

> The growth of business sponsorship has not just brought in useful cash, but expertise and experience too. This is now changing – and rightly so – into a two-way process. It has become clear that we also need to look at the benefits the creative approaches of the arts can in turn bring to business. Increasingly, the qualities demanded for business – such as communication skills, flexibility of approach, improvisational and creative thinking, working as a team so that the parts add up to a whole – are precisely those that can be inculcated through exposure to the arts (p54).

This goes beyond even the arts-meets-business policies established under Thatcher, taking the insights of the GLC cultural industries projects and deploying them according to an agenda which begins and ends with the pursuit of profit. This idea that 'the arts' can bring 'creativity' to business intersects with the perceived 'feminisation' of industry and with attempts to integrate signifiers of leisure into certain types of 'flexecutive' workplaces, as well as with the new-age discourse of holism in contemporary business practice that Karen Salamon explores elsewhere in this volume. It is also a key term for New Labour anti-politics; as Liz Greenhalgh astutely points out, in Blairite discourse, 'creativity is positive, light, the essential human spirit, boundless and free, whilst "ideology" is the old repressor'.[23] In a similar vein, the banal and ubiquitous phrase 'excellence' springs from the pages of 1980s management theory, particularly a book by Thomas Peters and Robert Waterman, *In Search of Excellence: Lessons from America's Best-Run companies*. As the self-help manual of radical democratic organisations, *What a Way to Run a Railroad*, commented as far back as 1985, it 'has seemed recently to be the fate of Excellence to be championed by the mediocre in the interests of the worst'.[24]

NEW LABOUR AND THE SENSATION GENERATION

I want to turn now to looking at New Labour's cultural affiliations in a more discursive sense by examining the politics of that much-discussed exhibition of 1997, *Sensation: Young British Artists From the Saatchi Collection*. Staged in the Royal Academy, traditionally the most 'Middle England' of metropolitan art institutions,[25] *Sensation* was easily able to bounce off the reflected dullness of the Academy's reputation to fashion and hone its avant-garde credentials. Indeed, this was necessary for both the display and for the institution. The main trope of both the exhibition's promotion and the media coverage it generated was that of the 'shock aesthetics' of its pieces, pieces including Marcus Harvey's image of Myra Hindley, *Myra*, Damien Hirst's stuffed shark, and Jake and Dinos Chapman's sculptures of children with penis-sprouting foreheads. Staging this event was guaranteed to alienate a segment (enough, but not too much) of the Royal Academy's steady audience and *The Daily Mail*; and simultaneously, and for exactly the same reason, it was guaranteed to expand vastly the host institution's promotional power. It worked, becoming the most profitable exhibition of the year, rescuing the supposedly ailing Academy from a considerable proportion of its debts.

The New Labour government lent enthusiastic support to the project. Tony Blair announced that a work by the artist Mark Francis, similar to his piece in *Sensation*, was to appear on his walls in Downing Street. 'He may' suggested a spokesman, 'use his office to promote works by British artists that are proving an international success'.[26] In *Creative Britain* Chris Smith praises the sculptor Rachel Whiteread (most famous for producing *House*, a temporary concrete cast of the interior of a terraced house in Bow) and refers to Damien Hirst as a good example of one of the 'skilled, creative people' that are, for him, reinvigorating Britain's cultural economy.[27] A Hirst painting even adorns the book's dust-jacket.

In several respects the government's endorsement of the *Sensation* generation was very easy to read. A publicity-seeking exhibition which hyped its 'youthful' identity, the 'BritArt' of *Sensation* was being heavily promoted by its network of vested interests as a ready and available signifier of national renewal. For the government, association with this helped to consolidate and amplify its keywords of *new*, *youth* and *nation* in that particular post-election moment. But exactly what set of values and interests were being promoted here? To understand what was at stake in this we can take a closer look at the cultural politics of the exhibition and its intersection with wider discursive formations.

SHARK AESTHETICS

Given that the artworks in *Sensation* were very visibly the property of Charles Saatchi, synonymous in British political culture with advertising (as co-founder of Saatchi & Saatchi) as well as with Thatcherism (Saatchi & Saatchi helped the 1979 election victory with their 'Labour Isn't Working' campaign), it is appropriate to consider further the discursive connections between the exhibition and the world of advertising.

A key cultural corollary of the exhibition lies in the 'shock' advertising techniques beloved of certain practitioners of second-wave advertising. Focusing on more closely defined niche-markets, 'second-wave' advertising marked its difference from previous advertising techniques by not so much dwelling on a product's unique selling point in adverts as marketing it through association with lifestyle aesthetics and cinematic or innovative visual effects. The clothing company Benetton became the arch example of a company using these shock techniques: shifting its advertising strategy in 1991 from one of multi-sweatered multiculturalism, its creative director and photographer Oliviero Toscani began to use a campaign based around controversial photographs, including images of a nun kissing a priest, a new-born baby covered in blood, a man who had been shot, black and white hands in handcuffs, and, perhaps most notoriously, an image of a man dying from AIDS.

The Benetton campaign interpellated two main consumer subjectivities: the media-savvy consumer, tired of conventional product advertising; and a socially aware consumer who might be counted on to appreciate the company's 'honesty' in displaying iconic images of contemporary suffering. As Carol Squires puts it, the campaign indicated that 'denial in the service of upbeat consumerism is no longer a workable strategy as we are continually overwhelmed by disturbing and even cataclysmic events'.[28] Benetton extended this into a moral justification, stressing that it was being socially responsible by presenting the 'realities of contemporary society', and the argument that it enabled images of cultural and political tragedy and oppression to be widely circulated gained the campaign high profile supporters such as Spike Lee. The campaign also addressed a section of the media who, successfully shocked, would seize on its controversial new strategies as newsworthy, thereby providing free publicity and boosting Benetton's brand awareness.[29] The discourse at work was one of shock aesthetics delivering a shot of *necessary truths* to its consumer constituency. In short, it offered a type of sensational, avant-garde realism.

We can see how this discourse worked its way through to the contemporary images constructed around an aesthetic of shock in *Sensation*. In Henry Giroux's critique of the Benetton campaign's cultural aesthetics, he writes that they offer 'a type of "hyperventilating" realism (a realism of sensationalism, shock, horror and spectacle)' in which 'they are stripped of their political possibilities and reduced to a spectacle of fascination, horror and terror that appears to privatise one's response to events'. It would not be far-fetched to say the same of *Myra*. Whilst *Sensation* differed on certain grounds (dwelling more on the attempt to upset what it imagined to be bourgeois sensibilities, and less on manipulating liberal sensibilities) it shared much of the same agenda. Both Benetton's advertising strategies and *Sensation* participated in a shared discursive formation of privatised immobility and an ethics of superior distance. For example, within the exhibition's promotional frame, Richard Billingham's photographs of his working-class family are rendered as an anthropological encounter, a curiosity validated through the viewpoint of an 'insider'. It is worth noting that there is no democracy of the gaze in the photographs; nothing is reciprocated.[30]

Labour's implicit or explicit support for the *Sensation* generation continued that of the Conservatives; Chris Smith's predecessor, Virginia Bottomley, had praised Damien Hirst's work on the grounds that 'All art is meant to disturb'.[31] The work was validated through the discourse that the function of art is to display and reveal unpalatable and necessary truths. What was being legitimated and reinscribed by both Bottomley and Smith's support, then, was the notion of the importance of an avant-garde.

Labour, however, became identified as sympathetic to this cultural formation to a degree way beyond that implied by Bottomley's taut message of approval. In doing so it legitimated a second key feature of *Sensation*, that of its populism: the exhibition was in part supported simply because of the breadth and volume of its coverage, because of its discursive reach. In an unprecedented move, the London listings magazine *Time Out* – one of the exhibition's sponsors – offered its version of a *Sensation* catalogue as a pull-out supplement. The exhibition also had a symbiotic relationship with the tabloid press: the dealer of the majority of the artists tipped off *The Sun* about its potentially offensive content, and in return *The Sun* gave the exhibition a barrage of scandalised coverage; as one commentator put it, 'contemporary art has grown both popular and deliciously weird from the tabloid's point of view'.[32] Going out of its way to disseminate an avant-garde discourse to a wider audience, the exhibition's visual jokes or concepts (Damien Hirst's shark, Sarah Lucas's kebab representing a vagina on a table-top) were easily accessible, not demanding the usual amount of cultural capital of its audience; the exhibition, as Angela McRobbie has pointed out, 'self-consciously staged itself as shocking but was also completely unintimidating'.[33]

But at the same time *Sensation* referred to little beyond its own shocking puns: there was little if any engagement with social issues, and an almost complete disregard for the cultural politics or histories of its subjects. The exception, out of this exhibition of work by forty-two artists, was Yinka Shonibare's post-colonial reworking of Victoriana, and while we might cite some artists' later output for evidence of more political engagement (such as Chris Ofili's painting about Stephen Lawrence's murder, *No Woman, No Cry*), it is important not to lose sight of the fact that it was the identity and branding of the *exhibition* which was influential. Here, as with the Benetton campaign, the 'necessary truths' it delivered were largely context-free. As Carol Squires has memorably pointed out, Benetton's uncaptioned images of social breakdown were reduced to icons of universalised contemporary tragedy, images pointing not towards understanding of their social and political context but to a privatised immobility to be participated in by a social group for which buying clothes is both signifier and consolation.[34] The Benetton campaign offered a kind of immobilising pessimism, smug in its apparently alienated knowledge, disabling to any kind of agency for positive change. It is no coincidence that Benetton is often invoked as a neo-liberal post-fordist company which has kept its overheads down by employing poorly paid female subcontractors, and that company head Luciano Benetton has doubled as right-wing senator in the Italian Parliament, vigorously promoting policies of deregulation of the marketplace and limiting state intervention.[35] The advertising discourse of privatised immobility is not accidental.

Likewise, *Sensation* marked a new use being found for contemporary visual arts; it functioned as a tool which:

> can now be relied upon to deliver particular audiences, broadly speaking the social categories AB and C1, and more specifically, the design and style-conscious young opinion-formers. The problem for businesses

trying to reach these influential but marketing-literate categories of consumers is that they do not respond favourably to conventional advertising and marketing techniques.[36]

In these terms, in its attempt to reach what Bourdieu calls 'new cultural intermediaries', the exhibition functioned as a type of conventionally delineated advertising, only with a displaced identity, all the more effective for its concealed status. In this sense, *Sensation* inversely paralleled adverts' like Benetton's attempts to claim the status of art. Just as 'art' adverts make little reference to the products they purport to advertise, the *Sensation* exhibits made no reference to the social world which avant-garde art purports to critique. The promotional network surrounding and constituting the exhibition meant that *Sensation* was a moment of synergistic marketing between those with vested interests in it, particularly Charles Saatchi, the YBAs, Christies, the Royal Academy and *Time Out*. This is not to say that there is anything wrong with marketing *per se* – it can be used, amongst other things, to market democratic ideas – merely that what was being marketed in this case was a politically conservative discourse, one which simultaneously swelled the ever-expanding wallet of Charles Saatchi and friends.

THE KEN SENSATION

But if the YBAs are so apolitical, in contrast to the offerings of the GLC's cultural policies, then what were they doing in the spring of 2000 explicitly supporting Ken Livingstone in his campaign to become mayor of London?[37] Is this not contradictory? Firstly, I would suggest that it was indicative of the politics of location: the YBAs displayed their identification with the metropolis in order to maintain an image of urban bohemianism. Secondly, the event of the Mayoral election itself was perceived as 'less political', offering minimal significant power, alongside the endorsement of 'personality politics' through the appointment of a 'face' for London. And thirdly, Livingstone enlisted their support because he was seen to offer an alternative to party politics. In one sense this is not a bad thing, since it demonstrated the enduring legacy of the GLC in reaching new constituencies of support and mobilising enthusiasm for a progressive agenda – an ability to reach parts that political parties failed to reach. On the other hand, the alignment of the YBAs with Livingstone occurred precisely because he was seen to be a 'rebel' against 'the system'; in short, it is an avant-garde politics of critiquing without participating.

However, and more worryingly, in terms of the policies of New Labour – or more encouragingly, should we choose to look at it in terms of the political 'maturity' of the YBAs – in one selective sense this critique is right: it rails against the rigid authoritarianism and managerialism offered by New Labour. Despite the affection of both for corporate cool, the libertarian ethos of the YBAs clashes with the authoritarianism of Labour's agenda. The mismatch between these discourses was one reason why 'Cool Britannia' looked so ridiculous so quickly.[38]

The unique selling point of *Sensation*, as many commentators have pointed out, was its perceived status as BritArt[TM]:[39] a symbol of the current 'state' of both British cultural practice and the new political culture. It was recognisably part of the same cultural formation as *Creative Britain* and Mark Leonard's *Rebranding Britain* report for the Demos think tank, thereby adding to its newsworthy appeal for the broadsheets.[40] Just as the exhibition promoted the 'mediators, brokers and diversifiers' of the *Sensation* generation, so has the keynote of the DCMS been to promote the popular-and-profitable, and so too has the mantra of *Creative Britain* been that 'the arts' are a resource to be exploited.

FROM 'HOUSE' TO POWERHOUSE

Culture and the State identified the emergence of a distinct mode of 'Culture' as coeval with the emergence of the representative modern state, with its more repressive, and exclusionary aspects. These legacies are apparent in New Labour's discourse in several ways.

Firstly, the liberal discourse of 'Culture' as constituting the under-standing of works of creativity and genius – a discourse which was deployed to separate the 'civilised' from the 'uncivilised' – still has its place in New Labour's understanding of culture. This discourse of culture as the 'fully human' is now, however, primarily deployed not as a means of social division but in order to assist the accumulation of corporate capital. New Labour's cultural field has been licensed to expand by virtue of its capacity to deliver economic profit: at the heart of this definition of culture is an equation in which 'culture' can now only qualify as 'culture' if it is corporate – priorities which fit snugly into a wider governmental agenda that Anthony Barnett has termed *corporate populism*.[41]

The deference towards corporations, and the acceptance and encouragement of the global economy as a force of nature, is New Labour's primary point of orientation, as a quick glance around the Millennium Dome – a showcase for assorted businesses and a material polemic in favour of 'flexible specialisation' – will reveal. Whilst the function of the nation state is now clearly very different from the 1950s, we might compare the Dome with the enormously popular 1951 Festival of Britain, which also had a trade function: sections of the South Bank exhibition were designed to improve the sales and image of British goods. The key difference between the Festival and the Dome, however, was that, firstly, in 1951 there was considerable government anxiety and direct intervention about the potential partisan promotion of products; secondly, commercial exhibitors were limited to a small element of the total display space; and thirdly, companies did not 'display themselves' – they did not have the governing principle and representational power over the exhibits. Rather than the individual companies autonomously bonding together to represent a fragmented commercial nation – which in some ways is exactly what the Dome does – it was for 'the nation' to decide how the individual companies were represented.[42]

In effect, the Dome formed what was rendered with a curious literalism at the Department of Trade and Industry's temporary showcase for British creative industries, the 1998 *powerhouse::uk* exhibition. Illustrating the theme 'Communicating' was a room-sized model of London made from a one-stop shop at Sainsburys. The miniature commodity-city was entirely constructed from branded goods – almost a sanitised, comic version of an anti-consumerist dystopia, complete with a baked-bean tin version of Battersea power station, in order to illustrate 'the city as a canvas for creativity as well as for inspiration'.[43] The exhibition was slightly more interesting and progressive than the Dome in its use of innovative display techniques, ergonomic designs, green solutions, and even a co-operative advertising firm, but the authoritarian discourse of facilitating corporate success remained.

The second point I have extrapolated from Lloyd and Thomas's analysis is how 'culture' became deployed as a separate sphere distinct from work. Under Blairism it would appear that we have the exact opposite of this, as the promotion of the term 'the cultural industries' – alongside the incorporation of signifiers of leisure and 'creativity' into certain strands of the workplace – illustrates. However, paradoxically, what remains is the discourse of culture and creativity as qualities which are both individual and *distinct* from that of wider social life. Consequently, there is little sense that the objects and aesthetics being promoted have a *politics* which connects to them. This, of course, is directly the opposite of the project pursued by cultural studies, which – in a genealogy we might trace in particular through the works of Williams and Bourdieu – took the expression 'there's no accounting for taste' and turned it on its head. There was *every* possibility of accounting for taste, and the importance of doing so was a critical and political necessity. Such insights, which appeared to be gaining ground in an earlier moment of Labour's cultural policies, have been explicitly marginalised.

Culture and the State also points to how 'Culture' became used as an authoritarian mechanism paralleling the rise of representative democracy in its structure of speaking *to* rather than *amongst* people, and marginalising Chartist calls for cultural activities which could be produced from, be integrated into and be relevant for daily life experience. Here we might cite that exhibition with its structure of self-absorbed statements, *Sensation,* which the government was so keen to promote, and Labour's constant addresses to 'the people'. Liz Greenhalgh, commenting on the frequency with which Blair has 'bolted the phrase "the people's" onto projects and princesses', has noticed that alongside the more egalitarian impulses inherent in the phrase, there also lurks a claim to *represent* the people reminiscent of Thatcher's authoritarian populism.[43] To apply the insights of Lloyd and Thomas, we can see in Labour the attempt to form a culture which is representative rather than participative. While its cultural rhetoric addresses 'the many rather than the few', New Labour promotes cultural forms which are authoritarian, rather than policies and discourses which are democratic in terms of participation and access. At present, 'culture' and 'creativity' mean little more than entrepreneurial brio inflected with some of the repressive seriousness of high art, a discourse more dependent on creative accounting than on an activated desire for democracy.

NOTES

1. Stephen Bayley, *Labour Camp: The Failure Of Style Over Substance,* Batsford, London 1998, p125.
2. See also Timothy Bewes, 'Truth and Appearance in Politics: The Mythology of Spin' in this volume.
3. Jonathan Glancey, in *Guardian Weekend,* 21 November 1998.
4. For discussions of the elision of mass consumption with the feminine and lower-class, see Andreas Huyssen, *After the Great Divide: Modernism, Mass Culture, Postmodernism,* Macmillan, Basingstoke 1988; Mica Nava, 'Modernity's Disavowal: Women, the City and the Department Store', in M. Nava and A. O'Shea (eds), *Modern Times: Reflections on a century of English modernity,* Routledge, London 1996.
5. Raymond Williams, *Culture and Society: Coleridge to Orwell,* Hogarth, London 1987.

6. David Lloyd and Paul Thomas, *Culture and the State*, Routledge, London 1998, p14.

7. For example, Ian Hunter, *Culture and Government: The Emergence of Literary Education*, Macmillan, London 1988.

8. Lloyd and Thomas, *op. cit.*, p42.

9. See, for example, Tony Bennett, *The Birth of the Museum: History Theory Politics*, Routledge, London 1995; Jim McGuigan, *Culture and the Public Sphere*, Routledge, London 1996.

10. McGuigan, *op. cit.*, p55.

11. Lloyd and Thomas, *op. cit.*, p58.

12. What is noticeable by its absence in *Culture and the State* – although the authors explicitly highlight this – are the gendered and imperial dynamics of this process. It is relatively easy, however, to see how such an account could be compatible with the slower incorporation of women into a system of representative democracy.

13. Alan Sinfield, *Literature Politics and Culture in Post-war Britain* (Second Edition), The Athlone Press, London 1997, p242

14. We could cite both 1970s community arts projects and the GLC projects discussed later in this chapter.

15. Chris Smith *Creative Britain*, Faber & Faber, London 1998, pp147, 23.

16. See Don Slater, *Consumer Culture and Modernity*, Polity Press, Cambridge 1997, pp38-9.

17. Sylvia Bashevkin, 'The Challenge of Personhood: Women's Citizenship in Contemporary Perspective', at *Women's Equality and Participation in Public Life in Canada and the UK* conference, Canada House, 21 October 1999.

18. McGuigan, *op. cit.*

19. See Chin-Tao Wu, *Privatising Culture: Aspects of Corporate Intervention in Contemporary Art and Art Institutions During the Reagan and Thatcher Decade* (DPhil thesis, UCL 1997; forthcoming from Verso).

20. Franco Bianchini, 'GLC R.I.P.: Cultural Policies in London, 1981-1986', *New Formations* No. 1 (Spring 1987).

21. *Ibid.*, p111.

22. Geoff Mulgan and Ken Worpole, *Saturday Night or Sunday Morning? From Arts to Industry – New Forms of Cultural Policy*, Comedia, London 1986.

23. Liz Greenhalgh, 'From Arts Policy to Creative Economy' in *Media International Australia Incorporating Culture and Policy* No. 87, May 1998, p89.

24. Landry et al, *What a Way to Run a Railroad: An Analysis of Radical Failure*, Comedia, London 1985, p56.

25. For accounts of the history of the Royal Academy see Gordon Fyfe, 'A Trojan Horse at the Tate: Theorizing the museum as agency and structure' in

Sharon Macdonald and Gordon Fyfe (eds), *Theorising Museums*, Blackwell, Oxford 1996, pp217-8 and Sidney C. Hutchinson, *The History of the Royal Academy 1786-1986* (Second Edition), Robert Royce Ltd, London 1986.

26. Dan Glaister, *Guardian*, 10 October 1997.

27. Smith, *op. cit.*, p147.

28. Carol Squires, 'Violence at Benetton', *ArtForum*, May 1992, p19.

29. Benetton's profits rose 24% when the campaign started in 1990-1, and its brand recognition rose sharply 'to a level approaching that of *Coca-Cola*'. See Henry A. Giroux, 'Consuming Social Change: The "United Colours of Benetton"' in *Cultural Critique*, Winter 1994, p9.

30. *Sensation: Young British Artists from the Saatchi Collection*, Thames and Hudson, London.

31. Bottomley is quoting Georges Braque. Cited in Andy Beckett, 'Shock Art to Shop Art', *Guardian* G2 28 August 1997.

32. Liz Jobey, 'A Rat Race' *Guardian Weekend* 4 October 1997.

33. Angela McRobbie, 'But Is It Art?' *Marxism Today*, November 1998, p56.

34. Squires, *op. cit.*

35. Robin Murray, 'Benetton Britain: The New Economic Order' in Stuart Hall and Martin Jacques, *New Times: The Changing Face of Politics in the 1990s*, Lawrence & Wishart, London 1989; Swasti Mitter, *Common Fate, Common Bond: Women in the Global Economy*, Pluto Press, London 1990.

36. Simon Ford and Anthony Davies, 'Art Capital', in *Art Monthly*, No. 213, February 1998, pp3-4.

37. Many young Britist artists including Tracey Emin, Damien Hirst and the Chapman Brothers donated works to auction for Livingstone's campaign. See Fiachra Gibbons, 'Brit art stars boost Livingstone campaign', *Guardian* 1 April 2000, p6.

38. Jeremy Gilbert has discussed a similar relationship between Britpop and Blairism. See his 'Blurred Vision: Pop, Populism and Politics' in Anne Coddington and Mark Perryman (eds), *The Moderniser's Dilemma: Radical Politics in the Age of Blair*, Lawrence & Wishart, London 1998.

39. William Feaver, 'Myra, Myra on the wall ...' *Observer* 21 September 1997.

40. Mark Leonard, *Britain^tm: Renewing Our Identity*, Demos, London 1997.

41. For a discussion of Anthony Barnett's use of this term and related themes see Michael Rustin, 'The New Labour ethic and the spirit of capitalism' in *Soundings* Issue 14 (Spring 2000) p116.

42. Letter from Gordon Russell to Gerald Barry, 20 April 1948, Council of Industrial Design Papers, Design Council Archive; Ian Cox, *The South Bank Exhibition: A Guide to the Story it Tells*, HMSO, London 1951.

43. Claire Catterall (ed), *powerhouse::uk*, Aspen Publishing, London 1998, p7.

44. Greenhalgh, *op. cit.*, p92

Beyond the hegemony of New Labour

JEREMY GILBERT

HEGEMONY? WHAT HEGEMONY?

New Labour has been criticised, especially in the issue of *Marxism Today* published in November 1998, and places close to it such as the journal *Soundings*, for lacking a 'hegemonic project'. But what does it mean to have a hegemonic project? In the loosest terms, a hegemonic project is what you get when one group in society sets out to convince a number of other groups that their interests will be well served by entering into a social coalition in which the hegemonic group is the leading partner. This process has been theorised in much more sophisticated terms by others, especially Ernesto Laclau and Chantal Mouffe,[1] but my definition holds good for the type of socio-political analysis with which I am going to begin.

For much of the 1980s, a particular section of the intellectual left berated the labour movement for failing to construct a hegemonic project, and had a reasonably clear idea as to what one might look like. It would involve the labour movement learning to speak the language of consumer society in order to talk to the public more clearly and convincingly about its core values of equality and democracy. It would use this language to put together a coalition much like that which was perceived to have been the basis for the electoral success of Ken Livingstone's Greater London Council, making people feel good about belonging to a multicultural democracy, channelling people's desires for material self-improvement into support for socialist policies such as the 'fares fair' campaign for cheaper public transport, generally making them feel that they would be better off and happier throwing in their lot with the sections of society which Labour had always represented than with the traditional, *Daily Mail*-reading Tory-voters of the home counties. Indeed, if only that small but influential section of the professional middle classes which had deserted Labour for the SDP and the Liberal Democrats could be brought on board, so went the argument, then we would never fear the Tories again: hence the many calls for a tactical alliance between the Liberal Democrats and Labour in the 1980s and early 1990s.

Labour's fundamental weakness, it was argued, was its failure to convince enough people that its world was anything to do with theirs. Its continued reliance, prior to the 1987-92 policy review, on an agenda dictated by the interests of industrial workers, was on a hiding to nothing when there were no longer – and would never be again – very many industrial workers to represent. The labour movement had to modernise, and in doing so to build a hegemonic project, to 'construct a politics, in the next twenty years, which is able to address itself not to one, but to a diversity of different points of antagonism in society; unifying them, in their differences, within a common project'.[2]

Much of the confusion that has arisen over New Labour in recent years can be attributed to the fact that New Labour has done precisely that, but not in the manner hoped for by the Gramscian left of the 1980s. For instance, the party has modernised, but has replaced the unwieldy and union-dominated bureaucracy of its old power-structures not with an expansive, inclusive, de-centralised, participatory and member-led form of organisation as many hoped for, but by a streamlined, centralised and wholly professionalised system of administration. More fundamentally, the social coalition which New Labour has articulated into a coherent formation, at least for the purposes of elections, is not one that anyone on the left had in mind when calling for a new popular front to turn back the tide of Thatcherism. It includes more of the people who had always voted Tory before 1997 than was ever envisaged as necessary to the success of that hoped for coalition, and it has appeared happy to exclude a large set of constituencies to its left: Labour's traditional working-class 'core voters', public sector workers, single parents, and so on. Indeed, one might observe that almost all of the groups who supported the Labour Party in 1983 – those six million who, in the words of Tony Benn, voted for socialism – are now excluded from the socio-political coalition which New Labour addresses as its own. This is partly because it has been assumed until recently that all of these groups will either vote Labour or not vote at all, so there is no need to court their support.

However, implicit in Blair's active hostility towards large sections of the public sector and the values which inform them is a further hope that New Labour can consolidate its support in the home counties to the point at which both the Tories and this broad left constituency become marginalised and isolated. In the wake of the European election results, when the Conservatives performed better and Labour worse than expected, we saw this emerging as the key point of debate within New Labour circles; implicit in the debate over how Labour's traditional core supporters could be enthused to turn out to vote is a deeper debate over whether or not New Labour can do without them altogether.

On the other hand, it is crucial to distinguish between New Labour and the Labour Party. New Labour is a formation comprising a section of the Labour leadership (most notably Tony Blair and Peter Mandelson), their institutional and intellectual allies (Demos, Anthony Giddens, etc.), the most right wing of the trade unions (e.g. the AEEU), that section of the electorate who prefer a managerialist government to either a conservative or social democratic one, and, importantly, those Labour Party members who have joined the party since Blair became leader and who have never participated in the structures, activities or decision-making processes of their local parties, whose main lines of communication with the leadership are the press, the broadcast media, and postal ballots. The Labour Party on the other hand is composed of that section of the party membership (including many members of the present government) which remains committed to social democratic ideals and institutions.

Furthermore, we can recognise that even these formations are not in themselves wholly homogenous; for example, the contest for London Mayor might be understood as one between a faction of the Labour Party (represented by Frank Dobson) which was committed to its coalition with New Labour and one (represented by Ken Livingstone) which had abandoned it to seek new alliances. The present government is underpinned by a balance between these two formations and those elements of 'Middle England' – the *Sun* newspaper, the voters of Enfield and Basildon – who deserted the Tories in the 1997 general election.

It is in the nature of hegemony that the articulations between the different elements of such a coalition transform the identities of those elements themselves,[3] and it is to be expected that the central and leading formation in such an articulation – in this case, New Labour – will work to break down the coherent identities of the others, drawing in elements which can be fully articulated with its own project and marginalising those which cannot. It is clear that at certain points, New Labour has regarded much of the Labour Party as incompatible with its project, and has seen the need to marginalise it under the label 'Old Labour'. However, recent developments – a warming towards the Tory leadership on the part of sections of the press such as the *Sun*, the growing fear that the mass abstention of the Labour Party from forthcoming elections may erode the government's electoral base beyond repair, the failure of New Labour to prevent Ken Livingstone from dominating and triumphing in the London Mayoral campaign – have demonstrated the continued, if reluctant dependence of New Labour on the Labour Party for its long-term stability. Treasury decisions such as the large cash injection into the coal industry announced by the government in April 2000, and the 'social democratic' Budget of the same year are direct results of this. All this should make us aware that there is still much to play for in the game of British electoral politics, and that the political character of the current government remains ambivalent. Furthermore, it may yet prove the case in the near future that those whose democratic ambitions run deeper, even in opposite directions, to those of New Labour, are left with no other realistic alternative to the increasingly racist and xenophobic Tory right. Nonetheless, it is important to appreciate the character of New Labour's project as it has emerged in the first three years of this government's life (while remembering that that project could change course at any moment), the logical aim of which can only be the marginalisation both of the authoritarian populist right and the democratising left.

THE HARD CENTRE

I would therefore suggest that Blair's claim to lead a government of 'the radical centre' should be taken literally and seriously. There is no need to interrogate the 'real' nature of the project lurking somewhere behind statements like this one. Rather, to take such statements at face value is to understand the politics of New Labour. What's more, to berate New Labour for failing to construct a hegemonic project is quite wrong. Just because it is not a hegemonic project led clearly from the left, as many had hoped for, or from the right, like Thatcherism, does not mean that it is not one. New Labour is a socio-political coalition which seeks to consolidate a solid centre-ground – socially, economically, politically, culturally – by excluding both the established constituencies of the radical left and those of the radical right. So overt racism is attacked as it never was under Thatcher, but radical anti-racist groups get none of the support they did from the GLC. (For example, and not untypically, the pioneering anti-racist group Newham Monitoring Project had its funding cancelled, interrupting over a decade of continuous service to the local community, following a Blairite take over of Newham Council's Labour group in 1997. Ironically, funding was restored via a National Lottery grant in 1999.) More money is spent on education, but progressive educational agendas are treated with even more contempt than they were under the Tories. The most recklessly destructive elements of finance capital – the currency markets – are threatened with being brought to heel by our joining the Euro, but beyond that the City is allowed to behave much as it ever did.

So what of those who, like Anthony Giddens, argue that this is all simply a rational and creative response to a changing world? The criticism which advocates of the 'Third Way' would make of my account is quite straightforward. They would point out that it is entirely predicated on the received view of politics which neatly divides the political spectrum into left, right, and things vaguely in between. At the beginning of the twenty-first century, Giddens would argue, such terms cannot cover the whole, if any, of the range of issues which politics decides.[4] Policy and politics cannot be seen in those terms; rather, creative solutions must be found to problems as they emerge, without being bound by the dictates of such old-fashioned categories as 'left', 'right' and centre. My account of politics harks back to a simple Marxist account of the relationships between politics, culture, economics and the social, dividing the entire spectrum of social, political and economic experience between left and right.

To some extent this criticism would be correct. However, although I do want to hold on to old notions of the difference between left and right and of the likelihood of respective social groups lending their support to one side or another,[5] I do not want to work with wholly standard notions of this distinction. Where I would agree with Giddens is in his claim that politics cannot simply be seen in terms of a left-right split with no distinctive middle position, and in the claim, made long before Giddens, that traditional Marxist categories cannot tell us all we need to know about politics. The unlikelihood of the imminent overthrow of the capitalist mode of production on the one hand, and the marked differences which are now discernible between different *kinds* of capitalism, some of which are decidedly more democratic and egalitarian than others, render the classical socialist version of this distinction irrelevant. Politics cannot, for the moment, be a question of being 'for or against capitalism' (although it can certainly be a question of being for or against the profit motive as the only determinant of public policy).

However, this is not to say that politics is now simply immune to classification. I would describe British, and to some extent global, politics as currently informed by three types of agenda between which there may be temporary alliances but which are always, sooner-or-later, irreducibly antagonistic. I will designate these agendas as democratic, anti-democratic and managerialist. An anti-democratic agenda is essentially hostile to attempts to break down existing concentrations of wealth and power or even to attempts to prevent such concentrations from intensifying; a democratic one is in favour of the redistribution of power, wealth and opportunity;[6] and a managerialist one is concerned with administering the status quo, such that some of the interests of the disadvantaged are taken into account while the overall distribution of social power is not threatened. To put it another way, the anti-democrat does not believe that people have any rights at all, so regards it as perfectly acceptable for government to be a means by which the dominant groups in society pursue their own interests unchecked (e.g. Thatcherism was informed by a belief that there is nothing wrong with the capitalist classes paying people low wages and using the machinery of the state to smash up their unions, making it impossible to defend themselves); the democrat believes that it is ultimately desirable for all groups and individuals to enjoy as much self-government and equality as possible in all spheres; and the managerialist believes that people have the right to be governed *well*, but has no belief in the desirability of them ever governing themselves.

Much of the rhetoric and almost all of the policy of New Labour is informed by this third position. Peter Mandelson is rumoured to have remarked to Anthony Barnett that Charter 88 should campaign not for better democracy, but for 'better government' (because the former sounded too archaic, too left-wing). Indeed, Mandelson's notorious comment that he believes the era of representative democracy to be at an end must be seen in this light.[7] By the same token, the government's position on the poor is that they are to be 'socially included', but never that they might actually be empowered: they should be invited to sit at the family table, even, perhaps, presented with some very limited menu options, but never offered a kitchen of their own. Unsurprisingly, I would suggest – *contra* Giddens – that it is still meaningful at the end of the millennium to declare oneself 'on the left', and that to do so is to commit oneself to that belief in the overriding value of democracy for which New Labour shows nothing but contempt.

It is crucial to understand that this contempt is not a simple matter of disagreement, or varying tastes. The managerialism which informs New Labour is not simply the product of a technical, political or ethical mistake. To see it as such has been, I think, the second great error of most of New Labour's recent critics.

THE IDEOLOGICAL FUNCTION OF THE THIRD WAY

So why is this taking place? Why are the agents of the New Labour project trying to convince the world that there is no left and right any more, that globalisation is inevitable, that political problems have to be dealt with one at a time, to be met by policies informed not by big ideas but by sound common sense efficiently applied? The answer, again, is simple and old fashioned: the people behind these moves are those who stand to gain the most from them: the 'technocratic-financial-managerial elite'.[8] New Labour is a project led by a specific class fraction of administrators and managers, drawn from the elite universities, the top ranks of the best-paid professions, and those sub-sections of finance, industry and the media wherein a technocratic approach to decision-making and problem solving, and a shallow but efficient approach to gathering and disseminating information, prevail. In a world where money is power – the world Thatcher wanted to maintain – such people are likely to find their authority dwarfed and distorted by the naked might of capital. In a democratic world this class of managers, advertisers and pseudo-experts would obviously be far less powerful than they are now. But in a world without politics the focus group replaces democratic consultation and the PR facilitator rules. In the world without politics, there is a right answer[9] to every social problem, and all it should take to sort it out is some young thing at Demos with a 2.1 in PPE and a nice line in graphs. In a world without politics, political activists – those hate-figures of the New Labour ideologues – are part of the problem and never part of the solution.

However, the situation is still more complex, and yet also simpler, than this. As the more astute commentators on the rise of the new managerialism have observed,[10] the forms of management currently being imposed by this government upon the public sector are in fact antiquated by the standards of contemporary business enterprises. For example, the government seems intent on squeezing all scope for creativity and flexibility out of the education system, filling our schools with OFSTED-harrassed, carefully-monitored, numerically-ranked teachers, forced to work to a centrally-devised national curriculum and paid on the basis of crudely-defined 'performance' (a kind of pedagogic piece-work). The individual which the government is thus trying to create, in the face of resistance which it defines only as 'conservative', is something akin to the industrial robot of the Fordist production line: standardised, atomised, stripped of all creative autonomy.[11] This person couldn't be more different from the autonomous, self-directed, multi-skilled, net-worker required by the theory and practice of post-fordist digital capitalism.[12] So why is this happening? More elaborated answers are hinted at elsewhere in this volume, but I will venture one, tentatively, here. Might it be that in the post-modern world of the global electronic economy and the network society, the most redundant figure of all will be the specialist 'manager'? For in this world of hyper-flexibility, where all of us act as unique nodes in myriad information networks, we must all be 'managers'; we must all exercise skills of information-processing and reproduction once typical only of the managerial class. Furthermore, in the knowledge economy, where ideas and information are the fundamental commodities of use and exchange, is not an 'intellectual', far from being the endangered animal which New Labour wants her to be, in fact that which every person must become? Under these circumstances, we might understand the rise of Third Way managerialism, with its constitutive marginalisation of intellectuals, as not the leading-edge of the Third Wave,[13] but the desperate last stand of a class which the rise of post-fordism is making redundant, clinging to power in the face of forces which threaten to sweep it away beneath a tide of creative thinking, flexible working, and decentralisation.

We might, if history were ever so legible, if the future ever anything but mysterious. But the fact is that there will never be a moment when we can know that the past, present and future have become so self-identical that we can be certain in which direction history is going. The meaning of the processes which are transforming our world is not predetermined, but precisely the object of political struggle. If we want to define the managerialist response as reactionary and redundant, then it is up to us to construct alternative narratives and to try to implement them. The observation that the rise of informational capitalism might as well result in a democratisation of the public sphere as in its crushing regimentation will be one, but only one, practical-rhetorical resource in any such struggle.

WHAT IS TO BE DONE?

So what exactly would be the shape of that struggle? What project should those of us who see our commitments to democracy as being thoroughly marginalised by New Labour actually pursue? I would suggest that the long-term task must be two-fold. On the one hand it would be to break up the existing social coalition which underpins New Labour, bringing much of it with us, and building a new coalition around a project which could genuinely deserve the name 'modernising left'. This would have to involve somehow convincing much or at least some of 'Middle England' that its interests can be best served by entering into a coalition with some of the most disadvantaged in society: no easy task. This was the function which the discourse of class struggle was once supposed to fulfil – calling as it did for the solidarity of all those who lived by selling their own labour – but clearly does not now. On the other hand it would mean convincing a largely sceptical public of the value of democracy itself. One thing which the left often forgets – and this is as true in Britain at the end of the twentieth century as it has ever been anywhere – is that very often people prefer being 'governed well' to governing themselves. This – more than anything – is still the great obstacle facing any kind of left project, modernising or otherwise: the need to persuade the public that their own material interests can, in the long term, only be served by they themselves taking control of their own lives and the institutions which govern them. Very few to the left of New Labour seem able to grasp this basic problem. The loose grouping which has formed itself around *Tribune* newspaper and the Grassroots Alliance (a network of anti-Blairite activists largely focused on getting left candidates elected to Labour's National Executive Committee) is already making the classic mistake of the British left, concentrating all of its efforts on winning over the Labour Party, and directing all of its anger at the leadership, while leaving the real fields of political combat – the vast and complex arenas of civil society – wide open to its enemies. The left won that battle in 1983, convincing the Labour Party to adopt a radical manifesto, and wholly failing to convince the public to vote for it. The result was another fourteen years of Thatcherism. This struggle is not about winning over the party: it is about winning over the country. Unless a modernising left can find a language with which to do that (and the work of writers such as Chantal Mouffe provides us with valuable resources with which we might do it, despite my criticisms elsewhere in this volume), then it has no future.

THE (ANTI-)POLITICS OF CULTURE

We can only come to a real understanding of this situation once we recognise that New Labour is, indissolubly, a cultural as well as a political and economic project – not only in the sense that it has a specific set of ideas about culture and cultural policy, but in the sense that there is a specific set of resonances between its political and social agendas and key phenomena in contemporary 'culture'.

The short-lived media discourse on 'Cool Britannia', despite its subsequent disavowal by all of its participants, remains a useful illustration. The assertion of a deliberately vague notion of 'British' cultural identity in fashion and the visual arts, and an explicitly conservative yet 'youthful' identity in music; the particular mechanisms for the elaboration and reproduction of identity mobilised within, for example, the Millennium Dome; the discourse on 'Re-branding Britain' initiated by Demos's Mark Leonard – all amount to a coherent discursive formation.

Consider the similarity between the techniques typical of the so-called 'Young British Artists' and those deployed by many of the exhibits in the Millennium Dome. The installations of Damien Hirst (such as his famous animals preserved in formaldehyde) provoke in the viewer casual meditations on mortality, corporeality, individuality and finitude which are ultimately devoid of any political content or historical specificity.[14] The empty reflexivity into which the viewer is encouraged by such pieces is very much the condition offered to the participating subject in many of the 'zones' at the Dome, many of which are best described as 'installations' in the same tradition of pallid conceptualism. 'Sensation' was the title of the key exhibition of these artists' work, and sensation (without any discernible content) is the apparent aim of its more populist counterpart in the Dome.[15] The participant in the Millennium Experience is constantly asked to wonder at and reflect upon the fact of her insertion into a world of digital technology, flexible work, lifelong learning, monetarist economics, environmental threat and community politics. Yet the scope offered by the various exhibits for drawing conclusions as to the nature of this world, its historicity, its possibility for change, its social differentiation, is negligible. We are all, according to the 'Work' zone, flexible workers now. What is more, we are all supposed to be happy about it. The image – characteristic of much YBA work – used to illustrate this fact is a battery of hamsters in row upon row of cages, followed by a similar bank of cages from which the hamsters have escaped, leaving their exercise wheels – symbolising the cast-off treadmill of a lifetime of secure employment – empty and abandoned.

The sheer intellectual vacuity of the Millennium Experience and *Sensation* is not, however, a mere symptom of mediocrity. Rather it is the expression of an explicitly anti-political ideology, geared towards the production of the type of subject required by information capitalism. This ideology is most clearly manifested in the output of New Labour's principal intellectual ideologues: the think tank Demos, and Anthony Giddens. Demos's major collection, published in 1997 – the year of the Blair's historic victory – was titled, simply *Life After Politics*, clearly implying (although, to be fair, many of the contributions did not) that 'politics', the process by which power relationships are historically contested, is finished.[16] This theme is made explicit in the assertions of Mulgan and Giddens that the 'left/right' distinction is of little relevance any more – in other words that the large scale inequalities of power which this distinction was always mobilised to address are either no longer existent or no longer relevant to the concerns of reasonable people.

The logical conclusion of this line of thinking is simple, and it is not one limited to this project or the present time. It was Marx and Engels who, in their most eschatologically anti-political moment, first imagined what life might be like after politics. In the Communist utopia, power itself would be abolished and the state would whither away.[17] Ironically, this is remarkably similar to the world which Demos insist we now live in, in which new technology, an inexorable force with a life of its own, has far more 'power to reshape governments'[18] than states have power over anything, and in which globalisation decimates the capacity of governments and other democratic institutions to act upon the world. However, let me point out again who must, of necessity, have power in such a world, when – contrary to Marx's vision – huge inequalities remain: the administrators, the technocrats, the managers[19] – in other words, exactly the people who are telling us that this is how the world now is.

We can see an example of the type of intervention which such a technocratic anti-politics generates in Mark Leonard's *Britain^tm: Renewing Our Identity*.[20] This extraordinary document includes chapter headings such as 'What is identity for?', 'What are the tools for constructing an identity?', 'Shaping our identity', 'Projecting a new identity' and 'Conclusion: Re-imagining Britain', without once acknowledging the existence of entire academic literatures on Britain, culture, nationality or identity. The reader is treated to one reference to Linda Colley, a Blair adviser, but never to the work on national identities of Benedict Anderson, Raymond Williams, Stuart Hall, or Slavoj Žižek. What Leonard doesn't know could fill a marvellous learning resource centre on the subject. So what does he draw on? His sources are, amongst others, 'Adrian Ellis, AEA consultants', 'Lord Archer of Western-Super-

Mare', and the British Tourist Authority. His method, using bullet-points, sound-bites and graphs to present as scientific and authoritative the most banal and worst-researched insights imaginable (apparently – wait for it – foreigners see the British as old fashioned! Hold the front page!) is precisely that of the stereotypical management or marketing consultant. The implication is that no more rigorous form of thinking is necessary, on issues so profound as these, than that capable of success-fully 're-branding' 'UK plc'. (Making our airports more appealing to visiting businesspeople is Leonard's number one policy recommenda-tion.) To be sure, there is a politics to Leonard's desire for the UK to project an image to the world which is cosmopolitan and forward-looking, and it is preferable to the politics of William Hague's attacks on asylum-seekers, but it is a politics which assumes without question that the only interests that matter are those of finance capital.

A similar politics is manifested in a slightly more complex way in the recent work of Anthony Giddens. Along with the German sociol-ogist Ulrich Beck, Giddens suggests that the processes transforming the developed world at the present time should be characterised as 'reflexive modernisation'. The best definition of the idea of 'reflexivity' as it features in their work is given by Scott Lash in the book he co-authored with them:

> 'First, there is *structural* reflexivity in which agency, set free from the constraints of social structure, then reflects on the 'rules' and 'resources' of such structure; reflects on agency's social conditions of existence. Second there is *self*-reflexivity, in which agency reflects on itself. In self-reflexivity previous heteronomous monitoring of agents is displaced by self-monitoring.[21]

A reflexive subject in a world of informational complexity where traditional political distinctions have no relevance; this is, according to Giddens, what each of us has become. Now, there is truth in this and there are problems with it, but the truth or otherwise of such state-ments is largely beside the point. As Lash goes on to point out (p121-40), the main problem with Giddens's account is that it over-looks the disempowering and immobilising effects the social processes he describes on those who do not possess the social, cultural or economic capital to take advantage of reflexive modernisation – but this is to criticise Giddens's account merely on the basis of its success or failure as *description*. When looked at alongside the other elements of the New Labour formation which I have described, we can see such statements to be not merely descriptive but *performative* in nature. Like the 'Work' zone at the Millennium Dome, like the installations of the YBAs, they exhort us to become the subjects of an empty reflexivity; in other words, subjects capable of and used to handling the complex and rapidly-changing flows of data which comprise contemporary capitalism (or post-capitalism), but without any reference points from which to challenge the source, direction, nature or effects of those flows and the concentrations of power which they reproduce. This is the politics of the Third Way: an insistence that there is no alternative to a global economic settlement in which the technocrats of the managerial class wield all power. What is crucial to recognise is the fact that the people telling us this have a vested interest in it being so. They are not merely reporting a situation, but creating one.

Finally, it is worth observing that the discourse generated by this formation is anti-political for two distinct reasons. On the one hand, presenting a particular set of actions and policies as not political but simply 'common sense' is the aim of all ideology. On the other hand, this particular ideology is particularly anti-political, because, unlike Thatcherism, with its explicitly named 'enemies within' (the trade unions, the left), the techno-managerial elite have a specific interest in promoting the idea that politics is a redundant concept best replaced by the efficient management of capitalism, of which only they are capable. The result is the very specific formation which has established itself as hegemonic within British political culture, which has New Labour at its core, and which looks more successful with every passing day.

BEYOND THE FRONTIERS OF THE PRESENT

The conclusion we should draw from this analysis should not be to berate New Labour for its failure to implement a democratic project. Why on earth should it? It has never promised to do so, nor would it be in its own best interests. Indeed, in the absence of any coherent movement for democratic transformation amongst the public at large, how *could* a group of professional politicians and career technocrats do anything *but* manage capitalism with all the skill at their disposal? Of course, this government cannot be absolved of responsibility for its anti-democratic tendencies. There have been numerous instances of it actively choosing to follow the least democratising course of action available to it, even when that went against the grain of public opinion (the debacles resulting from Millbank's determination to retain complete control over the Welsh assembly and the London mayoralty being the most obvious examples). However, it would be utterly paradoxical to criticise New

Labour for failing to engineer democracy from Whitehall: democracy can only come from below; and in those areas, such as Scottish civil society, where there has been an organised demand for democratisation, this government has not stood in the way. It therefore behoves those of us who accept the preceding critique of New Labour not to criticise the government for not being what it is not, but to try to build a movement, or even just a mood, in Britain and beyond which would make a public and manifest commitment to radical democracy an attractive option for such a coterie of professional pragmatists. Having established the nature of New Labour, the question must be how to build a powerful coalition in support of democratising alternatives. For the remainder of this essay, I will try to begin to answer this question by looking at things going on in the sphere of 'popular culture', and asking what resources there might be in already-existing structures of feeling for democratic political projects to draw on and learn from. Finally, I will sketch out some programmatic suggestions as to what such projects might actually include.

These are not easy questions to answer. They open up the issue of just what kind of questions, from what perspectives, and with what aims, the left needs to ask of 'culture'. (These have been some of the key questions which 'cultural studies' has existed to ask.) To turn the question around, we need to ask just what it is that the 'left' wants to be happening in the sphere of people's beliefs and self-images for its aims to have any hope of realisation, before we can consider the extent to which tendencies in contemporary 'culture' might be amenable or hostile to such ends.

I would identify three characteristics of a culture in which progressive, democratic politics can win popular support. Firstly, people need to believe that change is possible. The biggest problem facing democratic politics today is de-politicisation: the detachment of everyday culture from explicitly political concerns. The apathy and hostility which is a dominant feature of current attitudes to politics needs to be understood as functioning to secure the perpetuation of a political and social status quo. Even active support for a regime carries with it the possibility that that support could be withdrawn, while apathy implies a belief that there is no alternative. It is this belief which has to be overcome before any other progress can be made. There's little evidence that people in Britain today believe in the actual possibility of progressive social change. In Gramscian terms, such de-politicisation might be understood as constituting the deepest form of consent to a given social order. As we have seen, the function of much 'Third Way' discourse is to encourage this outlook, but it is also an attitude which is experienced at the level of everyday life, the inevitable result of decades of defeat for the forces of democracy.

Secondly, people have to believe that change would be in their interests. The New Right came to power at the end of the 1970s by convincing large numbers of people that many changes taking place in society were not in their interests; it is only when people take the opposite view that the left can make any progress.

Thirdly, people have to be convinced that change can only be brought about by them themselves. As has already been discussed, central to New Labour discourse is the belief in a technocratic notion of 'good government' – the belief that people have the right to be governed wisely and well, to have their tax money spent effectively and their services run efficiently – and a hostility to the democratic principle that people are better off governing themselves. For a more democratic outlook to win widespread acceptance, people have to believe that social, political, economic and cultural democracy are not just ethically desirable but necessary to the maximisation of their own material interests.

Historically, these themes were articulated and mobilised by the discourse of class struggle and the socialist movement. What was so effective about this discourse was that it brought together these three elements into a convincing narrative. The problem facing the left at the beginning of the twenty-first century is the fact that this narrative has lost its purchase on people's loyalties and imaginations, and nothing nearly so serviceable has replaced it. What we need to do now when examining contemporary culture and society is to try to pick out those radical constituencies and sensibilities from which we might build new coalitions, and articulate new structures of feeling, which might serve to carry out some of its essential functions.

So what might such phenomena look like? How would we recognise them if we saw them? The most straightforward and schematic way of answering this question was offered by Raymond Williams in the 1970s.[22] However, Williams's distinction between merely 'alternative' cultural formations which offer people limited space outside mainstream culture and truly 'oppositional' ones which offer a challenge to the existing distribution of power in society is not appropriate to the de-centred complexity of postmodern societies. Instead, I would suggest two or three issues to think about when considering the political significance of given instances of 'culture'. Firstly, we should ask what, if any, their democratising potential might be. Do they help to break down existing concentrations of power, or legitimate and reinforce them? Do they help to multiply the life options – material, intellectual, emotional – available to as many people as possible, or contain them? Do they challenge patterns of dominance or reinforce them? Secondly, we can learn a lot about a given cultural formation by considering what we might call its hegemonic potential. To what extent is it capable of expanding its frontiers to include as many elements as possible? Thirdly, it's worth thinking about the extent to which different cultural phenomena manifest quite different attitudes to the possibility of change, indeed, to the very notion of the future itself. No structure of feeling which is afraid of the future is going to be much inspiration for any progressive project.

A recent example of a cultural formation with seriously hegemonic ambitions was the set of bands and media practices (Radio One playlists, music-press manifestos, etc.) which went by the name of 'Britpop'.[23] The name said it all; this wasn't about defining a tiny little sub-section of popular culture, it was about defining the entire field of popular music in terms of a coherent and conservatively communitarian idea of what it meant to be British.

We can contrast this with the more pluralist and democratic dance music cultures which have been central to the lives of many people, especially young people, throughout the 1990s. If there's any clearly discernible ethic to this loose formation, it's a libertarian hedonism; this implies a very strong anti-work attitude which is obviously necessary to any culture that revolves around taking a lot of drugs at the weekend. This is radically subversive of the New Labour project, for the work ethic is a key element of New Labour discourse. Work is presented as the basis of citizenship, and the government's first priority has been to get those who do not work back into work, even when – as in the case of single parents – that might not be their first priority. Of course, libertarian hedonism is a value cherished by the most reactionary rock'n'roller, and it's worth considering the fact that the love affair between Britpop and Blairism ended precisely when New Labour's puritanism came into conflict with it – when the *New Musical Express* came out against the government over its plans to compel young claimants to work.[24] This goes to demonstrate the resistance to the work ethic across much of contemporary popular culture, but how that resistance will manifest itself in the future – whether by constructive politics or escapist nihilism – is an open question. What's particularly notable in the case of dance culture is the fact that its hedonism and democratic pluralism have more or less prevented it from exercising any hegemonic potential it might have had. In comparison to Britpop – which quickly received the widespread endorsement of powerful institutions, from the Labour Party to the BBC – dance culture's lack of interest in persuading those outside of it of its right to exist, let alone of its potential value, has made it vulnerable to numerous attacks from the state and to commercial exploitation so rampant that it often robs it of any radical potential it may have.

Another important tendency in contemporary culture is the common sense feminism of 'girl power'. As Angela McRobbie has pointed out,[25] it is clear from the success of magazines like *More* and *Minx* that if any constituency in recent years has undergone a radical transformation it is young women. Young women have developed an optimistic and assertive identity in recent years, as is borne out not just by the cultural phenomenon of the Spice Girls but by the increasingly well-documented success of young women in education and the workplace. It is interesting that while women have historically been less likely to vote Labour than men, at the last two general elections the Labour Party received its largest vote from women between the ages of 18 and 35.[26] We can safely assume that the willingness of young women to vote for the principal party of the left is motivated not by enthusiasm for its authoritarian model of modernisation, which has nothing in common with attitudes manifested in 'girl culture', but by their willingness to embrace the radical possibilities of a future which would be different from the present or the past.

At the same time we have seen the rise of a culture by and for young men which has less progressive connotations. The rise of the 'New Lad' – the hedonistic, consumption-fixated, anti-political, militantly infantile man behaving badly (and who knows he should know better) – is probably best represented by the phenomenal impact of the magazine *Loaded*. This cultural discourse is in part a response to the changes in the lives of many people over recent years which have dislocated old patterns of work, social and family life, and leisure, putting consumption at the heart of people's sense of self and posing particular problems for the identities of young men. In some senses it is a re-assertion of traditional masculinity against the advances of feminism and a reaction against some of the feminising 'loved up' aspects of dance culture. On the other hand, New Laddism is also concerned with providing an identity for young men that does not revolve around work. What *Loaded* culture really seeks to do is to articulate both the commodifying tendencies of late capitalism and the hedonism and anti-work attitudes of dance culture with more traditional (and sexist) ideas of masculinity, transforming every available aspect of social and physical experience – clothes, places, memories, music, women – into consumable commodities, combined with the refusal of any critical stance towards its implications.

Several key themes emerge. The first is the prevalence of hedonism and a resistance to work as a regimented and administered domain. The second, a crucial terrain of struggle at present, is sexual politics. There has been a widespread dissemination of some profoundly transformatory feminist ideas amongst young women, with potentially more serious implications than the popularisation of an assertive individualism. Opposed to this we see both a return to more traditional masculine values in certain spheres of popular culture and the mobilisation of traditional 'family values' by this and the previous government, with its imaginary effect of reasserting conservative gender roles. Thirdly, there is a strong liberal multiculturalism in some areas of popular culture, but the example of Britpop's successful, little-criticised (even in the supposedly left-leaning indie rock press) mobilisation of a whiter-than-white version of British identity demonstrates that this can never be taken for granted. Fourthly, there is an interesting set of attitudes to community and individuality in circulation. Britpop, for all its failings, was a strong attempt to re-evoke a notion of homogenous national community, which reveals the desire of many people to go beyond the culture of individualism inherited from the Thatcher era. Similarly, rave culture was constituted around the notion of different cultures and individuals sharing space, a belief in a democratic plurality of differences. What the two formations shared was an interest in elaborating new forms of community.

Presented with this collection of themes, we need to consider what kind of intervention might be useful and effective from the point of view of democratic projects. One of the most difficult and necessary tasks of any cultural politics today must be the articulation of a popular feminism which can include straight men; the disparity between the discourses of the New Lad and Girl Power demonstrates this clearly. It may be that dance culture can help by providing examples of different sets of ethics, different and more empathic modes of behaviour which can challenge hegemonic models of masculinity in a pleasurable way.[27] The novels of Irvine Welsh offer, largely from a male perspective, meditations on the relations between identity and consumption, work and community which are informed by an appreciation of the potency of pleasure and the limitations of politics, but also by a reflexive feminist sensibility quite different from that which motivates the New Lad.

The common sense feminism which is very strong amongst young women could be translated into something far more than votes for Tony Blair, but there is also a danger that the Conservatives will adopt a pro-feminist rhetoric of choice and self-determination in order to draw these women back. If this is going to be avoided, then these popular feminist sentiments need to be deepened and articulated with other traditional themes of the left. One aspect of this project would be to circulate a very different discourse on the family to that reproduced by the government and the *Daily Mail*. The left needs to do more than display perpetual outrage at Blair's social conservatism, and make a strident defence of women's autonomy. We need, for example, to find ways of representing single parents not as social problems or as victims who need our protection, but as heroic figures who are struggling against the odds in bringing their children up.

Thirdly, we need to recognise the importance of hedonism. People do not identify with their working life as much as they once did; they identify rather with their life as consumers. Trade unions need to adapt to this change and realise that many people have a largely instrumental attitude to work. They also need to be relevant for people who do not recognise themselves as victims of naked exploitation. Therefore, while it is vital to campaign against low pay and casualisation, unions also need to address relatively affluent people who have learnt to value the flexibility of certain new working arrangements. This means a change in how trade unions relate to workers, and the adoption of different kinds of campaigns. Of course, much of this is already taking place, and the new politics being conducted under the rubric of the 'New Unionism' deserves our full support. More than anything, though, recognising the potency of hedonist values means getting home the basic message that trade unionism, socialism, indeed the class struggle itself, is and always has been about one key goal: more money for less work.

Another important issue is that of political education. This country is almost alone in the developed world in that one can complete secondary education and not have a clue how laws are made, how parliaments work, how the government is run, how taxes work. Considering this, we can hardly be surprised if people are barely aware that change is possible. The exact content of the government's proposed 'Citizenship' element of the National Curriculum must be examined in critical detail while being welcomed in principle.

A further issue, typical of the emerging antagonisms of the new conjuncture, is drugs. There is an absolute refusal on the part of government to deal with the failure of prohibition as a policy, and this is symptomatic of the deep commitment of key elements in New Labour to the same ideological puritanism whence springs their moralising obsession with work. Millions of pounds of public money are wasted pursuing a policy which results in the incarceration of thousands of people for victimless 'crimes', while a large number of young people experience themselves as criminalised every day of the week. This does not just alienate them from the police and the legal system but from the political process altogether. It is wholly encouraging that figures such as Clare Short, Mo Mowlam, Ken Livingstone and Paul Flynn have taken a progressive stand on this issue, but we need to go further. There are simply no such thing as 'drugs' (a catch-all description which conveys no information), except in the paranoid fantasies of Jack Straw and Middle England, and this perpetual moral panic must be brought to an end.

Finally, in the formation of any popular movement one is always faced with the complex problem of inclusivity and exclusivity. For example, a significant failure of the environmental/'anti-capitalist' direct action movement is that it effectively values and perpetuates a high level of exclusivity. Activists tend to differentiate themselves sharply from the mainstream of society by abandoning the normal economy, and developing separate social structures and cultural activities. This separatism is forcibly communicated by visual differences in dress, hairstyle, etc. In contrast, I would argue that a popular movement can only succeed if it can be broadened through drawing in different constituencies and sensibilities in society at large.

Despite the media attention which the latest waves of protests against global capitalism has received, in the UK context the turn towards an extreme 'anti-capitalism' amongst sections of this movement is not a welcome development. Since a high-point in May 1997 – when the group Reclaim the Streets joined with sacked Liverpool dock workers to mount a hugely successful demonstration and street party in Trafalgar Square, bringing together anarchists, environmentalists, conservationists and trade-unionists – the turn towards more extreme and violent tactics aimed with an ever-greater sense of futility at ever-more inaccessible targets has resulted in the significant reduction in the actual numbers of participants.[28] The J18 'day of action against global capitalism', 18 June 1999, although a televisual success, brought together far fewer people than the May 1997 event, and the dual slide towards extremism and marginality has not been halted. This is the danger for any movement which becomes more concerned with self-definition than with expanding its own borders.

On the other hand, such expansion can never be continued indefinitely if a movement is to retain a distinct shape and meaning. Any movement needs to cohere around some common principles. With the collapse of the discourse of class struggle the left has lacked any unifying theme. There seems little hope of a similar 'grand narrative' replacing it, but in this postmodern context a generalised commitment to processes of *democratisation* is more likely than anything else to provide a successful alternative. It is a principle that can be transferred to a multiplicity of spheres – the family, work, sexual relations, leisure, education – in each of which the general aim of dispersing concentrations of power can be pursued in multifarious ways. However it is imperative to understand, at the crucial level of tactics, that the notion of democracy will rarely draw significant numbers of people to radical politics. People need to be convinced of more immediate rewards, defined by their existing sets of values. Only by convincing people that ongoing democratisation is the best way of realising their most immediate interests can the left have any hope of a future. Only by building coalitions and articulating shared structures of feeling around this theme – structures of feeling which make sense in terms of people's current experience – can we hope to bring that future closer.

NOTES

1. Ernesto Laclau and Chantal Mouffe, *Hegemony and Socialist Strategy*, Verso, London 1985.
2. Stuart Hall, 'Gramsci and us' in *The Hard Road to Renewal*, Verso, London 1988, p171.
3. Laclau and Mouffe, *op. cit.*, pp93-148.
4. Anthony Giddens, *The Third Way: The Renewal of Social Democracy*, Polity, Cambridge, 1998, p44.
5. See Chantal Mouffe, 'The radical centre: a politics without adversary' in *Soundings* 9, Lawrence and Wishart, London 1998.
6. One can cite no more eloquent description of such a politics than that offered by Giddens in his short essay advocating 'utopian realism' in Hall *et al* (eds), *Modernity and its Futures*, Polity, Cambridge 1992, p59.
7. Nick Cohen, 'New Labour... in focus, on message, out of control', *Observer*, 28 November 1999.
8. Manuel Castells, *The Rise of the Network Society*, Blackwell, Oxford 1996, p415.
9. James Donald has described this as 'the politics of the right answer' in a personal conversation.
10. See Tiziana Terranova in this volume. See also Wendy Wheeler in her *A*

New Modernity? Change in Literature, Science and Politics, Lawrence and Wishart, London 1999, pp103-31.

11. See Antonio Gramsci, 'Americanism and Fordism' in *Selections from the Prison Notebooks,* Lawrence and Wishart, London 1971, pp301-13.

12. David Harvey, *The Condition of Postmodernity,* Polity, Cambridge 1989, pp.141-97; Manuel Castells, *The Rise of the Network Society, op. cit.*

13. Alvin Toffler, *The Third Wave,* William Collins, London 1980.

14. See Julian Stallabrass, *High Art Lite,* Verso, London 1999, pp19-21.

15. See Jo Littler in this volume.

16. Geoff Mulgan (ed), *Life After Politics,* Demos, London 1997.

17. Marx and Engels, *The Communist Manifesto,* Penguin, London 1967.

18. Geoff Mulgan, *op. cit.,* pxiv.

19. A similar point was made of certain aspects of the 'New Times' projects by Michael Rustin, in 'The trouble with "New Times"', in Stuart Hall and Martin Jacques (eds), *New Times: The Changing Face of Politics in the 1990s,* Lawrence and Wishart, London 1990, p311.

20. Mark Leonard, *Britain^{tm}: Renewing Our Identity,* Demos, London 1997.

21. Ulrich Beck, Anthony Giddens and Scott Lash, *Reflexive Modernization,* Polity, London 1994, p116.

22. Raymond Williams, *Marxism and Literature,* Oxford University Press, Oxford 1977.

23. See my other chapter, 'In defence of discourse analysis', in this volume.

24. See Jeremy Gilbert, 'Blurred vision: pop, populism and politics' in Anne Coddington and Mark Perryman (eds), *The Moderniser's Dilemma,* Lawrence and Wishart, London, p86.

25. Angela McRobbie, 'Pecs and penises: the meaning of Girlie Culture' in *Soundings* 6, Lawrence and Wishart, London 1997.

26. P. Norris, 'Mobilising the women's vote: the gender-generation gap in voting behaviour' in *Parliamentary Affairs* 49, pp333-42.

27. See M. Pini, 'Cyborgs, Nomads and the Raving Feminine', in H. Thomas (ed), *Dance in the City,* Routledge, London 1977, p168; J. Gilbert and E. Pearson, *Discographies: Dance Music, Culture and the Politics of Sound,* Routledge, London 1999.

28. See Naomi Klein, *No Logo,* Flamingo, London 2000, pp311-24; Ernesto Laclau and Chantal Mouffe, *Hegemony and Socialist Strategy,* Verso, London 1985.

Notes on contributors

Timothy Bewes is Post-Doctoral Research Fellow at Liverpool John Moores University, and the author of *Cynicism and Postmodernity* (Verso, 1997). He is currently writing a book about reification and cultural anxiety.

Alan Finlayson is a Lecturer in the Department of Political Theory and Government, University of Wales Swansea. He has written a number of articles on political theory, New Labour, nationalism and political identity in Northern Ireland. He is co-author of *Contemporary Social and Political Theory: An introduction* (The Open University Press, 1999), and is currently writing a book on political theory and the media.

Jeremy Gilbert teaches Cultural Studies and Media Studies at the University of East London. He is the co-author (with Ewan Pearson) of *Discographies: Dance Music, Culture and the Politics of Sound* (Routledge, 1999).

Matt Jordan is a Lecturer in Literature and Cultural History at Liverpool John Moores University and the author of *Milton and Modernity: Paradise Lost and the Making of Man* (Macmillan, 2000).

Jo Littler is currently finishing a DPhil on exhibitions and consumer culture, and is a visiting lecturer at Sussex University and Middlesex University.

Martin McQuillan is a Lecturer in Cultural Theory and Analysis at Leeds University. He co-edited *Post-Theory: New Directions in Criticism* (Edinburgh University Press, 1999), and is co-author, with Eleanor Byrne, of *Deconstructing Disney* (Pluto, 1999).

Karen Lisa G. Salamon is a Research Fellow in the Department of Management, Politics and Philosophy at Copenhagen Business School. She has worked as a consultant on cultural affairs to public organisations and business corporations in Denmark, and is an editor of *RAMBAM*, a journal of scientific research into Danish-Jewish history and culture.

Paul Smith is Professor of Media and Cultural Studies at the University of Sussex. His books include *Millennial Dreams* (Verso, 1997), *Clint Eastwood* (University of Minnesota Press, 1993), *Discerning the Subject* (University of Minnesota Press, 1988), and he has edited *Men in Feminism* (Methuen/Routledge, 1987), *Madonnarama* (Cleis, 1993) and *Boys* (Westview, 1996). He is currently working on a Cultural Studies manifesto and a book about the political economy of the new media.

Tiziana Terranova lectures in Media, Culture and Film at the University of Essex. She is currently completing a book on networked intelligence and collective politics.

Index